Adventures in the Earth Game

Observations from the Asylum

Doug Michael

DEDICATION

This work is dedicated to my beautiful children, Darrion and Marissa, whose lives have touched mine in ways that words cannot describe. My existence in the Earth Game has meaning because you are here, and people like you prove that your generation isn't completely lost. May the light of the creation forever shine upon you and guide you into becoming the best that you can be.

CONTENTS

Forward...i

1. At the Crossroads...1

2. Distraction-Deception-Division...24

3. Captives of Ego...48

4. Comfort Zones: Human crabs and Self-imposed Buckets.................70

5. Ideological Subversion...84

6. Rectal-Cranial Inversion..112

7. Manufactured Crises...136

8. What Happened on 9/11?...191

9. Fabricated reality..209

10. The Fall of Civilization..238

11. Technology and Transhumanism..270

12. Game Over..299

Afterward..320

ACKNOWLEDGMENTS

To all who have stood by me and supported my efforts, I extend my deepest appreciation, thanks and heartfelt gratitude. Without your encouragement, my efforts would mean nothing, and I am truly grateful to all of you. A very special thank you and the utmost respect to: Yardley Pearson, Emerald Orchid, Heather R. Edick, Michael and Joanne Volosack, Paul Middleton, Greg Brewster, Cheryl Chances, Leonard Baldwin, Aaron Berry, Sarah Ebanks, David Michael Thomas, Cal Cummins, Eva McQuillan, Antony Mallace, Frank Carentz, Stephen Morse, Katrina Porter, Jane Gregory, Rich Burton, Kameron Evans, Tony Dejohn, Jay Freeman, Hank Johnston, Laurent Moret, Zach Orlowski, Laurie Burgess, Andrea Edick, Rock & Roll Rich, Jebus Fist, and to everyone that has assisted me in my endeavors and who have taken the time to read the books.

An extra special thanks to Yardley Pearson for the front cover image!

FORWARD

To know Doug Michael is quite an experience. I met him somewhere around 2005, long before the internet was so readily spreading the word about ayahuasca, the intricacies of the ego, the threat of domestic socialism or the possibility that the universe is a simulation. Doug introduced me to these, and many other amazing, baffling, challenging and sometimes frightening ideas. Then, over the next decade and-a-half (I don't know where the time went) I saw more and more of these topics, first on the internet and then increasingly, within mainstream media. Doug seemed to be ever a step ahead of the cutting edge of the most bizarre parts of our culture. I've always had an interest in the bizarre, starting from a very early age when I watched Leonard Nimoy on *In Search of,* and now here was someone who was way ahead of the curve when it came to all things strange and fascinating.

Doug's work resides at the intersection of epistemology and ontology. Not only is he able to illuminate historical patterns and hidden agendas, he is able to do this so compellingly that I am left wondering how I didn't see these things before. And then he is able to show us how these sinister events continue to repeat and re-manifest over and over, from year to year, decade to decade and century to century, as if the same template is being used and only updated with changes in technology and the geo-political landscape. As compelling as these examples of hidden-in-plain-sight crimes against humanity and decency are, they are all meticulously researched. As you read his work you are led as if by torch light that illuminates only the immediate area that surrounds you until Doug brings you to an insightful conclusion that draws together previous observations and examples. This is when you step into the dazzling light of a new reality. Things here are not what you might have expected, but they do make sense. Doug's logic reveals an astonishing landscape of hidden agendas and insidious plans.

However, unlike so many in the alternative media, Doug's goal is not to bewilder the reader and take them on a one-way trip that ends with inevitable doom and destruction. Doug reminds each of us that we have within ourselves the power to resist these sinister changes that powerful hidden cabals are imposing upon mankind. Doug reminds us that we still have the most powerful weapon of all at our disposal in this struggle for our future. We still have the truth. And while the truth may set us free, Doug shows us that the truth may also turn back the dark tides that threaten to flood our civilization.

Doug was there when I first started on my own spiritual journey. He pointed out some of the pitfalls and showed me the trap doors to watch out for. It was good to wake up to what was happening to our civilization, he told me, but it's also just as important to keep your head on your shoulders. Don't give in to the temptation of despair. Keep a sense of humor about things and remember to enjoy life. As Nietzsche said: *"when you gaze long into an abyss, the abyss also gazes into you."* Remember, there is more to life than just gazing into the abyss, Doug was telling me, and this advice has definitely come in handy.

In the last few years, our culture and our society has taken many strange turns. The definition of a man and the definition of a woman are no longer set in stone. We live in a society that allows and even encourages people to decide these things for themselves. And while gender may not be real, apparently UFOs really are. More and more government entities are admitting that they believe that UFOs are filling our skies and they are to be taken seriously. But Knowing Doug and his work has made living in these strange times more meaningful. He has always been there to remind me that there is a sleight-of-hand taking place. Look here, not there. Doug has been able to discern what is really going on and put it in a historical context that has been reassuring to me. So, whatever the future holds-and if the present is any indication of what's to come-then I know it's going to be even stranger. And I am glad to know Doug to help me put things into perspective and remind me that the truth will always belong to those bold enough to speak it.

David M. Thomas, 2019.

ONE

At the Crossroads

While it can no longer be denied, that humanity stands at the crossroads, faced with immense challenges, it is important to realize that where there is crisis, there is also opportunity. That being said, humanity is faced with an enormous opportunity, one of growth, true conscious evolution and the decision to once and for all take charge of our own destinies.

No longer can humanity walk the path that has been laid before us by the hidden rulers, the dark ones, the servants of evil, and expect the outcome to be anything but complete annihilation. Like it or not, this is the choice that we all now face: choose our own destiny, understand our interconnectedness to each other and to nature or simply march headlong over the cliff into our very extinction. There is simply no middle ground and this decision cannot be left to those in power who have sold humanity down the river long ago. The choice of course begins within the *individual* consciousness, within the heart and mind of the *self*.

We are in an age of apocalypse. This does not necessarily mean cataclysm or disaster; the word Apocalypse comes from the Greek word, *apokalyptein*, which means to "uncover," "expose" or "reveal." We exist within an interesting timeframe, in which the mask is being pulled away to reveal all that has remained hidden.

This unique time that we find ourselves within, signifies a peeling away of the veil to expose all which has been obscured, all that is false, all that is imbalanced and all that needs healing. This age brings with it a deconstructive force that will expose all that has been concealed in the shadows and it's important to realize that the peeling away of the masks of illusion will be felt first within one's own psyche and within people's most intimate and closest relationships.

Because of such a lack of understanding of what I consider to be natural, deconstructive processes and of the psyche in general, many people are literally suffering psychological breakdown thus we witness a massive proliferation in the widespread use of anti-psychotic medications, tranquilizers and narcotic pain medications that has reached staggering and epidemic proportions. The very nature of this deconstructive force brings to the surface all the repressed things about us to be cleansed and healed. By allowing this process to occur, one can be gifted with healing and liberation. Resistance to this natural process due to over identification with the roles that we play in life or with ego centered consciousness will bring suffering and dare I say, complete and utter psychosis.

One barely needs a modicum of conscious awareness to see this occurring all around us; it is ubiquitous and in our faces.

The unrecognized, behind-the-scenes, self-appointed overlords (The Consortium) and their lower level minions have become so arrogant and brazen in their actions that only the most hopelessly asleep and hypnotized people remain ignorant and unaware of the challenges that we face as a species. I believe that this willful denial of that which is so in our faces stems from a deep, existential malaise born out of an inability or unwillingness to face one's own inner fears and anxieties, an absolute dread of facing one's own darker emotions and repressed, inner trauma. Of course, this is understandable; for we are a deeply traumatized species.

When a person refuses to embrace these things within themselves, i.e. the things about themselves that they do not like or their deepest inner fears, the result is what is known as "shadow projection." All those inner traumas left undealt with are projected out onto our relationships and collectively onto the world at large. Thus, the dysfunction we witness in our lives and in the world reflects to us that which needs healing *within!* Relationships without solid foundations and those that seek external fulfillment from another, are doomed to failure from the very start. So many get into relationships and look to their partners to fill a void that is within themselves. As long as someone looks outside for that which can only be found within, they will flounder from one dysfunctional relationship to the next and this is another area where we witness enormous breakdown in today's world.

What if we were to embrace this breakdown and see it as an opportunity to create something new? The old systems and ways are collapsing to present us with a blank slate with which to create anew. Instead of embracing these changes, most react in fear and absolute panic and again, one barely needs a pulse to witness this. Most people turn a blind eye out of crippling fear which is simply a symptom of refusing to face their own *inner* fear. Of course, this begins with the individual and with a deep examination of our own inner darkness.

We are taught from the moment we begin to learn and develop as children, that we should fear what we call the "darker" emotions rather than embrace them. I assert that this causes so many of the world's problems, so many difficulties within our own intimate relationships, and within our very psychological understanding about ourselves. Embracing the dark side rather than denying its existence brings rewards and true psychological and emotional liberation. The nature of these deconstructive energies is to facilitate the surfacing of these repressed emotions, whether we like it or not.

Since so many do not understand what is occurring and cannot or *will not* face their inner fears, repressed emotions and shadow self, they will run to the nearest "expert" to willingly receive their prescriptions for mind destroying psychotropic, SSRI drugs or tranquilizers. You cannot numb away the dark side of life or your own psyche, but that certainly doesn't stop people from trying. The shadow, as Jung termed it, is a part of our psyche and numbing the portion of the brain that these dangerous "medications" target, simply destroys the totality of a person's being. All aspects must be embraced if we are to facilitate true transformation within ourselves and thus the outer world. It begins within; the outer will never change until the *inner* world is transformed!

From my perspective, this is the most important thing to understand about the timeframe we are currently within. These deconstructive energies will affect people on the deepest levels, and we can clearly observe the breakdown occurring in those toxic and lost souls that refuse to face the surfacing of these darker emotions and deal with them accordingly.

This apocalyptic age not only heralds a lifting away of the curtain so to speak, but also brings to the forefront the most astounding and amazing discoveries, or *rediscoveries* if you will. We are in an age where we are going to discover our true origins, who we are and where we came from and it is going to be quite a shock for many people. Almost on a daily basis, I read about the most amazing discoveries in the fields of genetics, quantum physics, astronomy, archeology, anthropology, and on and on the list goes.

This time signifies the end of an age. I believe that it may very well be the end of the world *as we have known it*. To me, the utter collapse of civilization is in plain view all around us.

Many seem to be expecting some great leap in human consciousness and I do not doubt for a moment that this time can absolutely facilitate a shift in consciousness; however, I don't

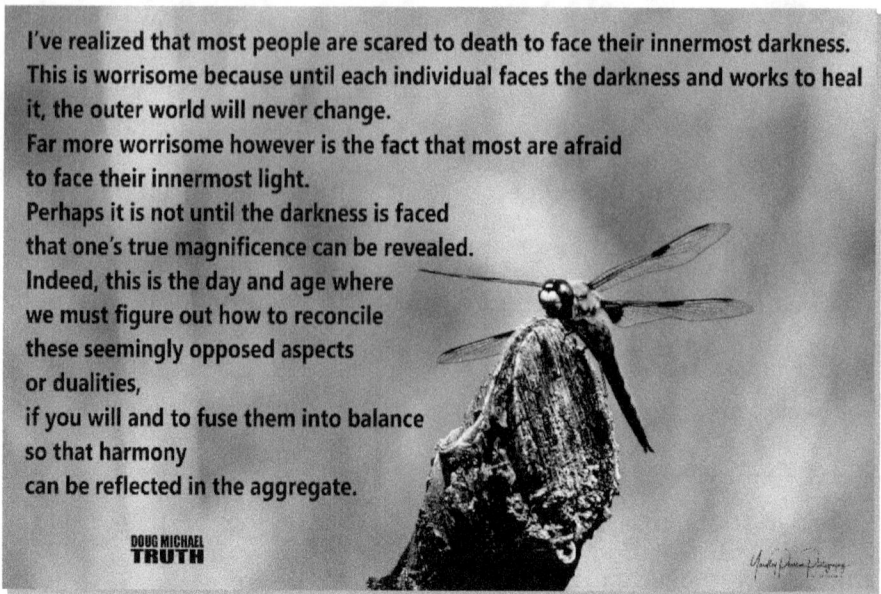

I've realized that most people are scared to death to face their innermost darkness. This is worrisome because until each individual faces the darkness and works to heal it, the outer world will never change.

Far more worrisome however is the fact that most are afraid to face their innermost light.

Perhaps it is not until the darkness is faced that one's true magnificence can be revealed.

Indeed, this is the day and age where we must figure out how to reconcile these seemingly opposed aspects or dualities, if you will and to fuse them into balance so that harmony can be reflected in the aggregate.

DOUG MICHAEL
TRUTH

believe it's going to just happen without considerable effort on the part of the individual and this means courageously facing inner fears and embracing the darker aspects of our psyches. I just can't buy into the idea that simply chanting, meditating and ignoring the immense challenges that we face, both inner and outer, is going to cut it. There are many that speak of this leap of consciousness but ignore all the "negative" things that we face. Where is the balance in that? From my perspective, those that simply turn a blind eye to what is perceived as negative are simply not balanced.

We must see reality in this world as it is, not as we wish it to be. That doesn't mean not focusing on the world we prefer to experience or contemplating solutions to these immense crises and challenges that we face; however, I feel that we must do this from a balanced perspective and that means facing all the darkness and all the negativity, as well as acknowledging the beauty and coming into the realization of our true interconnectedness to nature and to one another.

We are beings of enormous potential, if only we could challenge our own conditioning and reevaluate what it is that we believe about ourselves. If we could find the courage to deconstruct ourselves and tap into that vast potential, who knows what we may create? A person cannot face their innermost light, until they have faced their innermost darkness!

Humanity has been so conditioned to reject the so-called negative aspects of ourselves when in fact, they can be our greatest teachers. To attempt to medicate away the darker aspect of the self, as so many do, is to literally destroy the totality of the psyche. One cannot medicate away the darker aspects of the self and expect to ever be a whole and complete being.

This age that is upon us is bringing to the surface all that has remained hidden, both inner and outer, and the massively increasing energies seem to be too much to handle for those that refuse to embrace their inner fears and darker emotions. So many willingly embrace self-destruction, rather than looking within to where the true solutions lie. I would suggest, that in these times, refusing to willingly embrace the fears and repressed memories that are surfacing, will cause those who stubbornly refuse to do so to be dragged through the dark depths of their own subconscious to the point of literal, psychological and emotional breakdown. Again, we can plainly see this occurring all around us.

We stand at the precipice of the merging of silicon and carbon; the infusion of man and machine. This is known as the transhumanist movement, and the dark elites that operate from behind the thrones of power seek to create a race of literal automatons who will be in love with their slavery. The technology has increased so rapidly, that so few are even remotely aware as to how much it has advanced and the imminent threat that humanity faces as a result. A massive, technetronic control grid structure has been erected all around us, and so many remain completely oblivious to it.

The dark rulers, the hidden forces that operate behind the thrones of power in this world, the "Consortium" as I call it, are dangerously close to realizing their anti-human agenda of reducing humanity to the state of literal, robotic, soulless, walking dead androids. The servants of evil are very close to birthing a post-human dystopia. We stand at the crossroads, and each person's unwillingness to face this grim reality will seal the fate of their own extinction, but it doesn't have to be this way. If only the individual took the necessary steps to become self-actualized, to stand within the light of their truest potential and magnificence, to dismantle the cognitive fortresses that hold the ego captive, then perhaps we may create that which we prefer to experience. Sadly, when surveying the situation that surrounds us, it seems very far off, when in actuality, it is only a change of mind and a change of *heart* away.

The Consortium relentlessly and mercilessly guides humanity

along their devolutionary path into a mechanized, technetronic world completely devoid of any shred of humanity. We can plainly witness their efforts with the complete dehumanization through the psychological and emotional manipulation of humanity and the absolute disconnect that flourishes all around us. The next stage in their agenda is about to be realized if humanity refuses the enormous opportunity that it is faced with.

The mutation of humanity both on a psychological and biological level has been underway for a long time. Genetically modified foods, vaccines, fluoride in the water, aerosol concoctions sprayed from aircraft, massive pollutants and toxins in the environment, pharmaceutical drugs and so much more are methodically and specifically used to alter the DNA of human beings and to create an environment in which human beings must be merged with technology simply in order to survive the harsh conditions being created. Humanity and the ecosystems of the entire planet are being reengineered.

It has taken me a long time and many years of full-time research to arrive at the conclusion that the force that is behind this is not in any way human. We need not think of it in terms of extraterrestrial life forms; although, it may very well be. It is a consciousness that is simply alien to everything that it means to be human. It is too intelligent, too ancient, too organized and too inhumane to even remotely be considered human in any way. The elite, behind-the-scenes rulers and their willing, sycophantic servants believe themselves to be progenies of this alien force or "descendants of the gods," if you like. Whether or not that is true is irrelevant, *they* believe it, and one thing is certain, the self-appointed rulers of planet Earth operate from a level of consciousness that is so far removed from what it truly means to be human.

The actual rulers of this realm are psychotic in every sense of the word and they are working night and day to contort the Earth into a twisted expression that resonates with their low, vibratory frequency. Their contempt for nature and her creatures is appalling. Their plans to merge humanity with technology to create the posthuman era and reduce human beings to nothing more than machines is disturbing to say the least. The transhuman agenda is openly embraced by many in academia and those in the material sciences that have no sense whatsoever of the spiritual side of life. They are reductionists that already see human beings as nothing more than machines to be dominated and controlled. They view life in the Earth Game as bacteria on a petri dish.

I personally believe that the Earth is going to have something to say about this desecration at the hands of those not of this Earth and that she has already begun to awaken, and that very soon we are going to witness unprecedented changes in the form of earthquakes, tectonic shifts, magnetic reversals of the poles, volcanic eruptions, mass extinction events and much more, and that these events will increase as the days go by. Indeed, we have already witnessed these unprecedented changes and they will most assuredly continue to amplify.

It is my view that human beings need to actively participate in their own conscious evolution in an organic and pure way. The transhumanists believe that it is our destiny to merge the human vehicle with technology in an unnatural and completely inorganic manner. Creating and implementing this "super intelligence" into our world would be the final eradication of the very things that make us human, and that is the goal of these sick and deranged fuckers. We have been conditioned to accept this ever-encroaching reality and the primary means have been through the contortion and manipulation of human consciousness. We have been trained to accept this false reality, lock, stock and barrel for our entire lives through the predictive programming of television, the media and the motion picture industry.

Most people already operate on the level of a programmable robot, completely obedient and docile, and absolutely brainwashed into a subservient state of total unawareness, disconnection and detachment, and they've been trained to serve only material pursuits. Vast numbers of people seem to identify with the most anti-human paradigms and cultural memes imaginable and yet they believe themselves to be free and thinking independently. I contend that:

"If you are well adjusted to the sick and depraved lunatic asylum that we courageously and laughingly call culture, then you may be suffering from severe mental health problems. As the moments go by it seems the more that the insanity is on full display

11

for all to see, at least for those who have lifted their consciousness from the muck and the mire and aren't afraid to face it. Although there appears to be a stirring within the mass consciousness, I think that it's an appallingly few that can really put the pieces together and push forward in their perceptual and conscious advancement within this cacophony of bullshit."

Identifying with this dysfunctional and insane world and believing it to even remotely contain any semblance of normalcy, is in my view completely insane and yet, if you are an observer who points out the madness, well then, *you* are the insane one! I've been called a lunatic and nutcase so many times, and every time I thank the universe that I do not identify with these dysfunctional paradigms or those that are so quick to label others a lunatic for simply having a different perspective.

We are conditioned into conformity to the stifling system of enslavement, in which all individuality is shunned and mercilessly attacked from all angles. It is the outsider that is the truly sane person in this insane world; it is the one who does not identify with the masses, the dysfunction or the paradigms of control. It is my perspective that the energies that are coalescing now offer us all the opportunity to create ourselves anew, to stand as one and yet to stand as individuals in true selfhood. It is a grand paradox: individuality within oneness, or *wholeness* if you will. We are all connected as we indeed come from the same source; however, there is no energy signature, no perspective, no vibrational frequency that is quite like you. You are unique. We are bombarded from all angles with systems, ideologies, beliefs, memes, cultural paradigms, traditions, and a whole host of other things that seek to collectivize and make us all the same. Perhaps this time signifies the turning point in which we choose whether to stand in our own magnificence and uniqueness or be assimilated into a Borg type mishmash of collectivized *false* oneness?

Many that maintain "new age" beliefs talk about oneness but so few mention selfhood. The collectivized, one world order, hive mind mentality so promulgated in today's world is a warped version of the true sense of interconnectedness so desperately needed, and which is being built upon the ashes of true selfhood and upon the remnants of a dying world. Remember the paradox: *individuality within oneness.*

Have you noticed how the outsider children are at once drugged into complacency and compliance for simply not fitting into the systems of dysfunction? Do you observe how many parents simply go along with it on the say so of some "expert?" Make them like the rest of us! Stifle that kid! We can't have them thinking for themselves and being unique! Then they'll all want to do it! Individuality and uniqueness are the greatest threat to the system.

In my view, it is very important in this age to define our own uniqueness and yet also realize our interconnectedness to each other and to nature. So many have become so helplessly disconnected even from their own sense of self that they will rush into any distraction they can, whether it be mind-altering pharmaceuticals, booze, social mores, hyper overinvolvement in the lives of others and their dramas, false and highly dysfunctional relationships, or the obsession with fashion or with pop culture.

There are endless distractions to fall into for those who are lost and divorced from their own true sense of selfhood and uniqueness. The entire cultural paradigm is designed to do just that, to distract, to separate, and to fuel the fires of fear. The dark rulers work feverishly to maintain the illusion of separation and to create fear and we are encouraged to no end to fear our so-called darker emotions which can ultimately act as our greatest allies.

Humanity is attacked on every level but primarily it is an all-out assault upon human consciousness and that point cannot be stressed enough. I believe that this is the age where we must consciously decide to facilitate our own upliftment, our own evolution, our own leap in consciousness and that if humanity stubbornly refuses this great opportunity, that life as we have known it will cease to be, as we march into a post-human, dystopian, technetronic nightmare.

The gathering energies that are so apparent now can absolutely help to facilitate the changes we need to embrace in order to achieve this shift; however, it must be stressed that this is to be done on an individual level. I have stressed this point time and again and this also cannot be overstated. The decision must be made within the individual heart, mind and spirit and no one can do it for you. In my view, the whole collectivized mindset must be cast aside. This does not mean that we don't reconnect, and support and love one another as each goes through the process; it simply means that the choice lies *within* you!

One can never hope to affect any change in their personal lives or in the wider world without first affecting change within their own being. The outer reflects the inner, so all change begins within! We can either create a new paradigm that works in balance with nature and begin with ourselves or allow the dark Consortium to continue to manipulate the course of human affairs into *their* vision of a new paradigm which will in no way reflect anything in accordance with what it means to be or experience as human beings. The dark, hidden masters have been guiding the course of human history according to their vision and we have finally arrived at the time where the opportunity has presented itself to put an end to their plans once and for all. It is time to face our innermost fears and the gathering energies can assist in this if the individual is willing to embrace the darker aspects of their own self and deal with the repression. The very nature of these facilitating energies is to bring the repression to the surface to be dealt with and it will not be easy, but to resist this change will only bring more needless suffering.

There are countless examples of how the planet is being literally destroyed right before our eyes and the time to become aware has run out. I'm of the mindset that if by now, a person is unaware of these immense challenges, it is because either they choose to remain ignorant or they are simply not meant to know.

For those that can face the challenges and not be crippled by fear, get ready and stay centered, because what is about to occur across this planet will shake it to its core!

I believe that this age signifies a gathering of energies if you will. Hold close to those in your circle that you resonate with, for like attracts like and we are going to need to lean upon each other very soon. Let the false relationships fall away and let those of incompatible energies go with those of like energies. Many will fall in the days ahead and I don't believe that it's the job of those who are consciously moving ahead to try and hold up those who are falling. Perhaps to fall is just what they need to facilitate their advancement? I choose to stay close to those who are moving in a similar direction while always remembering that this is my own, personal journey. No one can walk the road for you, but we certainly can support one another as we create ourselves anew.

Celebrate uniqueness! Gather with those of like mind that are also redefining themselves and support them! Above all, fear no evil, because you are about to come face to face with it! In fact, it is the dark ones who are truly in fear. The age we are in has them trembling. They are the most disconnected and the most lost within ego consciousness. Their arrogance has them blinded. Evil harbors within it the very imbalance that will ensure its own destruction. From my perspective, it is very important to look within and to know where you stand, and to hold close to those who stand there with you.

No longer can the blame be cast outside of ourselves. We have

LIKE ENERGY ATTRACTS LIKE ENERGY
AND THOUGHT THINKS AND CREATES.

IF ONE'S BELIEF ABOUT THEMSELVES
IS THAT THEY ARE A POWERLESS VICTIM
THEN THAT IS THE EXPERIENCE
THEY WILL ATTRACT AS WELL
AS VICTIMIZERS TO FULFILL
THAT IDEA THAT THEY HOLD ONTO.

THEY WILL ALSO BE SURROUNDED BY FELLOW VICTIMS.

WHEN BILLIONS OF PEOPLE ARE LOCKED
WITHIN THE LIMITING COGNITIVE FORTRESS OF THE VICTIM,
WHAT KIND OF EXPERIENCE WILL THAT MANIFEST?
HOW COULD THE OUTER WORLD EVER CHANGE?
IT CAN'T!

NOT UNTIL SUCH A TIME AS HUMANITY DECIDES
TO RISE ABOVE THE NARROW CONFINES
AND THE STIFLING VICTIMHOOD MENTALITY,
CAN WE EVER HOPE TO REALIZE OUR FULLEST POTENTIAL
AND STAND FORTH WITHIN A GREATER EXPERIENCE,
NOT ONLY OF WHO WE ARE,
BUT WITHIN A WORLD THAT REFLECTS THAT.

DOUG MICHAEL
TRUTH

allowed evil to flourish by our own failure to acknowledge that which moves all around us. Granted, there is an outside, manipulating force that has worked through human consciousness for many millennia; however, we have willingly bought into all of the lies and only each individual can correct it through a conscious shift of their own attitudes, beliefs and conscious awareness and this begins by looking *within*. The energetic changes can absolutely assist in that process, but it must be embraced willingly. Again, those that refuse this opportunity will suffer grave trauma, and they will fall. Let them!

I think that it's important for those who are consciously choosing to recreate themselves, to stop looking to the outer world to give them meaning and instead, to begin bringing *your own* meaning to the world. So many of us run around frantically, looking for that next big fix, pursuing outer stimuli, but I truly feel that the significance of this age is an urging to embark on an inner journey. We are encouraged for our entire lives to seek outside of ourselves and to ensnare ourselves and each other within the very traps provided by the cultural engineers to further divide ourselves *from* ourselves and also from one another. In my view, a complete detachment from all that is false and a conscious turning within is the only way to begin to facilitate the shift in consciousness that so many have spoken of regarding this age of apocalypse that we are now immersed within.

True anxiety arises within an individual who is living a lie, one who is not living true to *oneself*. So many seek the approval of others and when they don't get it, a deep discomfort is felt which can serve as a warning sign that the individual is not in accordance with their true purpose. Instead of examining the true cause of their suffering, so many instead turn to escapism or simply give away more of themselves to try to gain that approval. Very few seem to be even remotely aware of that understanding. We are taught to be "selfless," that being selfless is some holy, virtuous ideal. I would suggest that it is the selfless one who will be in the most trouble in the not too distant future.

Operating within selfhood does not mean that one is selfish. In fact, it is the narcissistic, selfish person who is perhaps the most disconnected from their true sense of self. Remember that we exist within a control structure that has been built upon the bones and the ashes of individualism and true selfhood. A person in true selfhood knows who they are and acts with true compassion. They also know and set their boundaries and never become the martyr or the victim of those selfless ones who are disconnected from their source and their center.

The selfless one never seems to be able to say no and so often becomes the doormat for others who are also divorced from their own sense of self. They become the victims of others needs at the expense of their own needs and we have been taught that this is somehow virtuous.

I think that one of the prime lessons of this age is the return to selfhood and authenticity. So many seem to be living false lives, caught up in roles, and living to please others while seeking their approval. They are lost and looking outside for that which can only be found within. Then, when the anxiety arises, they run to the nearest expert to try to fix them, and they try to medicate away the anxiety which is simply trying to warn them that the temple is collapsing. **You** *are* the temple! The only god that should ever be sought is the true self, which is GOD, and which is not separate or apart from you. Haven't the greatest teachers always tried to impart to us that the kingdom of heaven is within? The following passage is from a profound work titled *Becoming*:

"God is not a focus of personality, individual thought processes or a benevolent creator separate from you. God is the combination of the focus of all Its parts coalesced into the

19

composite of all. Each awareness is blocked from being a part of that composite until each realizes that it is a part of this composite. Being told that it is, means nothing at all. It is the realization that one's self is a viable part of that composite that encompasses the totality of the being, that is what 'becoming' is all about.

One must become that reality and realize it is a viable aspect of the totality of God and that its input to that reality is the truth of who they are. It is not a mental realization, but one that registers total agreement within the mental, emotional, physical and spiritual levels of the total self. In other words, the spiritual aspect that focuses each into manifested reality finally gets the message through to the rest of its focus that is walking around in the body. The body must register this understanding through the totality of its brain-nervous system resulting in what is called a realization that then registers as a sudden feeling sensation accompanied by an all-encompassing understanding. It allows for a total change in perception with regard to the self and how this self fits into the composite picture of experience. This results in a change in the perception of 'God'' which suddenly allows for an understanding that 'God' equates to cosmic/galactic citizenship rather than a father/child relationship. It is a shift from 'being or experiencing as powerless' to the awesome responsibility of being a contributing portion to the totality of what constitutes 'God', or the creative energy of potentiality being focused into experience in order that it can be defined and understood."[1]

I believe that this age can signify and act as a catalyst for the return to this understanding but only for those who are ready and willing to make the conscious choice to divorce themselves from all the nonsense, to challenge one's own beliefs and to willingly turn within fearlessly.

There is no such thing as some mystical day or event that will magically awaken people and bring automatic transcendence. If you're waiting for that to happen and you have not embraced the repression within and the shadow side of your own personality, well good luck with that. Self-examination of your own dark, inner psychic content is not an easy task to be sure, but it is highly rewarding. It brings liberation and opens the door to the temple within where the answers you seek truly lie.

Look around at all the dysfunction, the malaise and the sickness of the outer world and then realize that it is a direct reflection of a bruised, imbalanced, toxic, and disconnected, collective consciousness. So many are not even willing to accept that the world is wall to wall filled up with imbalance, horror, evil, greed, and just plain insanity. I believe that this directly reflects a stubborn refusal to look within. Most cannot even get that far as they seek their next fix of idiotic, political theater, some new TV show, or whatever nonsensical bullshit they seek to distract themselves with while the world falls dead all around them. The only way to affect positive change in the world or in your relationships is to first cultivate that positive change within yourself! The temple is haunted and in disrepair and one can only exorcise and repair the temple oneself; no one else can do it for you! So, while you turn to the outer, to the priest or psychologist, the guru or the minister to fix you or give you the answer, you will forever be lost and divided within. It is time to become your own shaman, your own teacher, your own guru, your own leader! But how? No one can tell you. You already know the answer; it lies within you! How could it be considered selfhood if someone else tells you how to do it?

I feel very deeply that this age brings a deep, inner calling for the return to selfhood. I feel that those firmly rooted in their center have absolutely nothing to fear and although the ride may get a bit bumpy and at times be uncomfortable, that this age and the shifting energies will bring healing, transformation, creation, balance and cleansing. There is simply no more time left to wait for someone else to do it for us. There will be no rescue from benevolent ETs, no intervening savior god, no magical ascension. One thing is certain, things simply cannot go on as they are if humanity is to have any future at all on this planet. Each individual must stand within the light of their own magnificence and their true selfhood and consciously choose to create the future that they prefer to experience. Leaving this choice up to the dark ones will only ensure humanity's downward spiral into oblivion. It really does begin with you. We must each, within our own individual power, stand together in unity, peace compassion and love, and vanquish this dark consciousness from our home once and for all. Failure to do so would create a literal hell on Earth and would certainly not be a place in which I would wish to live.

We are at the crossroads. We have arrived. We can choose to create a new paradigm for human experience and expression or allow the dark Consortium to continue in their plan to create a mechanized, dystopian hell on Earth. The feeling that one is small, insignificant or powerless in the face of this great challenge is nothing more than false ego illusion. Where do you stand? Let us rise together and once and for all get this right. Failure to take advantage of this opportunity will result in the destruction of everything that it means to be human. Which will it be? Rise or fall?

TWO

Distraction-Deception-Division

At every turn in this wasteland of what we call culture, or society, humanity is distracted, deceived and divided. This is how the controllers, the dark manipulators, your unseen and unacknowledged masters guide your life, your very reality, and remain undetected while the majority continue to exist unaware and blissfully content within their own enslavement. I understand that this may sound harsh but that is exactly what is occurring and exactly how it is whether we like it or not.

For this situation to continue unabated as it has for so long, the seeds of division have had to be sown and cultivated over and again, generation after generation. The illusion of separation has had to be promulgated and reinforced constantly as over and again, humanity has been manipulated into hating and killing one another, destroying each other from time immemorial, so that the ones manipulating this situation can continue to plunder and steal from them what is theirs by their very birthright. It's more of the

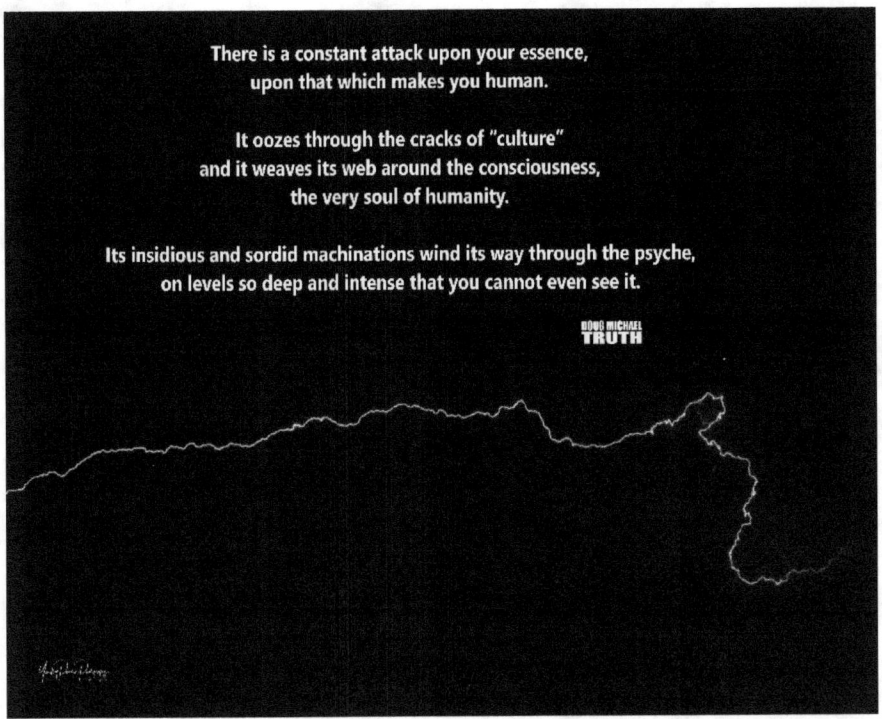

There is a constant attack upon your essence,
upon that which makes you human.

It oozes through the cracks of "culture"
and it weaves its web around the consciousness,
the very soul of humanity.

Its insidious and sordid machinations wind its way through the psyche,
on levels so deep and intense that you cannot even see it.

DOUG MICHAEL
TRUTH

same old same old and human beings just seem to keep doing more of what has never worked and what never will.

Here we stand amidst enormous change, on the cusp of a massive transformation, that is, if we *choose* to claim the golden ring. The saddest thing is that here we are and yet so many will simply bow and acquiesce, kneel and conform, and simply go along to get along within their cognitive, emotional and spiritual prison cells, forever estranged from their own potential and spark of creativity that has been stolen from us since we were children. You must understand that what you are, your very spark, your very self, your *essence* is under attack from the moment that you are born into this world, this twisted insane asylum of the surreal. Can you see it? Do you even want to? I can't blame you if you don't; however, turning a blind eye and embracing the denial that you were coerced into accepting is your very downfall.

We are distracted in numerous ways, particularly today with the massive proliferation of technology and the advent of social media. The rapid increase in advanced technology seems to have placed a lid on human consciousness for the average person, rather than being utilized as a tool for expansion. It's become an escape into the virtual non-reality and antisocial media has become a pulpit and a platform for the mundane and it is also a major tool for data mining and psychological profiling.

I'm not against technology, not at all, but what I am critiquing here is the way in which it is used as a distraction as opposed to being used as a tool for gathering information, increasing knowledge and manifesting creativity. Of course, many people do use it in this way, but the vast majority it seems, simply use these tools to unplug from life and plug into the virtual nonreality matrix. Tablets and smart phones are given to toddlers, even infants, to distract them and plug them into the virtual world before they have even really begun to develop. People sit across from one another in restaurants and don't even talk to each other; they sit glued to their smart phones and have forgotten how to interact.

Social media is used as a platform for people to share their dirty laundry with the world or to cry for attention. People seem to live their lives through the phony virtual world and present a fake image in the quest for approval from others that are doing the same thing. It's an amazing thing to observe. I've seen on more than one occasion, single mothers with multiple kids from multiple fathers that love to advertise on social networking just how much they love their kids and what great mothers they are when in real life, they are anything but what they advertise themselves to be on Facebook, the ghetto of the internet. They present an image that isn't real and prop up their ego on a digital pedestal to gain the approval of their virtual friends or, digital acquaintances if you like.

The overall collective consciousness has been dumbed down so comprehensively that it defies belief. Facebook has become a great way to observe how infantilized the average mind has become. It's astounding! The number of grown adults that display the mentality of a cognitively arrested child is unbelievable. People seem to have no problem sharing their intimate, personal details on public platforms such as Twitter or Facebook and show not even the slightest concern about being completely monitored. Intrusions into their personal lives do not bother them in the slightest, and they have no problem airing their dirty laundry to the world and engaging within their silly, cyber drama. A very childlike mentality has gripped the mass consciousness and it's been all according to a specific strategy that's been wildly successful. This is what happens when people refuse to educate themselves and instead use the tools available simply for distraction and entertainment, trained like the obedient, Pavlovian dogs that they've become.

The fact that Facebook has recently come under fire for its widespread theft of data and privacy violations doesn't seem to be a concern for very many people at all. In fact, so many willingly give up their personal information and have no care or concern that they are being spied upon and psychologically profiled. This is the downside to technology, the vast and pervasive surveillance network that has been erected all around us. It has advanced tremendously, and so few even realize how far the technology has expanded.

What really gets me is that many people seem to have the attitude that if they have nothing to hide then it's perfectly OK to be watched and have their privacy violated. This is the mentality of a willing slave and unfortunately, it's pervasive and ubiquitous. People are tracked by their smart phones, surveilled everywhere they go, spied upon by their smart TVs, have their every keystroke and searches recorded and monitored by Google, and seem to have absolutely no problem with it. People have been so cognitively arrested and dumbed down and the high-tech world that has emerged has played a major role in this. It seems that so few even see this or would even bother to be the least bit concerned about it. It's Orwell's 1984 on steroids!

The public pays no mind to the destruction of their freedom as the spy machine expands and intrudes into their personal lives. They willingly give their personal information to data-mining social media platforms that resemble a CIA dossier. They are monitored and psychologically profiled in ways that they cannot even imagine while censorship increases dramatically in the politically correct landscape. The manufactured, perceptual illusions keep the consciousness in lockdown as the population spirals downward into oblivion without complaint.

Video games are another major distraction. Now, I'm not knocking video games or gamers, but again, it has become such a detachment for so many people. Games have become very realistic and graphic and even very young ones immerse themselves in games that are extremely violent, and many parents seem to have no problem with this at all. In 2017, I was at a party where there were adults and young children in attendance. There were a few kids gathered around a TV playing a video game called *Friday the 13th*, in which, the object of the game is to hunt people down and murder them in sadistic ways. The oldest kid couldn't have been more than ten-years-old, and they were having a ball hacking and slashing the characters in this very adult-themed video game. You cannot convince me for one second that these graphic games do not have an influence on a young mind; they desensitize. One of the adults turned to me and said: "no wonder kids these days are going crazy and killing." He may have been onto something.

I've suggested for many years that we are living within a modern-day version of Ancient Rome, just prior to its collapse. We have an American empire that is in a constant, perpetual state of war, just as Rome was prior to its fall. Also, the middle class is diminishing at an alarming rate, just as it did in Rome and there are many other parallels. The very few get obscenely wealthy at the expense of the many. It's the same tired old story, as history repeats itself, over and again.

One very major distraction is sports. The sports junkies can sit around and talk all kinds of statistics and display amazing knowledge of their teams but seem to lack even basic knowledge and understanding of current events or even very recent history. They're not stupid, it's just that their intelligence is applied in ways that are well, irrelevant. If you can name all the players on your favorite team, spew out statistics or recite figures and data but don't know who won the Civil War, you just may be cognitively distracted. Again, there's nothing wrong with being a sports fan and being involved with it but when it remains at the forefront of your consciousness, to the exclusion of things that truly matter, it definitely diminishes your understanding of what the hell is going on all around you but then again, so few actually care anyway, and that is the truly sad thing.

To point out a completely mindless display of idiocy: in February 2018, the Philadelphia Eagles won their first Superbowl in their history. For my readers that may not be familiar with American football, the Superbowl is the biggest game of the year. It's huge and many people consider it to be a national holiday. Anyway, the Eagles won their very first bowl that year, and in celebration of the victory, fans took to the streets and rioted, vandalizing and destroying property in their own city. What if the Eagles had lost? They just may have burned the city to the ground. It was an open display of mindlessness at its worst. What will people like that do if there is some sort of national emergency and the grocery stores run out of food? Think about that for a minute.

One of the greatest distractions and deceivers in today's world is the television, especially when taking the media into consideration. The media is nothing more than the propaganda, spin machine for the ruling oligarchs and all mainstream media in the US is owned by only six mega conglomerate corporations. It's important to understand that essentially, it's only really *one* corporation. The fact that corporate news shapes and influences the opinions of so many people certainly explains why so many remain so woefully misinformed and ignorant of history.

As has been pointed out on many occasions, media ownership in the US is consolidated into very few hands. All the major media outlets will have representatives within organizations such as the Bilderberg organization, the Council on Foreign Relations and other enclaves of decision-making power. Their agents occupy positions in think tank groups such as Tavistock and many other powerful organizations. The media is the propaganda machine for this Consortium network and its purpose is to literally shape reality for droves of people through the manipulation of consciousness and it has been extremely effective for decades. The six main media outlets in the US are:

Time Warner: The world's largest media conglomerate, its holdings include CNN, Warner Bros. Pictures, AOL, *Time Magazine,* HBO and many others. Time Warner's revenue in

2017 was *$41.8 billion*. Time Warner recently merged with a company called Spectrum and its parent company is Charter Communications.[1]

General Electric: G.E. owns major networks such as NBC and owns Universal Pictures. Its revenues for 2017 were *$120 billion*.[2]

Disney: The Walt Disney Company generated *$59 billion* in revenues in 2018. Its holdings include ABC, ESPN, Touchstone, Mirimax, Pixar, and many others. It owns radio stations, theme parks and several publishing companies.[3]

CBS: CBS owns 30 television stations, 130 radio stations, Showtime, Simon and Schuster Publishing and many other holdings. CBS revenues in 2017 were *$13.4 billion*.[4]

Viacom: With 2017 revenues of over *$13 billion*, this corporation's holdings include Paramount Pictures, MTV, Nickelodeon and many others.[5]

NewsCorp.: This conglomerate owns Fox broadcasting, The Wall Street Journal, The New York Post, Harper Collins Publishing, and 20th Century Fox among many other holdings, and generated revenues of *$9.2 billion* in 2009.[6]

Since the mass majority of those in the more technologically advanced cultures rely so much on television to dictate to them world events or a specific version of reality, it is certainly no wonder that so many remain so oblivious to what is actually happening in the world or to ideas that lie outside of the tiny, narrow perspective that television and its sorcerers and media manipulators present. Many people's entire worldview is shaped by the faux reality that TV perpetuates. Television has become a massive instrument for corporate advertising, influence of public opinion and for complete manipulation of the consensus reality. In order for the Consortium to successfully steer the consciousness and shape public opinion, information must be controlled and regulated very tightly. All platforms of information, and that certainly includes, Google, Youtube and Facebook are completely regulated and monitored.

Psychological conditioning of the perceptions begins in school and follows us throughout our lives. Edward Bernays, dubbed the "father of public relations," was the nephew of Sigmund Freud. He was a member of the very influential Tavistock Institute and specialized in what is called crowd psychology. A basic idea of crowd psychology is as follows:

"Crowd psychology, also known as mob psychology, is a branch of social psychology. Social psychologists have developed several theories for explaining the ways in which the psychology of a crowd differs from and interacts with that of the individuals

within it. Major theorists in crowd psychology include Gustave Le Bon, Gabriel Tarde, Sigmund Freud, and Steve Reicher. This field relates to the behaviors and thought processes of both the individual crowd members and the crowd as an entity. Crowd behavior is heavily influenced by the loss of responsibility of the individual and the impression of universality of behavior, both of which increase with crowd size."[7]

The *Tavistock Institute* is a major think-tank organization based in Britain, which was involved with psychological warfare during WW II. It was a creation of the influential Fabian Society. Its purpose was to infiltrate the collective consciousness to effectively shape and influence public opinion through propaganda and downright brainwashing and it has been enormously successful. Edward Bernays was one of the major affiliates of Tavistock. Sometimes we can get a glimmer of truth right from the horse's mouth. Bernays stated:

"The conscious and intelligent manipulation of the organized habits and opinions of the masses is an important element in democratic society. Those who manipulate this unseen mechanism of society constitute an invisible government which is the true ruling power of our country. We are governed, our minds are molded, our tastes formed, our ideas suggested, largely by men we have never heard of. This is a logical result of the way in which our democratic society is organized. Vast numbers of human

beings must cooperate in this manner if they are to live together as a smoothly functioning society. Our invisible governors are, in many cases, unaware of the identity of their fellow members in the inner cabinet."[8]

Bernays was an expert in propaganda and his methods of crowd psychology have been employed on a massive scale. The term propaganda was abandoned in favor of the term "public relations," to soften the language in typical, euphemistic fashion that we can clearly witness occurring all over society today. Bernays was telling the truth when he said:

"In almost every act of our lives, whether in the sphere of politics or business, in our social conduct or our ethical thinking, we are dominated by the relatively small number of persons who understand the mental processes and social patterns of the masses. It is they who pull the wires that control the public mind, who harness old social forces and contrive new ways to bind and guide the world."[9]

And further:

"If we understand the mechanism and motives of the group mind, it is now possible to control and regiment the masses according to our will without them knowing it."

Just take an honest look at the world all around you in this day and age. Humanity's perceptions are manipulated on such a massive scale that most live within a cognitive prison and never notice it. It truly is a simulacrum, that is to say, an artificial, superimposed, cognitive and perceptual facsimile, a pseudo reality if you will. The Fabians infiltrate cultures with propaganda and slowly and methodically, drip feed their poison into society. We clearly see this all around us in today's society with the transgender agenda, political correctness, the attacks on the language and of course through the media and television programming in general. The average American watches between four and five hours of TV every day! What may seem harmless has been weaponized as a tool for psychological manipulation and it has been extremely effective.

Many will seek all manner of stimuli or escapism including simply indulging in self-induced brainwashing by the number one hypnotizer of human consciousness, television. So many people's entire worldview is dictated and shaped by this medium and it isn't the medium itself that's the issue, it's the amount of pure, grade A, unadulterated shit that accounts for about 99.9% of broadcasting. Since so many people's entire reality is shaped by what they are indoctrinated with from TV, we can clearly observe the correlation between TV programming and the unbelievable level of unawareness present within the average minds of those that consume their daily dose of propaganda and mind-numbing banality.

I would suggest that TV is the ultimate distraction that exists in our culture and the fact that so many people's entire worldview is shaped by this medium is a very telling sign of how things have gotten the way they are. Most people's entire perspective is twisted into form by this most effective form of abject mind control. The mass majority are TV educated. This has been one of the most powerfully effective weapons of the dark Consortium network in their war upon human consciousness. Television is the one-eyed, flickering, high definition sorcerer that takes residence in virtually every home in the industrialized world. Just observe most of the content on television, especially advertising, and it becomes patently obvious that it is directed towards the lowest level of intelligence.

Very few people these days seem to have the desire to read anymore. The seductive technology has induced cognitive laziness and has caused a massive dumbing down of the average mind in society. And my goodness, do they love to display their arrested development all over social networking and advertise their foolishness with unapologetic zeal. It's sad and disturbing and it seems that the most ignorant are the loudest and the proudest. These days, it appears as if the majority wants their information delivered in 30-second sound bites or short video snippets. They don't want to have to think too much. When you read you need to take the time to process and absorb the information, to ponder and engage your brain but it's become an archaic chore for so many people. Alexa or Google will tell me all that I need to know and there's such little effort required. The Chinese philosopher Confucius was claimed to have said:

"No matter how busy you may think you are you must find time for reading or surrender yourself to self-chosen ignorance."

I love that quote because it is so true. Whether you like to read or not, it is the basis of how we learn in this world. Ask a physicist or a microbiologist how much reading was involved for them to get to where they are in their level of understanding; I can assure you; it was an awful lot!

According to official statistics, roughly 21% of Americans operate with only a fifth-grade level of reading and comprehension. Think about this for just a moment. Almost a quarter of the population, when it comes to understanding and comprehending the language, are basically operating with the mentality of a ten-year-old child! Just observe social media and witness the infantilized mindset of the average adult.

We are deceived from the very moment that we begin to learn and develop. Many are deceived by religious mythologies that are presented as literal, historical fact. Then, children get pushed through an educational system that from its very inception, was created as a propaganda machine, a robot factory if you will, to train people to become debtors and to shape their perceptual reality. The educational system is one of Fabian indoctrination and it was not infiltrated with Fabian Marxism, it was the very creation of these mind doctors. The early warnings in the beginning of the 20th century, that those responsible for the inception of public education were Communist sympathizers, particularly warnings given by the American Legion, of course fell upon deaf ears and now we have generations that have been effectively indoctrinated with Marxist propaganda. The results speak for themselves with the puke-inducing display of neo-liberal Marxists clamoring for their own enslavement.

The absolute mind doctoring, and brainwashing has taken on a whole new level of indoctrination in today's educational climate. College-aged young adults are provided with "safe spaces," comfort dogs and coloring books so that they don't get their precious little feelings hurt. A politically correct, gender neutral, completely pussified situation now exists on campuses across the country in this sickening display of childish nonsense. The politically correct garbage being spouted everywhere is nothing less than thought control. Since we think in terms of language, if you control the language, you control the mind. We are witnessing the absolute destruction of our youth and the fact that so many will turn a willfully ignorant, blind eye to this atrocity and instead remain more concerned about who won the basketball game, speaks volumes about where we are and where we are headed if the people either cannot or *refuse* to lift their consciousness out of this psychological tyranny. Rome is fallen!

What happens when the young men of a nation become distracted, confused and emasculated? You will get a nation of docile, non-critically thinking robots who will not stand up against tyranny and will instead embrace their own enslavement. Unfortunately, this endeavor of penetrating the culture with Fabian Marxism has been enormously successful. It's up to the individual to educate themselves and deprogram while they still can and I have to tell you, if that is what one desires, it will include a lot of reading, and the desire to read and expand one's knowledge base is something that the educational system has basically bred out of people. Sadly, far too many would rather remain as automatons, plugged into the virtual world of the plastic nonreality.

I suppose it's very difficult for people to come to terms with the fact that they've been manipulated and lied to for their entire lives, but there is a freedom in doing so, and then taking the necessary steps to deprogram oneself. It's not exactly easy but it is highly rewarding. The level of deception is so deeply ingrained within the mass consciousness that so many will never come to terms with it. Why bother anyway? The latest celebrity scandal is far more interesting than the realization that I've been screwed my whole life. It's difficult for an ego to admit that it's been tricked. "Not me!" "I'm too clever, you can't get one over on me!" The truth is that we've *all* been bamboozled and hoodwinked and the sooner an individual can come to terms with this, the better off they will be. If in their steadfast denial, they refuse to do so, then they will simply spiral downwards into cognitive oblivion that of course will lead eventually to physical ruin. Oh well, fuck it! The game is on dammit!

I think that what is necessary much of the time is to unplug from everything in the external circus carnival, silence the mind chatter and go deeply within. I feel that underneath all the layers of indoctrination and programming, the truth is there and that it's just a matter of clearing the debris to reveal it. That of course takes work, a strong willingness and unwavering intent. It's a difficult process of deconstruction but it is possible to achieve, and achieve it we must, if we are ever to transcend this lunatic asylum.

United we stand, divided we fall. Well, this nation has never been so divided and disunited. The manufactured divisions are numerous, thoroughly destructive and absolutely fucking childish. The unfortunate thing is that when the mindless buy into all this shit, it manifests in the outer world in horrific ways, hence all the violence and slaughter. Examine all this completely nonsensical racial division. People overidentify with the physical to the point that they will hate and kill someone because of the color of their skin. How absurd! The body is the least of what you truly are. Yeah well, tell that to someone embroiled within hatred and see how far you get. To me, thinking of someone as lesser because of their skin color is like hating someone because they painted their boat green and you hate the color green; it's stupidity in action! The physical body is simply a vessel for consciousness to experience this dense, third dimensional world but people want to hate and kill one another because your vessel is a different color than my vessel. Complete and total spiritual ignorance is on open display for all to see. One thing that this world is, currently, is a

41

smorgasbord of observation. I think that if those observational skills are really honed and developed, that perceptual growth for an individual can be rather immense in this day and age.

Then of course, there's all this political division, which is utter nonsense based upon complete illusions. I see these simpletons on social media arguing over which figurehead would better represent them, as if any damned one of them ever represents the people. Do they not notice that whichever one gets into power that the wars keep on occurring, the surveillance grid keeps expanding, freedom keeps diminishing while the middle class continues to be raped without mercy? No, they don't notice because the illusions that prop up their cognitive fortresses are too strong and too deeply solidified.

I don't know why it is so difficult for so many people to grasp that the political puppets are beholden to the lobbyists and the international banking network. It's not that difficult to understand and why am I considered a "conspiracy theorist" for simply pointing out the obvious? The only difference between the political figureheads are minor surface appearances and one herd will hurl abuse, even violence at times against the other herd as they are polarized and divided, and they are too brainwashed to see it. To keep the masses divided is crucial for the ruling elite so that it can maintain its power and advance its agenda while the people fight each other over which political ideology is better, meanwhile they are all controlled by the same force, the same invisible puppeteers.

What to me is plainly obvious seems impossible to grasp for

so many people and what awaits those who refuse to pull their consciousness out of these distractions is destruction and utter annihilation. *No one* gets into the CEO position of corporate America without enormous financial backing from the big money interests or the nod of approval of enclaves such as the Council on Foreign Relations or AIPAC (American Israeli Public Affairs Committee) the Zionist lobby in America. A CEO is always beholden to the shareholders and that means the financiers that back them. It's a scam, and droves of people keep falling for it, repeatedly, every four years. So, while the clueless bicker on social media over which puppet they believe better represents them, they remain divided and conquered as their nation sinks deeper into decadence, despair and ruin. But go ahead and vote because it will be different this time! Meanwhile, the wars and coups keep expanding and the people's taxation pays for it all, as the expansion of the surveillance network tightens its grip like a barbed-wire noose around the necks of the gullible. Isn't it so great to be free?

You'd be hard-pressed to find something that deceives and divides quite as comprehensively as religion. What a useful tool this has been in the hands of the controllers. Europe is exploding in a clash of civilizations right now with religion as the main underlying theme. My god is better than yours and so I'll kill you to make a point. Nonsensical, mythological and archaic nonsense divides people so thoroughly, and the blood and tears span the ages. It's amazing to me that in the 21st century, masses of people are still willing to kill and die over varying religious beliefs, which are nothing more than historicized mythologies. My book of fantasy and fairy tales is the correct one, yours is wrong! Now die infidel! Nothing has kept the human mind bound within cognitive chains as much as religion for a very long time, and I'm incredulous as to how this bullshit still ensnares the minds of so many after all these centuries.

Certain countries such as Saudi Arabia employ religious police forces to "defend the faith" and they do it brutally and violently with reckless intolerance; it's a theocratic dictatorship. Religion is perhaps the thing that human consciousness needs to transcend the most if we are ever to exist in a world without tyranny. People also need to stop bowing and kowtowing to pseudo spiritual leaders like the Jesuit, Marxist Pope or the Marxist Dali Lama, and instead trust their own inherent guidance and intelligence. People need to take their power back, that is, unless they choose to remain as slaves, oh wait, they do! I suppose you get what you deserve.

Religion is a scourge and a plague upon humanity and if human beings don't outgrow it, they can *never* be free. In this world, especially in the west, freedom is nothing but tyranny *disguised* as freedom; it's an illusion! So, while masses of people bow their heads and bend their knees to the external, invisible sky daddy, powerful forces hell-bent on destruction steal your future and enslave your children. Religion is an awesome tool for the controllers to regiment the herds and keep them at war with each other. Well, it's worked for centuries so why fix it if it isn't broken? It should be flushed down the toilet with all the other shit!

There are countless ways in which humans remain divided. Race, religion, political affiliation, where they live, how much money they make, sexuality and on and on the list goes. The thing to realize is that the divisions are manufactured deliberately to keep the herd divided and at war with each other. People cannot see past the prison bars of their own cognitive fortresses as their consciousness remains firmly rooted within perceptual illusions. When you reach a point of observation where you have divorced your consciousness from all this nonsense, you can see it for what it truly is, a sick joke. If it weren't so tragic it would be hysterical!

Look at how much this last American election has divided this country. Elections are irrelevant, they exist simply to convince people that they have a choice. They don't! Voting for carefully selected and vetted CFR and AIPAC figureheads is no choice at all. This entire charade is scripted theater and I have never seen so much division over a meaningless election in my entire life. Did you see the film clips of grown adults brought to tears crying over Clinton's loss? If that is not a display of complete and abject ignorance, then I don't know what is. I would suggest that:

"You have to wonder what goes on within the psyche of a person that can look up to a completely amoral, corrupt, mass murdering psychopath and see them as a virtuous and honorable human being."

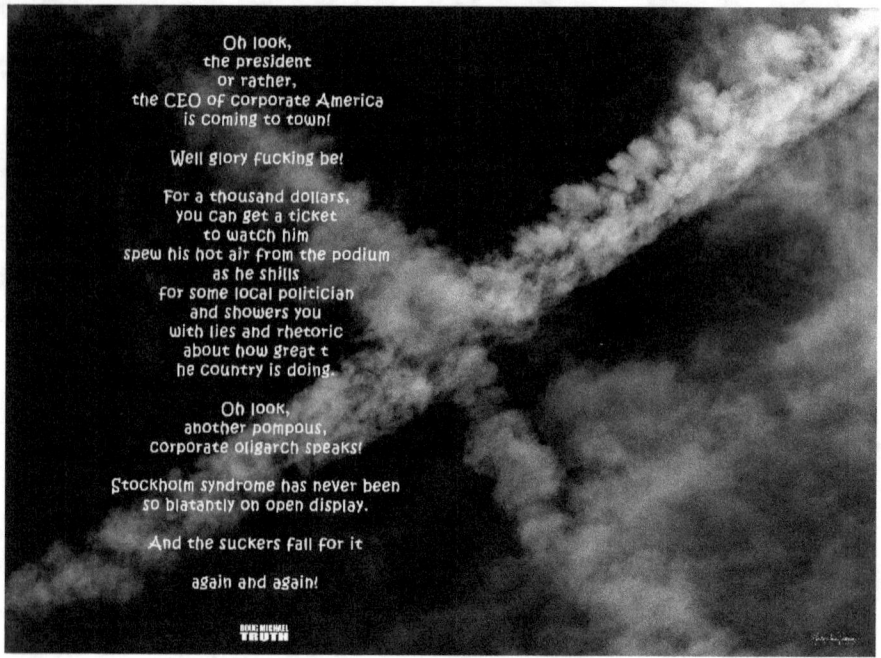

Oh look,
the president
or rather,
the CEO of corporate America
is coming to town!

Well glory fucking be!

For a thousand dollars,
you can get a ticket
to watch him
spew his hot air from the podium
as he shills
for some local politician
and showers you
with lies and rhetoric
about how great t
he country is doing.

Oh look,
another pompous,
corporate oligarch speaks!

Stockholm syndrome has never been
so blatantly on open display.

And the suckers fall for it

again and again!

Droves of people do, and it is sad and disturbing to say the least. Have people become that detached and far removed from what is occurring in plain view all around them? Apparently so. People wailing and weeping over a career criminal not being placed into the CEO position of corporate America is a sure sign of how far we have fallen. Just for the record, I don't support the other clown either! The politicians are nothing more than the elite's wind-up toys, bought-and-paid-for figureheads and self-serving sycophants.

What is this idea of looking outside of oneself for someone to lead you? The lowest of the low rise to positions of power in this asylum, and people think they represent them? You think that some figurehead, puppet is going to lead you to safety, freedom and prosperity? Humanity needs to lead *itself*, but at this point, I think it is so far removed from that concept that the good and decent people are going to have to rebuild from the smoldering ashes. How lost and broken have people become psychologically? It's on a level that defies belief.

Keep this in mind when observing cults of personality, so-called leaders, academic pundits, egotistical potentates, political parasites, celebrities, journalists, or any one of these dark sorcerers that are experts in the art of the misdirection of consciousness:

"A devilish person does not wear horns; she wears a false crown of thorns; darkness cloaked behind counterfeit light, his charm a charade, her goodness a falsehood."

Rome is fallen!

THREE

Captives of Ego

What defines you? Is it the roles that you play in life, the social personas, the titles and labels? Is it the master's degree or the impressive letters that follow your fictitious name? Do you define yourself as the aspect that thinks, with the mechanism that produces thought, the endless mind chatter of the ego? Do you define yourself as a purely physical and material being, a biological meat bag of flesh, bone, atoms, cells and molecules? Do you search for the meaning of your life outside of yourself, in a dysfunctional society, deliberately structured to prevent you from ever remembering who you truly are?

The greatest enemy you will ever face is the tyrant that exists within your own mind. To conquer this enemy takes great fortitude, nerves of steel, unwavering resolve, bold courage and unbending intent. You are born with it, many will die never even knowing that it exists, because it grows like a tapeworm, a parasite on the primary consciousness, suffocating and strangling the true self while using any tactic that it can to keep you from discovering it, all the while convincing you that it *is* you. It is a liar, a chameleon, a shapeshifter.

Call it what you will, a foreign installation, a superimposed consciousness, a mind parasite, a facsimile, an overlaid program or an ego. This tiny aspect of the psyche runs amok and seeks to operate in the capacity of captain of the vessel, when it's really only a deckhand. Its function is to maintain the ship, to keep it seaworthy, but it neglects its duty and tries to be captain, so the ship steers towards the rocks. The true navigator is bound and gagged, tied up in the hull. "I'm captain," shouts tiny little king ego. "Follow me!"

We are encouraged at every turn, beginning from the day of our arrival in this Earth Game, to see ourselves as small, insignificant and powerless. We are pushed to fit into traditions, to conform to consensus "norms," to buy into all manner of false ideals and outright lies. Ultimately, the system is designed to disconnect you from the realization of your own being, your own self, and it does an astounding job at doing so.

The need for approval from outside of self to determine a person's worth is like an epidemic, a Cancer spread through the collective consciousness of humankind. We are encouraged at every turn to seek outer stimuli to fill the *inner* void, to look without instead of within, to give away our most precious gift, the gift of selfhood, to the outer world of imbalance and collectivized insanity, and to conform to the herd mentality of the consensus trance. The mass majority are all too willing to externalize because the inner road to selfhood and individualism is a difficult and lonely road to walk. The slave mentality is willingly embraced as it is far easier to be told what to think than to serve truth and stand alone to define and create oneself. The fear of what others think is enough to keep people in line, blissfully grazing in the mental and emotional sheep pen where it is far less likely to be hassled.

The deeply ingrained fear of simply being an individual, and instead embracing the collective, has created a system of control and enslavement of human consciousness that has persisted for literally thousands of years. The stubborn refusal to live authentic lives, true to oneself and one's purpose, keeps the mind and emotions in a constant state of intense stress and anxiety. Ignorance is willingly and happily embraced to avoid the awesome responsibility of self-examination, personal responsibility, self-determination, self-definition and self-actualization.

Standing apart from the crowd has always been a challenging position to maintain and history has shown us that the courageous few that do, are often met with fierce opposition and all too often, death. Over identification with the mechanism that we think our thoughts with, the ego, encourages and sustains inner division. Human consciousness is extremely dissociated, inwardly split and divided. The ego, while maintaining the position of dominance, is but a tiny aspect of the psyche, and this idea that what you think with is the totality of what you are, feeds the inner division. Fear, doubt, rigidity, self-importance, pity, shame, guilt; these are the tools the tyrant king uses to keep the cognitive fortresses in place and firmly rooted. So comprehensive is its dominance over the psyche that most will never reach the point of observation to recognize the inner schism or split. Schism is defined as:

"Division or disunion, especially into opposing parties."[1]

This is precisely the psychological state that most humans operate within, and so few reach the point where they can see this split. The false king will do anything that it can, sometimes even die to prevent one from discovering the greater aspects of the self/psyche. Just look at the zealots who are willing to kill and die for some manufactured ideology. These are the extremes that an ego imprisoned within cognitive fortresses will go to in order to protect its perceptual stronghold, its hallowed ground so to speak. To observe and acknowledge the inner conflict is the first step to spirit reclaiming its rightful position, but so many are so hopelessly lost in the world of the illusory, secondary, overlaid consciousness, that they simply cannot see it. It is their only point of reference. It is who they are within their own minds; it is their very identity.

Think of the comic book character Superman. The geeky, nerdy, Clarke Kent is the ego. Superman is the true, self-actualized, cognitively aware being. The only difference in this analogy is that Superman *knows* it. He knows who he is underneath the mask of the Clarke Kent persona. He must wear the mask of

Clarke Kent to navigate through the world and to protect his true identity from his enemies. Most will never know their true magnitude because they have allowed Clarke Kent to completely consume their true identity and have forgotten the true extent of who they are.

Ego does serve a necessary function, but the problem is that ego believes itself to be the king of the castle, while its true function is as a servant. The falsely enthroned king believes itself to be the totality of the self and doesn't realize that it is but a relatively tiny aspect of a greater whole. The overinflated ego acts as a veil, separating itself from the other aspects of the being. The current, cultural paradigm caters to ego consciousness and feeds the beast in this decaying culture of separation and me-ism.

Many never even get to the point of identifying with their thoughts because they don't think. They simply operate as automatons, empty vessels drifting aimlessly. We're programmed to distrust our own inherent, inner intelligence or "knowingness," in favor of what the system wants us to think, gift wrapped nicely and presented by one of its gatekeepers, be it an academic type, a politician, potentate or priest, an alleged journalist, or anyone that is presented as possessing some kind of authority on truth and knowledge. As we are relentlessly encouraged to seek externally, selfhood is willingly given away to the occult mind doctors that perpetuate the system through an absolute, full on assault on human consciousness. The consciousness is manipulated to project the collective reality that we experience, which resonates with the manipulator's imbalance and psychopathy. They cannot create, and thus manipulate the collective mind of humanity to manifest, project and create the low-vibrational cesspool that matches their frequency and that they feel comfortable within. They are misguided, psychopathic, consciousness parasites that conduct and play humanity like out of tune violins in a discordant orchestra of utter insanity.

Many never even get so far as ego identification; they are locked within identifying with social personas, or the roles which they play. Persona is defined thusly:

1. *A character assumed by an author in a written work.*

2. *a. An individual's social facade or front that especially in the analytic psychology of C. G. Jung reflects the role in life the individual is playing.*

   b. the personality that a person (such as an actor or politician) projects in public.[2]

They identify who they are, with what they *do*, as the primary aspect of the self remains hidden and veiled, as they exist on the outskirts of themselves, lost in illusion, buying into innumerable, external distractions and allowing them to define who they are. This identification with the persona, or mask, and the identification with ego, causes division and creates so many problems in the world by fostering the illusion of separation. Billions of people live their lives oblivious to their own nature, a stranger to themselves, enslaved by limiting ideas, thoughts and patterns of behavior.

Then, there is the hyper, over-identification with the physical, which is of course encouraged at every turn within the Earth Game. Just look at corporate advertising, media and television. It's come to the point, where if a person doesn't resemble the Madison Avenue idea of beauty, (the airbrushed model in the magazine advertisement) or if they don't wear the correct designer apparel or the latest fashion, then they are somehow less of a human being. This physical identification stagnates the development of the psyche and the spirit, as the body is the least of what you are. The body is merely a vessel for consciousness to experience the physical.

Think of a scuba diver, that must take on the burden of all the cumbersome and heavy equipment in order to experience the dense pressure of the dep sea environment. The diver is using the equipment to experience and observe the foreign environment that he's navigating. The scuba gear are merely tools that the diver uses to immerse himself in the underwater realm so that he can survive while he explores.

Imagine driving around in a car and believing yourself to *be* the car and not the driver. Obsession with youth, and a completely superficial standard of beauty encourages an extremely shallow view of the self and of the world. Look at the lengths people will go to in order to maintain specific appearances, i.e. plastic surgery,

Botox injections to the face, sex change operations or whichever way that identification with the body manifests. It's like the diver believing himself to be the wetsuit. We don't normally tend to think of living, breathing people as being dead, but those immersed within these false paradigms are just that, spiritually dead and emotionally and psychologically arrested.

This massive over identification with the ego and with the physical, drives materialism, encourages belief in the illusion of separation, and caters to the survival drives and instincts, to the lower, base consciousness. This identification with the survival instincts is greatly amplified by things such as manufactured scarcity, plunder-produce-discard, complete and willful misuse of resources, engineered crises and the suppression of technology that could end or seriously curtail the abuse and plundering.

The distractions are numerous and widely varied, and the system cares not which you buy into, as long as you buy into something that keeps you from looking within, be it a religion, obsession with pop culture, pharmaceutical drugs, acquisition of stuff, the erroneous belief in authority or any number of distractions designed to keep you looking outside of the self. It's a manufactured reality, and most are so helplessly caught up in the illusions, that they will live their entire lives as a stranger to themselves. That is the idea. Ultimately, becoming aware of the present situation humanity is currently embroiled within, leads to looking within and facing one's own inner darkness. It is essential to embrace one's shadow as the outer world of manifested reality

Lack of care, compassion and empathy is what is wrong with the world. Obsession with outer stimuli and over identification with the external is marching us straight into collectivism.

The entire cultural paradigm speaks to survival instincts and promotes over identification with the mechanism that we think our thoughts with, what is called the ego.

Division and separation are the calling cards of this faux paradigm.

DOUG MICHAEL
TRUTH

is in a symbiotic relationship with the inner world of the psyche. Attitudes, beliefs, opinions, systems of thought and the actions based upon these, create the reality we experience, and this is done individually and *collectively*. The outer reflects the inner in your personal life and on the global stage.

The mass majority flat out refuse, or remain unable to do the inner, deconstructive work because it is a difficult process, requires enormous effort and forces one to examine themselves, which means looking at all the things that they have allowed to shape their identity. There is an enormous amount of fear that is present regarding this process, but it is the only way out of the mess. Over identification with the ego creates a barrier to the other aspects of the psyche and most will live their entire lives oblivious to that understanding.

Rather than looking within and embracing the darker aspects of the self, the overly egoic mind will avoid that process at every turn and instead willingly embrace ignorance over truth. Our culture, especially here in America, is one gigantic, in-your-face example of this. The overwhelming majority will willingly turn away from a painful truth, disengage their thought processes, and willingly choose to remain ignorant, as long as their little comfort zone is not upset and their physical needs are met, which breeds a society of narcissistic, selfish, me-ism. So blinded and hypnotized by false paradigms, ideologies and belief systems, they cannot, or deliberately will not see the snake coiling around to bite them on the ass!

Willful ignorance is defined as:

"The state and practice of ignoring any sensory input that appears to contradict one's inner model of reality. The practice can entail completely disregarding established facts, evidence and/or reasonable opinions if they fail to meet one's expectations."[3]

The act of willful ignorance includes the rejection of any information that contradicts what one *thinks* they know, and without consideration. This is a blatant example of an unhealthy and over inflated ego and it causes enormous problems in the world and also in personal relationships. An ego trapped in this way of thinking has absolutely no concept that it is a part of something much greater. It is the courageous and strong spirit that will willingly challenge everything it thinks it knows and strive to walk the inner road, and through self-realization, define oneself.

People seem to avoid self-examination and instead immerse themselves into the collective. They despise truth and the messengers that bring it. It is easier for them to allow the system to do their thinking for them, than to engage in any actual thinking of their own. They believe in the illusion of authority, and give their minds away willingly to it, be it in the form of a god, guru or government; a belief system, or simply complete immersion into the outer distractions and stimuli.

I contend that:

"You have been trained your whole life to silence your inner voice. You have been conditioned to distrust your own inherent intelligence, to externalize to find that which can only be found within. You have been hypnotized to believe that you are only the thinker, not the perceiver, that you are powerless, weak and small. The lies must be put to rest, and you must stand within your own magnificence if you are ever to affect change in your life and in the world."

Being bound within ego consciousness keeps the mind locked into a lower state, and this is deliberately encouraged, primarily through the manipulation of the emotion of fear. Again, the survival instincts are catered to; humanity is kept imprisoned in the lower centers, the R complex of the brain. Of course, the system would not work for the controllers without the *illusion* of freedom. As the German novelist Von Goethe said:

"None are more hopelessly enslaved than those who falsely believe they are free."

We have entire populations existing within a "group think," slave mentality while believing they are free. In fact, most do not want real freedom, because true freedom entails personal responsibility; what they want is freedom *from* freedom and they will immerse themselves within the collective to avoid the responsibility that comes with being truly free.

In observing people, I've noticed that there seems to be a profound detachment from a sense of wonder about life. Even in the very young, it seems as if imagination is in its final death throes. It's become more about entertaining and distracting the mind as opposed to seeking knowledge and growth of the mind, and the willing adoption of this attitude is what will ensure absolute slavery.

I notice people all the time who seem to be proud of their ignorance. They know a lot about nothing and advertise it loudly. Any person that shows intellectual interests is shunned and ridiculed by the willfully ignorant. For instance, I am weird, or strange because I watch very little TV and instead read, study and seek to expand my knowledge. In these days, the person who does such things is considered a weirdo by those who follow the collective herd. This is another reason why so few avoid the path of selfhood; fear of what others will think. I say, stand within that uniqueness that defines you; for a tiger does not give one shit about the opinion of sheep! I contend that:

"Ignorance has become the new cool. These days, if you show even a semblance of intelligence or hold interests beyond the distractions and absurdities manufactured by this dying culture you are at once looked at with suspicion. Having intellectual pursuits makes one a threat and invites merciless ridicule by those who exist on the outskirts of their own being, lost within the confines of their mental and emotional prison cells, influenced by Hollywood, Madison Avenue and a completely defunct public [mis]education system. Every depraved meme, ideology and false reality is paraded as normal and woe to those who refuse to buy into the lies or to expose them for the nonsense that they quite obviously are. What is the rationale of a person that will willingly embrace ignorance and shun wisdom and knowledge in favor of outright stupidity? Perhaps those few who haven't completely given away their minds and souls can build something new from the ashes."

Again, the reason so many will never step out of ignorance is because that requires hard work. It requires self-examination and a willingness to challenge one's beliefs. People have this erroneous notion that walking the spiritual path is one of just love and light and very little challenge, when the opposite is true. When one makes the commitment to step into the light of truth, all hell breaks loose as belief systems are turned upside down and false ideas fall away. It is very uncomfortable for most and so many will fight with every ounce of strength to avoid facing themselves at all cost. It also involves saying no to systems, ideas, beliefs and people that no longer serve you or your experience.

The reason there is so much imbalance in the world and why it remains largely unrecognized, stems from an unwillingness or an inability, to face one's own dark side, or shadow self. We have been taught our entire lives to look away from the so-called "negative" emotions, even to the absurd point of attempting to drug them out of existence. The repression of the darker side of the self builds up, causes intense anxiety and is projected outwards collectively, so manifested reality can reflect it back to us. These so-called darker emotions can be our greatest teachers. The whole idea is to cause extreme imbalance within the collective psyche, to project a world of imbalance into manifestation. There is a symbiotic relationship between the energy of the psyche and the causal factors that manifest reality into existence; they are intimately linked, and the forces that operate in the shadows understand this well and are absolute experts at manipulating human consciousness to manifest the world they desire, a world of utter imbalance and darkness, a world devoid of one of the true human elements, compassion.

It is our own unwillingness to face ourselves and our fears that creates so many of the problems that we face. Couple this with over-identification with the ego and you have a recipe for disaster. We are about to see the results of our refusal to face the inner darkness and it will not be pretty. It can still however, I believe, be turned around but it would take a willingness on the individual level, to look within and take the necessary steps to participate in, and facilitate one's own conscious evolution, and sadly, so few seem to be even remotely interested in that; therefore, humanity is facing cataclysm. The majority will never look within and do the necessary homework until they are faced with disaster, and that opportunity has certainly arrived.

Our refusal to embrace the darker aspects of self, individually and collectively, has allowed evil to rise and flourish in the world. Our continued stubbornness and refusal to face this fact, has brought us to this sad state of affairs that we are now engulfed within. Humanity is inwardly divided and split, and the manipulators know all too well how to encourage this inner division; they are masters of psychological manipulation. The prize is selfhood, the very soul of humanity. Some have referred to this as a spiritual war and they are absolutely correct. The solution can be boiled down to two words: know thyself.

In my view, it's not the dissolution of the ego but rather the embracing of the ego by the higher self that needs to occur. Ego needs to be put in its place and allowed to function as it is supposed to. Ego has a necessary function, so all this new age claptrap about killing the ego is nonsense; the ego needs to be embraced and its function understood. Again, the problem is that ego thinks it is the boss, the captain of the ship, but that is not its function and purpose.

Beginning in 2010, I had three major experiences with an ancient, shamanic medicine called, Ayahuasca. It showed me what I've described here in a very real and dramatic way. Ayahuasca is one of the most potent psychedelic substances known to man, and its use has been effective in treating depression, PTSD, addiction, Alzheimer's, Multiple Sclerosis, and many other ailments. This medicine radically alters the state of consciousness and can provide profound breakthroughs in the user. I trained myself how to make this medicine, which consists of two plants boiled and fused together to create a rather foul-tasting brew. The experiences I had with this substance were so profound that words cannot describe it, but I will try to sum up my experiences:

As the medicine kicked in, the ego put up a fight, and that other (higher) aspect of the self actually thanked the ego. When you enter that state of consciousness, a voice speaks to you. The higher voice said to the ego: "your function is honored and necessary, thank you." It also said: "you are not the boss here." I was led to understand that the ego's purpose is to act as sort of an anchor for this reality, and that its job is to put things in neat little boxes, like an efficient stock clerk if you will.

The first profound experience I had with the Ayahuasca showed me so much about my own psyche. As the medicine began to take hold, I asked myself if I was going insane, to which the voice responded: "the ego does not go willingly." Ayahuasca is considered an "entheogen." The word entheogen means: "the divine generated within." I feel that it's more accurate to say that entheogens *reveal* the divine, not generate it; it is already inherent within you. The medicine pierces the veil of the ego and reveals you to yourself. The ego feels isolated from the totality of the self; it thinks it is alone and it is the ego that buys into the false notion of separation.

Because of this ego isolation, we have masses of people that believe that the thinking aspect is the totality of what they are, and this is a major cause of so many problems in the world. The control system absolutely feeds this type of consciousness.

A false reality has been superimposed over the true reality. Masses of people buy into lie after lie and believe them to be true. Now so, more than ever in this technologically advanced culture, we are encouraged and conditioned not to think but to blindly accept. Those who question or present a different perspective are at once attacked and ridiculed and thus, humanity keeps itself in a psychological and emotional prison cell.

The false, consensus reality presented to us is designed to create a low vibrational state through collective projection. This is why I suggest that it is crucial for each individual to strive to

Does not the entire
universe dwell within?
How can you possibly
place infinity into a box?
The labels, the "trends,"
the division and
separation,
the cultural memes and
false ideologies which all
serve to distract,
are nothing more than
psychological prison cells.

DOUG MICHAEL
TRUTH

correct their own inner imbalance and face the dark side of themselves. We can facilitate our own conscious evolution, but it is very challenging; it takes great courage and an unshakeable resolve to face one's own inner darkness, embrace it and learn from it.

This begins with an unlearning process and a negation process by facing what is untrue. The ego has defense mechanisms and resists the challenging of what it thinks it knows which is why so few ever engage in the process. We are at a crucial time; whereas if we refuse to do this necessary, inner work, we will march headlong into the arms of extinction. Even if not a physical extinction, the very things that make us human are under enormous threat. So many people willingly embrace their own destruction. This refusal to see things as they are allows the prison paradigm to thrive and actually gives rise to it in the first place. I think that it's imperative for humanity to come into the understanding that their names, their physical body, their belief systems, their jobs, their thought processes, their social personas, their titles and their perceived social status, have nothing to do with who they ARE! The body is a vessel for consciousness to experience this dense, low vibratory, material reality; it is the temple that contains the unique aspect of the infinite consciousness, the true self.

Once a person can gain even a tiny glimmer into the true self, beyond the veil of the ever-present internal monologue, the ongoing conversation and its heavily fortified cognitive fortresses, one can strive to reach the observational perspective to really see the conflict within them. Then the battle can begin. You cannot negotiate with the tyrant, I tried that, it does not work; you will lose every time. You cannot make nice-nice with the schoolyard bully; it will only stab you in the back. You must put it in its place with fierceness and ferocity, for that is the only language it understands, just like any tyrant.

When I use this metaphor of going to battle, I don't mean to suggest that you should kill this aspect of yourself. Rather I would suggest, reconciling the inner divide, recognizing the conversation (the chatter of the ego), seeing it for what it is and allowing it to function in the capacity that it's meant to, as the deckhand. For a while as you reach towards a broader perceptual realization, the gateway into higher awareness, ego will try its best to reassert itself as captain of the vessel. Its greatest fear is being discovered because then its power is threatened. Look at the outer world, look at how the Consortium hides in the darkness, terrified of being discovered. As within so without. Realize that those tyrants are the most infected with the parasite and they are the ones that are truly in fear. Why is there so much division, war, imbalance and strife in the world? I would suggest that it's because those things exist within us.

So then, naturally the question will arise: how do I discover it? How do I defeat it? Or how do I put it in its place? This is the difficult part. We are talking about *self*-realization and *self*-actualization so no one can really tell you, or else it's simply following some other authority, something that so many seem to revel in. No one can tell you who you are except you! If you think about it, would you want someone else to? Shit, we've lived our entire lives like that and look where that road leads, down the dark corridors to oblivion! On the other hand, those who have walked the road of self-actualization and self-creation can act in an advisory capacity. History is loaded with examples and usually, we kill those people. Or, their teachings get turned into a religion to be used to control and fortify the cognitive fortresses.

So instead of asking another, how do I do it? Ask yourself! Shut down the chatter for just a moment and let your own inner self guide you. Is it easy? Hell no! The deckhand will throw every curve ball at you to derail you. That path to self-discovery is the road that leads within. All the brush that must be cleared and hacked away is the psychological and emotional debris i.e. fear, doubt, self-deprecation, victimhood, powerlessness, superiority, self-negation and all the rest of it.

One piece of advice I would give, is to become aware at how the tyrant shows up and to be aware of the cognitive fortresses in which it likes to reside. It wears many masks. It is like a stage actor that constantly changes costumes. Step back from your thoughts and observe without judgement. I think being fluid and not too rigid is a good idea. And don't forget to laugh!

The first step in reconciling the schism is to recognize it. Remember, others may advise or share their experiences, but your path is unique. Ain't nothing to it but to do it! Fear will be your greatest challenge in this endeavor. Detach and observe. Detach a bit from your thoughts and emotions and observe the inner workings of this mechanism. Again, don't judge! Simply observe. See it first! Know thy enemy or else you cannot go into battle! I've seen the enemy and it is me (or false me, if you want to be precise about it) Perhaps better to say: "I've seen the enemy and it is what I *thought* was me."

Remember that the superimposed consciousness wears many costumes. "Poor me" is just as much a display of ego as the puffed up, arrogant jackass that thinks his shit doesn't stink. The "compassionate," "selfless" caregiver that constantly acts as a toilet for others to dump their crap in is another example. Think about it; if you are "selfless" that means lack of self and that is no way to live because without selfhood, you are nothing more than a marionette on someone else's strings! No one can give you your selfhood, umm, expect yourself, otherwise it isn't selfhood.

Another suggestion would be to look to no one to lead you. Lead yourself! Be your own authority. The word authority comes from the Latin word which means author. So, are you the author of your experience? Or, do you let someone else write the story? Will you write it? I'm interested in the story that you write for yourself, not the one that has been written for you. That one ends in tragedy.

One more suggestion I can give is to try, I mean really put effort into shifting from the victim mentality to the victor mentality. The victor writes the script. The victim is well, a victim of it. That my dear friends, is naught but a choice, it is an attitudinal shift and well worth the effort. Little tyrant deckhand loves to play the victim, or play the victimizer but can we get past this duality? Yes, certainly one can do so if one puts in the effort and overthrows their tyrant.

Once you reach a point where you can see the schism you may reach a point where you can reconcile the great divide and operate within a more holistic level of consciousness, free from the prison of the cognitive fortresses. Claim who you are or better yet, create it! Be willing to die and be reborn with each moment. Why does the hanged man smile? In the Christian metaphor, why did Christ go to the cross willingly? Because he knew that his death would mean rebirth. The ego is not the self; it is the straight jacket that binds the self unless the split is reconciled, and the deckhand allowed to function in the capacity that it was meant to. The me that I see is not *truly* me, you see?

FOUR

Comfort Zones: Human Crabs and Self-imposed Buckets

As a child, I would often accompany my family down to the pier in the Patchogue area of Long Island, on the Great South Bay, to catch crabs. At the time, back in the early and mid-1980s, the blue-claw crab population in that area was absolutely abundant. It isn't these days anymore, and people are restricted to how many they can catch and threatened with hefty fines for taking more than the limit.

Crabbing is easy, you simply purchase a wire/steel mesh trap, bait it, and cast the trap down into the water. When the trap hits the bottom, it unfolds, leaving only the top and bottom fixed, while all four sides open to allow easy entry. Just wait about 10 minutes, and then pull the trap up. When tension is applied to the cord, the sides of the wire trap fold up, encaging the crustaceans inside. The larger crabs are removed, and placed into a pail, while the small ones get thrown back.

After a few hours, and with little effort, if the tide was right, you could have an entire bucket-full of blue-claws, which make for some very tasty eating. I've always been amazed at observing the caught crabs that were placed into the pail. Whenever one crab tried to escape, the others would pull it back into the bucket. If another tried to escape, the same thing would happen. Over and over, one or several crabs would try to escape their fate, and the others would pull it back into the bucket. It was never necessary to place a lid on the bucket.

In this analogy, the crabs represent the human race. The bucket represents beliefs, traditions, ideologies, worldviews, opinions etc. Simply, the bucket represents the very confined, narrow and accepted ideas about reality, normality, or comfort zones or what I refer to as cognitive fortresses. When one crab, (human) attempts to break free from the limiting confines, (think or express itself differently than the norm) the others pull it back in, (ridicule, condemnation, out casting, etc.) The crabs seem to keep each other in line, and this can be applied to humanity in this analogy. Just watch what happens when you begin to think and express yourself differently to the status quo norm. Watch all the other crabs tug and pull at you, to bring you back into the confines of the pail.

Control takes so many forms and permutations. It seems that so much of our lives operate within parameters and paradigms that seek to control, force conformity and create uniformity. Just look around at today's world with this massive push for homogenization and collectivism, within this atmosphere of political correctness and total censorship. Of course, so few seem to realize this; however, it does seem as though growing numbers are starting to ask questions and realize that there is so much more going on underneath the veil, behind the movie screen of life, hence this dramatic push to stifle individualism.

From the moment we begin to develop and learn, we are bombarded with societal norms, manufactured versions of how things should be and dogmas that surround us and follow us right up to the present moment. For most people it seems, these doctrines and ideas of normalcy follow them to their very graves.

Who sets the norms in any given society? If you could control what people view as sane or insane, true or untrue, possible or impossible, real or not real etc. you then could ultimately control their reality, or at the least, how they *see and experience* reality. This is ultimately how it's done, through cognitive misdirection.

What is occurring is primarily a perceptual or *psychological* manipulation. The norms are set, and then the encouraged, accepted, and ultimately self-imposed concept, that thinking, acting or expressing outside of those norms makes one wrong, bad, crazy, dangerous, insane, etc. is what keeps billions of human crabs within the bucket. These days, it's getting ridiculous with what you can or cannot say, simply because someone just might get offended.

In essence, humanity keeps *each other* in line, by immediately attacking anyone that dares to challenge the accepted beliefs, conditioning, perceptions, ideologies, etc. Once one crab (person) tries to escape from the bucket, (belief systems, norms, dogmas, etc.) then the other crabs will tug and pull at the one trying to escape, pulling it back into the pail. Well, you know what they say, misery loves company.

To me this analogy speaks volumes about how humanity is controlled by regulating each other. We seem, (or most do) to exist within very narrow and limiting "comfort zones." Once anyone expresses his or herself outside of the zone of normality, they are immediately attacked, and brought back into line by those who are conforming to it without question.

We see this happen all the time. I've personally experienced this many times, simply by expressing ideas that are different to the "normal" or readily acceptable ones, as I'm sure many of my readers and listeners have as well. I can't tell you how many times I've heard, "you're nuts," or "that's crazy," or "well I've never heard of that," or any of the other blather offered by unknowing crabs. The ones who blindly conform to the norms, always seem to insist that everyone else conforms also, rather than opening their minds, thinking in terms of possibility and simply allowing others to freely express themselves. They never seem to have the courage to think for themselves, so why should *you* be allowed to? Then comes the ridicule, condemnation, and the proverbial crabs tugging at one another, displaying the ultimate ignorance.

But, for those few crabs that do escape, they are now labeled "insane," "stupid," "crazy," "wrong," "nuts," or whatever, simply because they have chosen to no longer conform to the narrow confines of the bucket, the comfort zone. And the ones who remain in the bucket, continue to wallow in the misery that is conformity, condemning you for your courage to think outside of the box, and to dare to express yourself differently, or to challenge conventional thought; oh, what a horrible human being you are, for expressing your own uniqueness.

What is it that keeps the crabs within the limiting confines of the bucket, tugging and clawing at each other? What is it that keeps the human sheep monitoring each other? I would suggest, ultimately, that it is the grand tool used on every level to control masses of people around the planet each moment, fear. What are they afraid of? I think that ultimately what most fear, is what *others will think of them,* if they dare to think and express themselves differently to the norm. These days, outright hostility and often violence will be directed towards someone who just may have a differing view.

Nobody likes to be ridiculed, vilified, ostracized or condemned by those they are close to, so rather than rock the boat, so to speak, they don't dare step outside of the boundaries that have been set up for them. Here's a great example: I know a person who is a hard-working man, intelligent and friendly. He attends church, and is bringing his children up within a belief system that he himself does not even remotely believe in.

The reason he does not express himself, as to how he really feels about this particular religion he's participating in, is because he's afraid of what his wife or mother-in-law would think of him if he said how he really felt. This is a typical example of someone conforming to something out of fear of what other people think. I would suggest, that if his wife or mother-in-law have a problem with how he really feels, then it is truly *their* problem, not his. If they were to be disappointed, because of his refusal to no longer conform, then it would serve them right, for their refusal to allow someone else the freedom to express themselves in their own uniqueness.

You see, people who conform, always seem to insist that you conform to what *they* are conforming to, in effect, forcing their will upon another, and what's more, they never even seem to realize it. On the other hand, if this person refuses to have courage enough to stand up to those people, and dare to express himself freely, without fear of condemnation, then he will get exactly what he deserves, his place within the narrow confines of the bucket, stuck in a belief system that will never bring him fulfillment.

I can tell you from personal experience, that the fear of what those close to you are going to think of you, once you step outside of the comfort zone, is very real; however, in exercising the courage to stand up and live your truth anyway, despite that fear, the rewards far outweigh the limitations of choosing to remain in the bucket with the rest of the conforming crabs. Moreover, when you continue to walk your truth, eventually, the crabs are going to stop tugging at you. Either they will accept your example of courage, and love and accept you for who you are, or they will write you off, condemning you, labeling you, and as was the case with me, speaking badly about you behind your back. In that case, fuck 'em!

If they cannot see what freedom can mean, by your example, your daring to be different, then who the hell needs friends or family like that anyway? I can tell you; I've lost many so called "friends" once I began to outgrow the bucket, think for myself, and display the audacity to express myself differently to the norm. Even my own mother condemned me, ridiculing me behind my back literally for years, but she did start to finally come around on her deathbed. Better late than never I suppose.

I noticed also, that others within her sphere of influence, be they family, or friends, would take her side, without even speaking to me about it. Their views were shaped by what they were told by my mother, and I've even had some things said to me that were entirely untruthful, but these crabs just *assumed* it to be true. At first, this was hurtful to me, but as the fear of what others think lessened, it just became laughable. Of course, now my attitude is: fuck the conforming little crabs that can't think for themselves. People that pass judgment on others, based on what *other people say*, are beyond ignorant, they're just plain stupid and lost souls.

Most people who are quick to condemn a new idea rarely engage in any research of their own, they look no further than what they already *think* they know, they refuse to peel off the blinders, and they ridicule anything outside of their narrow and limiting beliefs. So many condemn outright, and on knee-jerk reaction before they even investigate things for themselves.

So many people say they don't concern themselves with what others think, but deep inside, they really do. It's quite evident in their actions. They give lip service to it, but in truth they are hiding behind the fear of what others will say about them. I see it so often, when they have the opportunity to speak up and don't do so, because they know that the people around them will have something negative to say. I say, speak up; let these crabs show their ignorance! Here's a simple formula that I feel would be a great step in the right direction:

A) Everyone expresses themselves freely, without fear of condemnation, or what others will think, do or say if they do so. We *dare to be different*. We speak our minds and walk our truth regardless of the other crabs in the bucket. We consciously walk each moment outside of the comfort zone of normality.

Now, here's the catch:

B) We allow others to do the same! We respect the right of everyone else to express their uniqueness, without ridicule, without condemnation, without insisting that they conform to our comfort zone. We honor diversity. We respect each other's right to be different. We consciously climb out of the bucket, and instead of tugging at others, pulling them into the normality zone; we *help them escape* from the bucket. We respect each other's right to free expression, even if we disagree with it! As long as we do no harm in the process, why not stand within uniqueness?

Sadly, when you look around, it seems a bit far off, doesn't it? Although it is a simple formula, so many people refuse to let go of their programming, and since that conditioning begins the moment a child begins learning and developing, the perceptual illusion is set in place very early, and it seems so difficult to climb out of the bucket of normality. In actuality, it's just a change of mind away.

All that we really need to do is to refuse to allow the will of others to be imposed upon us. We refuse to allow the "values" of others to determine our own. We refuse to be programmed any more, be it by religion, political dogmas, outmoded ideologies, what we've "learned" in school, from our parents, or from what we see on the TV. We grow up and begin to think for ourselves, regardless of what others might say, or think if we do. In other words, we become self-actualized. That's *true* courage. We begin to question, and even engage in our own truth seeking, be it through study, research, contemplation, meditation, etc. and then we begin to *live and express* that truth, again, contrary to what others might say about it, as long as we don't seek to impose our will upon another; that would not be freedom, that would simply be another bucket to confine ourselves and others within.

We stop insisting that others conform to our way of thinking, and refuse to conform to theirs, all the while respecting their right to be different, and honoring diversity. If we all did that, it would be impossible to control the world on the scale that it is being manipulated today. Diversity is a nightmare to control; uniformity on the other hand, is a piece of cake to control and regiment.

Here's another example of the power of conditioning: have you ever had a conversation with someone, in which an out of the ordinary topic came up, and immediately, the other person, instead of opening their mind, at once displays their programming by saying: "well my doctor says this," or, "in college, the professor said this," or, "well, I saw it on the Learning Channel," or "everyone knows that's not true." I'm sure you can think of many other examples. So, who's really doing their thinking for them? It's sad that so many will never look past the bucket to see if there may just be some truth out there.

OH MY GOD! A doctor said it. Well, he's an expert. We wouldn't want to question the doctor. You know, something like: "you need Statin drugs because your cholesterol is high." He's gone to med school, and gotten a degree from a prestigious university, he must know exactly what he's talking about, can't question him! And what would my mother say if I did? Oh no! Blah, blah, blah, blah blah. Incidentally, almost every time I've been hospitalized for something serious, these know-it-all doctors have misdiagnosed me. Recently, a doctor I was seeing for some testing, was trying to get me to agree to getting the flu shot. He was adamant and tried using guilt and fear to get me to comply. I remained calm and simply refused. I said: "I'll take my chances." I'm sure that the fact that doctors receive kickbacks from the pharmaceutical companies had absolutely nothing to do with his disapproval of my decision.

I've seen people, sometimes in their late 20's or early 30's and even much older, that still allow their parents to do their thinking for them. How sad. Even in many cases when they don't agree, they dare not speak their truth, out of fear that their parents may be "disappointed." Well, my dad says this, my mom says that, well, what do *you* say? And for the parents that expect their children to conform rigidly to their ways of thinking, shame on you! Let them be themselves. Let them express their unique individuality. If you're going to be disappointed because they think differently than you do, good! Maybe it'll do you some good to be disappointed. I've always encouraged my children to think for themselves, it builds character. And I will certainly never seek to impose my beliefs on them, or anyone else for that matter.

My father suffered from know-it-all syndrome. His mind was closed like a steel trap. I see so many parents like this. They think that only *they* know best. They think it's impossible to learn anything from someone who is younger than they are. It's a shame, because you can learn so much from simply observing children. They live in the moment. They have no preconceived notions or prejudices. They must be *taught* those things. I'm not saying don't give guidance and discipline, but for goodness sake, let them be who they are!

I've observed people defend literally ridiculous ideas, based upon what they learned from some teacher in high school or college. Well, she *is* a teacher. She must know what she's talking about. We wouldn't want to question her. She's gone to the university and she's obtained a degree. And we all know that paying thousands upon thousands of dollars to the system to obtain that worthless piece of paper equals intelligence, at least, that's what they've told us.

Who am I to question? Blah, blah, blah, blah, blah. Crabs in a bucket. Stay in that comfort zone, you won't get hassled in there. We've been taught to not question any outside authority, regardless of whatever twisted, false or ridiculous form it may take. In other words, just swallow all the bullshit and don't ask questions!

One of the most controlling buckets for the human crabs, to me, is religion. People base their entire beliefs, and spiritual concepts upon what manuscripts, often thousands of years old say or on how some authority is interpreting it for them. Anything outside of those scriptures or documents, which just may challenge the authenticity of those beliefs, could not possibly be true. So many of these crabs, never even study *their own* bibles or doctrines, let alone anything outside of them. They believe them because they have been *told* to. They don't question, because they've been told it was wrong to question the often ridiculous scriptures and doctrines. Yeah, that makes sense: God gives you a free-thinking mind, setting us apart from all other species on Earth, because of our ability to reason, but then makes it a sin to use that ability to question. "Have faith" they say. Fuck faith, I want the truth! Well, my minister says it's true. Wouldn't want to question him. He's been to the seminary, he must know what he's talking about, blah, blah, blah, blah, blah.

Regarding religion, we really have little choice in the matter. People are born into their religious beliefs, and they are enforced, often very strictly, through upbringing and tradition. When the few courageous ones dare to ask questions, especially if they are children, they are shot down before they even have a chance. They are forced into conformity, through fear that a god of love will punish them for all eternity for daring to have doubts or questions. How absurd, and yet, so many well-meaning parents-who themselves were never able to break the cycle of indoctrination-enforce these narrow and limiting beliefs on their children. Meanwhile, more blood has been spilled upon this Earth because of religion, than by any other force humanity has ever known. Catholic churches have paid out well over *3.5 billion dollars* in pedophilia cases, and even though this is now widely known, people still attend the churches, insisting that their kids also conform to the stunning hypocrisy called Catholicism, and many times, look down upon you because you don't!

I'm sure that you could think of many more examples of buckets used to confine human crabs. There are many normality zones that appear different on the outside, but overall, they serve

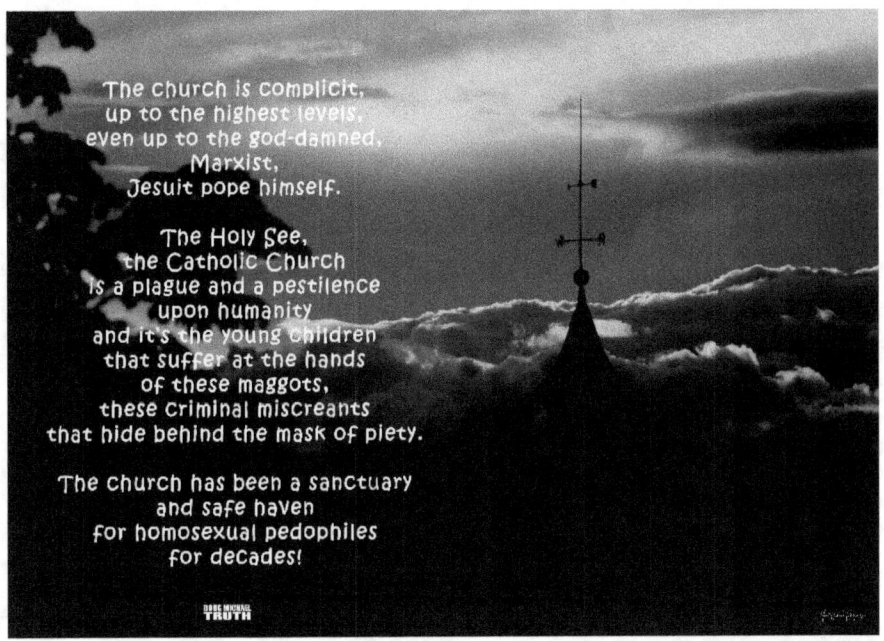

The church is complicit,
up to the highest levels,
even up to the god-damned,
Marxist,
Jesuit pope himself.

The Holy See,
the Catholic Church
is a plague and a pestilence
upon humanity
and it's the young children
that suffer at the hands
of these maggots,
these criminal miscreants
that hide behind the mask of piety.

The church has been a sanctuary
and safe haven
for homosexual pedophiles
for decades!

TRUTH

the same purpose: to confine humanity within very narrow and limiting belief structures. Belief systems are just that, systems of belief, nothing more.

Not until we can unlearn everything that we think we know, not until we can seek answers beyond the mundane, not until we can step outside of the comfort zones, escape the confines of the buckets and help others to do so, can we be truly free and begin to learn. And especially, not until we can allow others to express themselves differently than the normality zones demand, can we experience a true revolution in consciousness that is so desperately needed at this point in human history.

FIVE

Ideological Subversion

Everything that has any value is contorted. Everything is twisted, distorted bastardized and then sold back to you. Everything is warped into a decrepit form and then offered up for mass consumption. Fabian, Marxist propaganda has set its hooks firmly within the minds of large numbers of people, even the young and they aren't even aware of it. They have taken the divide and rule bait. They have embraced warped ideologies and have very little basic understanding of history or even what is occurring all around them.

They are locked within the technetronic control grid and remain blissfully unaware, enslaved like prisoners to the mechanized, digital godhead. Powerful people have infiltrated American and western culture with Marxist ideology, and we need to really begin to become aware of this and how it's been achieved. Psychology is used as a weapon and the Consortium's agents that operate behind the thrones of power are absolute experts at manipulating human consciousness through propaganda, crowd psychology, language, symbolism, education, media and various other methods and infiltration tactics.

Yuri Bezmenov was a Soviet agent who worked for the KGB and defected to Canada in the 1970s. He came forward giving lectures and interviews concerning Soviet subversion of the American political system. He explains that the primary method of Marxist infiltration used by the KGB, was not so much in espionage, but in psychological warfare. We can refer to these methods as perceptual sedition. It's a war waged upon on the very consciousness. This is how the Consortium operates, it's a cognitive battle, a perceptual game of psychological manipulation. Once your eyes are opened you can see it everywhere and the truly amazing thing is that you will be thought of as a lunatic for simply seeing the obvious. This is how comprehensive the mind manipulation is. Masses of people will defend utter illusions, many times to the death. Ideological subversion consists of four key components:

1. Demoralization
2. Destabilization
3. Crisis
4. Normalization.

Demoralization is defined as:

1. *To deprive a person or persons of spirit, courage, discipline, etc. to destroy the morale of.*

2. *To throw a person into disorder or confusion, to bewilder.*

3. *To corrupt or undermine the morals of.*[1]

We can think of this as an attack on the moral ideals of a society, a contortion of values if you will. Respect for your elders? Gone! Manners and politeness? Gone! Compassion, care, kindness? Flush all of that right down the toilet. This attitude of indifference will always lead to cultural collapse as history has proven again and again, over and over throughout the blood-splattered corridors of time. Where do you suppose that we are within this repeating cycle?

One needs only to be barely conscious to see the demoralization that has taken hold in this country and around much of the western world. What would never have been tolerated just a decade or two ago, is perfectly acceptable these days. Moral relativism runs rampant and every sick and depraved cultural meme and ideology is paraded right in front of us and in many cases accepted as normal. A case in point is the recent push by certain organizations to normalize pedophilia. Some groups are even relabeling pedophiles as "minor attracted persons."

Powerful enclaves such as Hollywood and the Vatican are infested with sick and depraved sexual deviants, so it's no wonder that we see this occurring. This is happening whether or not the people are aware of it. If you are aware, what I would suggest is within your own consciousness, withdraw your consent with anything that insults the spirit. Stand up within your own being and reject evil. For those who are just clueless but decent people, educate them, if you can. If they are too far gone to even wrap their minds around the truth of what is occurring, plant the seed and move on. What else can you do? If they don't have the fortitude and courage to face things as they are, then they will fall and there's nothing you can do about it. It's very sad indeed but there are many casualties in this war; it's sad but it's true.

Organizations of pedophiles want to be welcomed into the LBGTQ community. They want to be accepted and certain organizations support them in their endeavors. You can bet that Consortium controlled front organizations will provide funding to push this agenda as part of the cultural subversion that's infiltrated this country and much of the western world as well.

Look at what's happening in much of Europe right now. Men are being marginalized and emasculated and it's accepted with very little protest. It's happening here too, but Americans and Europeans alike refuse to see it. Hand your children over to the mind doctors. Their very consciousness is being raped; their very spirit imprisoned. It's as if some sort of collective denial has taken hold of the mass consciousness. What happens when the men of a nation become emasculated and turned into metrosexual, spineless bimbos? They will be too coerced and too afraid to stand up against tyranny and they will let the government take their children, twist their perceptions and they will remain too stupefied to be any the wiser. Well, this is where we are.

And to those few who can actually see it, I understand your frustration, and you should feel angry and frustrated. If you're not pissed off and frustrated, you may want to check to see if you still have a pulse. The same group of Fabians, bankers and corporate oligarchs financed the feminist movement and the social justice warrior nonsense, and it's all designed to infiltrate and overthrow a nation, and unfortunately, it's been very successful.

We're done here! Unless we make a conscious decision to create something new. At this point, because most are so dumbed down and so comprehensively clueless, nothing short of cataclysm will shake their cognitive chains to the ground. Personal responsibility is just so much more difficult than being a pampered little slave don't you know? I will never understand the lack of desire for true freedom and sovereignty and the denial of will, instead of embracing self-ownership. Well, to hell with it! Feed and water me and provide for my creature comforts. Give me my booze, sports, drugs, sex, my TV, my external stimuli and my distractions. I will willingly kiss the devil on the tongue, her poison tastes so sweet, but there's a price to pay, and it's a heavy price.

Your slavery comes with many enticing rewards that satiate

the senses, but is it worth it? Only individuals can decide that for themselves. If you allow someone else to make that choice the outcome will always and inevitably lead to slavery. The conundrum is that people are all too happy being slaves and moreover, they don't even know that they are! Many people in very high positions of power including within the Vatican and Hollywood *are* pedophiles, so watch this agenda unfold; it already is. The sickest and most depraved amongst us have the power to push this and if the people just blindly accept it, then they deserve to fall, and they will. If people lack the courage to stand up and speak out against evil, then what else would you expect?

Tolerance is a good thing, but certain things should never be tolerated. Where is the line in the sand? The fact that there is a push for the normalization of pedophilia should have people up in arms; however, care has been so bred out of the majority, that they just turn a blind eye to the destruction of their country, remaining blissfully content in their slumber. What intrigues me is that they think they will skate through life unscathed, while they cling onto willful ignorance, but the truth is that they will pay a hefty price for their complete lack of concern. The hammer is going to come down hard. Brace yourself, get ready for it.

Another issue that needs to be addressed is all this politically correct nonsense. Since when does a person have a right to not be offended? The whole thing is ridiculous. Have you noticed that people these days will find anything to get offended about? They want to create or join movements to force acceptance or to change the language, and this is another prime example of the subversion that has taken place. They are lost and completely emotionally reactive and ego driven.

We need legislation enacted to force people to use "gender neutral pronouns" so that others don't get offended. I'll tell you what, I want to identify as a helicopter, and I demand that you use only neutral, helicopter friendly pronouns when you address me. I want the government to pass legislation that protects helicopter identified people. In today's climate, I could probably win a court case claiming discrimination against my right to identify as a helicopter. It would most certainly make the news media and we could celebrate another mockery.

They got your kids! Do you understand this? They have our children! They've taken over their minds through the educational establishments, and now college campuses all over the western world have the kids completely propagandized and brainwashed, and for those who refuse to see this, that refuse to stand up and speak out, they deserve what they get. They've enslaved the children and most people were too blind to see it or too cowardice to stand up against it, so they let their kids become cannon fodder for the system, the very same one that enslaved them.

One idea for a solution to this would be to home school children, while it's still legal. For goodness sake, parents should stop allowing the government to twist the minds of their children with Marxism. Step up and be responsible and stop making excuses. Freedom does not come easily, and it's never handed to

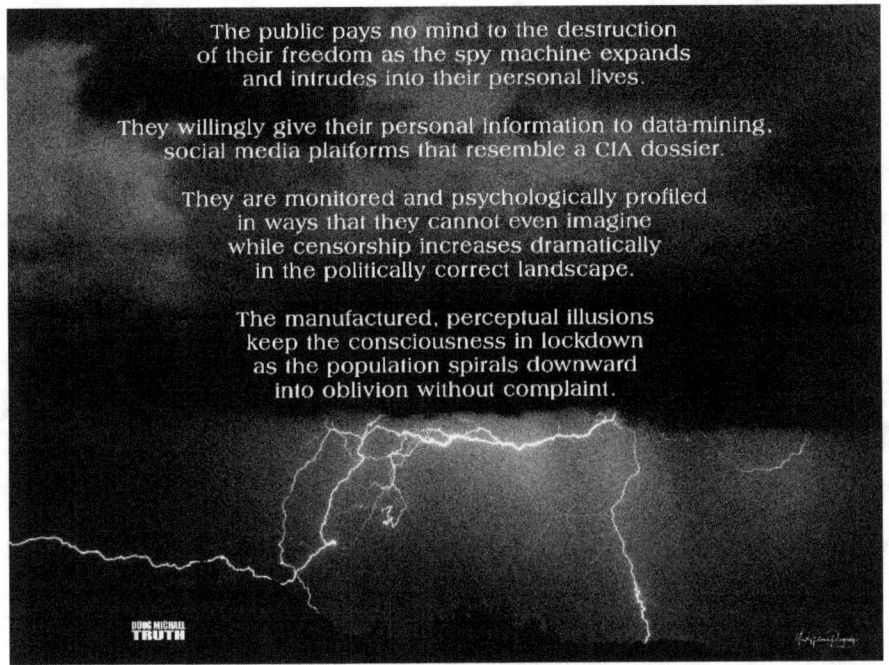

The public pays no mind to the destruction
of their freedom as the spy machine expands
and intrudes into their personal lives.

They willingly give their personal information to data-mining,
social media platforms that resemble a CIA dossier.

They are monitored and psychologically profiled
in ways that they cannot even imagine
while censorship increases dramatically
in the politically correct landscape.

The manufactured, perceptual illusions
keep the consciousness in lockdown
as the population spirals downward
into oblivion without complaint.

you on a silver platter. When you send your little ones to the government indoctrination centers, how many vaccines are they required to get, before they are even allowed into the brainwashing facility? What is it these days? 20? 30? The psyche, the spirit and the physical vessel of a child is murdered, and we allow it. Government knows best right? What the fuck is wrong with human beings?

You can believe all that you want to that going out and voting will make any difference at all, that you will ever affect any sort of positive change by using the system itself to try and change anything, but ultimately, this whole voting thing is kind of like masturbation, in the end, you're only fucking yourself. You're voting for your jailer, your enslaver. They don't represent you.

They represent the corporations, the lobbyists, the Zionists and the bankers. How is it that so few people in today's world understand that it's the same force, the same behind-the-scenes players that control both sides of the equation? And they call you a lunatic for pointing out the obvious. They are caught within perceptual illusions and by God they will defend those false realities with tenacity, sometimes with violence.

You are at once an enemy if you dare to challenge the consensus, perceptual reality, you're a threat, you're a fly in the ointment. Well keep doing that! Make waves, rock the boat, be that disturbance! The world needs rebels dammit! Let me tell you what needs to be transcended if humanity ever even has a chance of any semblance of freedom: money, religion and government. I would suggest that these are the three things that enslave us the most, and if you still have invested faith into any one of them, then you have some serious work to do, inner work, conscious advancement, perceptual expansion. Do it! Walk the road willingly, see the illusion for what it is and let the lie crumble. Walk in the fire.

It's amazing, the kids go into massive debt to go out into a world of ever-shrinking opportunity, and they pay through the nose for their own brainwashing. Public schools and colleges have become indoctrination centers for Fabian Marxism, and so many don't even have a clue of what Marxism even is; it's astounding. Marxist philosophy is the basis of Communism and this twisted ideology put into practice has seen well over 100 million people put to death and slaughtered all over the planet, and now, this disease has taken root in the western world. We've got people preaching this philosophy and professors shoving it down your children's throats in schools and colleges and no one seems to be any the wiser. If you do not see the sickness it is because you deliberately and willingly choose not to because you're scared. Now, it's OK to be afraid, but don't let that fear cripple you; your freedom is at stake!

The entire transgender movement is another example of this cultural subversion. How can anyone for a moment think that there isn't an agenda behind this? The idea is to demoralize and create conflict and it's working rather well. The Consortium and their sycophantic underlings attack the children, and no one seems to notice or care in the slightest. A culture or a society will fall into decay, morally, socially and spiritually in direct proportion to what it's willing to put up with. Regarding all this silly transgender, pangender, nongender or whatever, let's just look at this in simple biological terms, just for a moment. Let's restore some sanity to the equation. Now listen carefully guys and girls, here's your biology lesson for the day: all sexuality aside, it's quite simple but pay close attention because apparently, growing numbers of people fail to understand this: if you have a dick and balls, you're a dude; if you have a vagina and breasts, you're a lady OK? This simple equation should clarify things a bit:

$$\text{penis} + \text{testicles} = \text{male} \qquad \text{vagina} + \text{ovaries} = \text{female}$$

If you're gay, transsexual, bisexual, pansexual or whatever, that has no bearing on physical biology. So, all this crap with gender neutral pronouns, and this manipulation of the language is just absolutely stupid; it's fucking ridiculous! On a spiritual level, I don't identify who I am, with the physical vessel. The way that I see it, I am my spirit, I am my consciousness, which is beyond gender; in fact, I think that spirit is a perfectly blended balance of the feminine and masculine aspects of nature and creation. However, in this particular incarnation, I just so happen to have been born into a male body, a masculine expression. That's just nature. All this whining about gender is just another distraction and another inversion to confuse the young ones. It's hyper overidentification with the physical and it neglects the spiritual. Mission accomplished!

The Consortium are contortionists. They distort, twist and contort reality and perceptions. Their twisted ideologies are like a cancer and a parasite on this world and upon everything that it means to be human, and your kids are their primary targets.

Bezmenov basically stated that demoralization is the goal to change the perception of reality, to the point that people would be completely bewildered in the face of defending their country, community and families. He also claimed that demoralized people are unable to distinguish true information from the fictional reality.

Now of course, just like anyone else who has ever tried to warn people, this man's words have fallen upon deaf ears. It's like some sort of quirk within human psychology that can't accept a painful truth if it upsets the perceptual comfort zone. I have always been intrigued by that.

Step two in the subversion process is destabilization. We can clearly witness numerous examples of this. The migrant crisis in Europe has left many regions destabilized. It's an engineered, cultural war that's being manipulated into place leaving many areas in complete chaos and utter ruin. The planned destabilization of the European continent and the North American continent through forced multiculturalism is part of a long-standing plan put into place by the Fabian Society and the Jesuit Order.

The Fabian Society, which was founded in 1884, and its sister organization, the Milner Group, were created to operate together to infiltrate societies with Marxism through a process of gradualism, to slowly chip away at the foundations of cultures and incrementally infiltrate them through divide and rule, demoralizing, and setting the people at war with each other, destabilizing and causing the destruction of entire nations. Rather than quick and violent revolution, which traditional Marxism advocates, Fabian Marxism takes a gradual, step-by-step approach, and in Europe and North America, we can plainly witness the results of their long-standing agenda coming to fruition.

The Fabian Society has many offshoots, including: The London School of Economics; the British Labour Party; The Institute of International Affairs, and its sister organization, the American Council on Foreign Relations (which plays a huge role in American domestic and foreign policy) and many other organizations. It also played a key role in the establishment of the United Nations. It is like an octopus that spreads its slimy tentacles across the world, influencing or outright controlling areas such as trade, transportation, education, political parties, and big industry and it has penetrated into many nations. The entire US educational system was conceived, promulgated and set into motion by Fabian socialists. John Dewey, a Marxist Socialist, was considered the "father of American Education" and was an admitted "democratic socialist." Dewey and his Fabian cohorts had tremendous influence in what has become modern education. He played a major role in teacher training and the development of curriculums which would be used create the foundation of the educational establishments with Fabian propaganda. The results speak for themselves when we witness the current [mis]educational climate in America.

Waves of migrants have invaded and continue to invade many European nations. Many countries including, Greece, Germany, Sweden, England, Finland and many other European nations, have seen a massive increase in violence and brutality, due to the political leaders of these nations, selling out their own countries and opening the floodgates of immigration.

The ultra-liberal attitudes of misleaders such as Angela Merkel, Chancellor of Germany, and the open-door policies of such traitors, is condemning Europe to an absolute living nightmare, and will plummet European culture into a new dark age if this continues for much longer. This forced, multiculturalism, a complete failure, is actually part of a much more sinister agenda to incite a cultural war and to further divide and rule humanity in this destabilization process, and it's working.

The Consortium's endless wars destabilize entire regions fomenting hatred amongst the populations that have been bombed into oblivion, and then droves of asylum seekers, mostly military aged, young men, flood the countries whose leaders supported the destruction of their nations. This is done deliberately to create this clash of civilizations.

Two powerful groups are behind the immigration influx. *The United Nations Refugee Agency*, under the direct influence of a Muslim, supremacist organization called: *The Organization of Islamic Cooperation*[2] choose where refugees are relocated from and where they will be resettled.

In far too many cases, refugees are resettled in areas that simply cannot accommodate them and this is done deliberately to disrupt those areas and ultimately, to create destabilization of civilizations. Overwhelmingly, migrants come from countries that have been bombed into oblivion and the seeds of hatred have been fomented, therefore, people who hate us and despise western culture are being relocated to cities and towns across North America and Europe. In the US, 190 cities and towns are currently used for relocation.[3]

Throughout Europe and increasingly in North America, refugees simply create their own cities within cities, with no intention whatsoever of adapting to western culture and society. The ultimate goal is to infiltrate western societies and establish

Islamic, Sharia law. Strict, Sharia abiding Muslims do not assimilate into western culture; western values and Sharia, religious law is diametrically opposed.

This colonization is referred to as the Hijra, which means "migration." The whole idea is to migrate to non-Muslim areas and establish Islam in those areas. During a Hijra, Muslims are encouraged to take on multiple wives in order to breed out the enemy. This is precisely what is occurring, and I've watched several imams on European TV claiming this openly. As we witness in Europe, this is not being done peacefully. There is a rape epidemic in many areas of Europe, including Sweden, Germany, and basically everywhere the migration crisis is unfolding. In Sharia law countries, their own women are beaten or put to death for being rape victims, so the fundamentalist believers in Sharia think nothing of raping European women. I've watched films of imams openly claiming that many will take several wives and have many children and breed with westerners, in effect, breeding out Europeans.

Under strict, Sharia law, any opposition to the faith is met with intolerance, often, extremely brutal intolerance, such as public beheadings or the hanging in the streets of those who have committed the crime of being homosexual, which occurs in Saudi Arabia on a regular basis. Islam, under strict Sharia law, is a totalitarian, oppressive political entity cloaked behind the mask of religion. Religion is the law and it is an oppressive and intolerant law. What is occurring in many areas of Europe, and is also happening in North America, is a massive influx of illegal migrants that refuse to be assimilated into the cities and towns where they are arriving. Actually, it's been going on for quite a while.

Under Sharia law, if a woman is raped, she must have four male witnesses against her attacker or she will most likely be charged with adultery and punished, which usually involves being beaten publicly or even put to death by stoning. This occurs all over the Middle East in countries that practice Sharia, particularly in places like Saudi Arabia, an absolutely brutal regime, which coincidentally is a major ally of the US. If too much of a woman's skin is showing, often under Sharia, she is lashed, abused and publicly shamed for such a wicked crime as not being covered up completely. Sharia law also allows for the taking of child brides.

This "refugee resettlement" has been going on for over 30 years, but lately, it has really been increasing dramatically and so have violent crimes against European people not least, women who are being raped and sexually assaulted all over Europe in increasing numbers. In Sweden, since its adoption of multiculturalism forty years ago, the nation has seen a 300% increase in violent crimes and a whopping increase in rape by 1,472 percent![4] Sweden was once considered one of the most peaceful nations in all of Europe.[5]

The Consortium stooges in positions of political power are selling out their own respective nations in support of this insidious, ultra-liberal agenda to destabilize Europe and to create a cultural war, further dividing human beings from one another.

This open-door policy of simply allowing anyone to flood across the borders is destructive and insane and I don't care what anyone thinks about me stating this plainly obvious truth. The politically correct, liberal minded sleepers, existing within a cognition of pure fantasy, will perhaps wake up when it is their city being destroyed or their daughters being raped. There have been numerous cases where people have welcomed migrants into their homes as a charitable gesture, only to be robbed, or to have their wives or daughters molested or raped.

I've heard many liberals declare: "well this country was built on immigration." Yes, it was built on the backs of hard-working European immigrants, that underwent a stringent system of checks and balances. My grandmother stepped right off the boat onto Ellis Island from Sicily in the early 1900s and it took her years to gain citizenship. There was also no welfare system in place back then, and many of the immigrants that arrived on American shores returned to their respective homelands because they simply could not succeed in building a new life here. The European migrants came here for a better life and worked very hard for it. The migrants flooding into Europe and America now expect everything to be handed to them, and it is being done and exhausting the social systems at the expense of the citizens of those nations.

Allowing illegal immigrants to simply waltz right into the US has already created serious problems, as with the growing gang violence in areas such as Los Angeles. Homeland Security, and all the oppressive laws that have passed since the engineered 9/11 attacks has nothing to do with protecting Americans, and everything to do with initiating the Fabian Society and the Consortium's agenda to destroy US sovereignty and freedom. In February 2019 alone, over 76,000 migrants crossed the southern US border.[6] In April, close to 100,000 migrants were detained.[7]

Marxism gained a strong foothold in Latin America, under the banner of "Liberation Theology." The smokescreen is that this movement sought to apply religious faith by aiding the poor through involvement in political and civic affairs. The KGB was behind the creation of this movement and its dispersion through Latin America, which caused massive destabilization in many nations. Although on the surface, the Catholic Church claimed to be opposed to this theology, it is intertwined with it. Anything that can be adopted or supported to uproot nations and create cultural wars is useful to the Vatican, its Jesuit controllers and the Fabian Society, in their endless quest to infiltrate nations with Marxist, Ideological subversion. The current Pope played a major role in supporting Marxist ideologies in Latin America. In fact, the Vatican owns and controls *all* of Latin America.

In many European countries such as Germany, Sweden, Greece and many others, police are ordered to stand down when crimes such as rapes or assaults occur. German police have come forward claiming that they are not allowed to detain migrants or prevent suspects from escaping custody.[8] Many of these criminals that commit these violent atrocities go free without charges as the courts are protecting them which in itself, is very telling. The brainwashed and numbed out liberals refuse to acknowledge this for fear of being labeled "Islamophobic." Can you imagine, your "elected representatives" selling you out in this manner while preaching tolerance and multiculturalism? Another thing to consider is that in many cases, the media is completely silent about these atrocities occurring all over Europe.

Despite the unfolding crisis in Europe, the great and pious Pope, is urging European nations to take in even more migrants. The Marxist Pope is just a front man stooge for the Jesuit Order, a military order which operates behind the throne of the Vatican. The Fabian/Jesuit/Marxist agenda is to destroy European culture and replace it with oppressive and tyrannical Sharia law. The Vatican, and the dark Jesuit force behind it have no problem destabilizing Europe and destroying its culture in favor of an oppressive system of open totalitarianism; it's how they have operated through history, and you can bet your life that the Vatican and the Jesuit manipulators operating behind the dark throne, are absolutely behind this. These Consortium puppeteers will pit one collective, religious ideology against another.

Relatively few have ever heard of the Jesuits or their general, Adolfo Nicholas, a man referred to as the "Black Pope." Their influence has been understood for centuries and even a few of the American founders warned about it. In a letter penned to Thomas Jefferson in 1816, John Quincy Adams, the 6th American president had this to say concerning the Jesuit Order:

"This Society [Jesuits] *has been a greater calamity to mankind than the French Revolution or Napoleon's despotism or ideology. It has obstructed the progress of reformation and the improvement of the human mind in society much longer and more fatally."*[9]

Marques de LaFayette, the French statesman and member of the Continental Army during the revolutionary war, had this to say concerning Jesuit power:

"It is my opinion that if the liberties of this country-the United States of America-are destroyed, it will be by the subtlety of the Roman Catholic Jesuit priests, for they are the most crafty, dangerous enemies to civil and religious liberty. They have instigated most of the wars of Europe."[10]

Migrants arriving in Europe are demanding that the cultures of the nations they are invading, bend to fit to *their* cultural systems and the vast majority have no intention of assimilating into European cultures, they want to take over, and of course, this has the full blessing of the Vatican and its Jesuit controllers. This of course is occurring in North America as well, and it is becoming more readily apparent. Illegal migrants from Islamic nations are being smuggled into America and granted full asylum.

Despite Trump's agenda to build a wall along America's southern border, he recently signed an amnesty bill granting asylum to illegal immigrants as a bargaining tool in "negotiations" with the Democrats.[11] The Consortium is playing chess, and when European culture is decimated, a more centrally controlled system will be built upon the ashes. It's a repeating pattern of destruction and restructuring of whole societies and this pattern will continue to repeat until humanity reaches a higher level of consciousness, or it allows itself to be destroyed.

We have reached the decision point. Unfortunately, it is damned near impossible to reach someone who has been indoctrinated for their entire life into a specific ideology and who is anchored firmly within their cognitive fortresses. A mind so trapped and lost within ideologies will murder, rape, torture and die for its erroneous beliefs, failing to ever see the cognitive manipulation that has ensnared their own minds; therefore, we will see many casualties in this war as one culture destroys another in this historical cycle of destruction. Of course, the Jesuits and the Fabians will clank their glasses of the finest champagne and revel in humanity's stupidity.

Take into consideration also, the fact that the US government is heavily allied with Saudi Arabia and Israel, the two biggest violators of human rights in the world. We have these scumbag, Consortium serving politicos claiming things like: "we don't support terrorists," and yet are in bed with the Saudi royals and the Israeli Zionists, the personifications of terrorism. Maybe it's the oil eh? That's part of it but it's far more than that; it's a mutual agenda of Consortium puppets enacting an itinerary to destroy cultures and build their globalist, totalitarian system of slavery upon the ashes, and if humanity does not wake up to the realization of how they are being played, we will witness our own demise. Saudi Arabia, with their flagrant disregard for human rights, was selected to oversee a United Nations panel on human rights![12]

Totalitarianism is defined thusly:

"a political system in which the state recognizes no limits to its authority and strives to regulate every aspect of public and private life wherever feasible. A distinctive feature of totalitarian governments is an 'elaborate ideology, a set of ideas that gives meaning and direction to the whole society.' Totalitarianism is the most severe and extreme form of authoritarianism."[13]

The modern dictionary definition is:

1. *Centralized control by an autocratic authority.*

2. *The political concept that the citizen should be totally subject to an absolute state authority.*[14]

The media has been complicit in this current divide and rule situation that we see occurring in America. Elections are meaningless, so while Americans fight and bicker over all this manufactured nonsense, the same, one world agenda keeps unfolding. Then, there are groups such as *Antifa*, and *Black Lives*

Matter, which are infiltrated with agitators to incite violence and agitate the herds. Billionaire, globalist Marxists such as George Soros, who was largely responsible for funding the crisis in the Ukraine,[15] provide the funding for such subversive organizations.

Idiot, Hollywood celebrities that haven't a clue, publicly vilify the current CEO, and either wittingly or not, contribute to the divide and rule destabilization process. It would be so much more useful if they used their platform to explain to people how this game really works, that it's the same big money and corporate interests that control both parties and that your vote means nothing. Along with the media, these neo-liberals contribute to the problem. This country has never been so divided and it's all over meaningless nonsense.

The next step is crisis and we could go on and on with this one. Many of the events that occur are manufactured crises, or false flag attacks that all lead to the normalization of tyranny.

False flag is defined thusly:

"A political or military act orchestrated in such a way that it appears to have been carried out by a party that is not in fact responsible."[16]

There are numerous examples of false flag events and manufactured crises including: the bombing of the Alfred P. Murrah building in Oklahoma City, on April 19th, 1995; The Gulf of Tonkin event which led America into the Vietnam war; the sinking of the luxury liner, the Lusitania, which garnered support for American involvement in WW I; the 1993 bombing of the World Trade Center; the massacre in Waco, Texas, on April 19th, 1993; the London bombings of July 7, 2005; and of course the key event which changed the face of society, forever, the attacks in New York, Washington DC and Pennsylvania that occurred on September 11th, 2001.

The events of 911 set into motion open-ended wars and an absolute militarization of the police. The march towards a total police state has continued unabated and the open-ended wars have escalated exponentially. Police forces across the US have become completely militarized, heavily armed and equipped for urban combat. The open-ended "war on terror" is a masquerade for empire building and the procurement of strategic lands that are rich in natural resources. It is a scam that has caused untold misery and by now has claimed well over a million lives.[17]

While the polarized herds fight each other over manufactured illusion, political theater and engineered division, the war machine expands, and the militarization of police forces domestically increases dramatically. In 2017, The Donald announced his plan to send more troops to Afghanistan in this long-standing, open ended war of terror.[18] At the same time, he lifted a ban on the transferring of military gear to police forces, which will aid in the further militarization of an already militarized police.[19] This decision will allow local police agencies to access heavy weaponry, including grenade launchers.[20] All to keep you "safe and free" of course. This is all part of the final phase of the four-step process of ideological subversion, the normalization of a military police state and the acceptance of oppression and tyranny.

Americans have accepted infringements on their freedom in exchange for the *illusion* of safety. They have accepted massive surveillance technology being implemented everywhere; no-knock SWAT team raids that have killed many innocent people;[21] entire cities being placed in lockdown and martial law, as with the aftermath of the Boston bombings;[22] the passing of freedom-destroying legislation such as the NDAA, (National Defense Authorization Act)[23] which basically makes everyone a potential suspect; the skies being filled with spy drones and the massive militarization of domestic law enforcement; in short, they have embraced with open arms, an invasive, technological police state.

While the grip of oppression tightens in America, the war drums beat and the saber rattling continues under the current administration as it advances the neocon agenda, setting its sights on Iran and North Korea.[24] By executive order, economic sanctions have been imposed on Venezuela,[25] and now a US sponsored military coup is underway in that country, which I'm sure has nothing to do with the fact that it contains the world's largest oil reserves.[26] Iran is number four on the list of largest oil reserves, which I'm certain is also purely coincidental.

Meanwhile the corrupted, completely bought-and-paid-for misleaders in the district of criminals, continue to support Israel and Saudi Arabia, two of the most brutal regimes on the planet. The Donald has already shown his allegiance to AIPAC and the CFR so what else would you expect than the continuation of the agenda set into place by the Consortium and carried out by his neocon predecessors?

To those who are opposed to Trump but believe that Obama was any better, they have fallen for the divide and rule game. They have been polarized and cognitively manipulated to believe that there is any difference between the puppets that are placed into the CEO position of corporate America; there isn't! One serves the left, one the right but both the left and right are controlled by the same ruling oligarchs, and it is so imperative that people begin to understand this.

While the polarized herd bickers over whether or not a wall should be built, if Trump paid hush money to a porn star, the government shutdown, or any other of a myriad of distractions in this political theater, the agenda of tyranny rolls on, full steam ahead!

Another thing I'd like to mention is the whole Q Anon phenomenon. Q is an entity that provides data dumps online claiming that sealed indictments exist, implicating powerful people in high political positions, and that arrests of the criminal elements are coming. The alternative community has been making similar claims for over a decade, so I wouldn't count on that happening. This is one that I will file in the "I'll believe it when I see it" category.

The events of 9/11, 2001 were the catalyst that is pushing America into what is rapidly becoming a completely militarized, **totalitarian super-state.** The TSA (Transportation Security Administration) is an agency that was established directly as a result of the 9/11 attacks and its purpose is not to protect citizens but to desensitize them into accepting infringements upon their freedoms, all as part of the normalization process. There have been numerous reports of TSA agents harassing people, including the elderly and disabled, even children.[27]

A surveillance grid control structure has been erected all around us and again, tyranny has become normalized and so few even seem to be remotely aware or care in the slightest. The cultural subversion has been effective in this country and much of the western world. The Pentagon cannot account for trillions of dollars, and I would suggest that much of the missing money gets funneled into black budget operations to develop technology that will be used to further enslave.

AI and the untested 5G system are being rolled out, and the potential dangers of this technology are very serious. Now we have organizations that want to normalize pedophilia as just another sexual preference. Corruption, tyranny, totalitarianism, decadence and depravity have become normalized. How many people will turn a blind eye and just go on, oblivious? Business as usual. Now it's reached the point where this agenda is right out in the open; it's no longer in the shadows, and still, so few can even see it. Such is the power of total psychological mind conditioning and cognitive programming.

The solution lies in the individual's willingness to free their consciousness and deliberately withdraw their consent from all this lunacy, to stop complying with their own enslavement. First, one must acknowledge the situation as it is and shift their perspective accordingly. In this final hour, it's beginning to look as if it may be too late. I still maintain a shred of hope, that when push comes to shove, humanity may finally get it right, but again, it comes down to the individual's willingness to be a part of the solution, to dismantle their cognitive fortresses once and for all and step into the light of their true being and potential. There is no other way.

SIX

Rectal-Cranial Inversion

There is currently a major epidemic sweeping across America and Europe that has claimed the minds of many people and it appears to be spreading exponentially with no ending in sight. It can be recognized by one or more of its many symptoms, including but not limited to:

1. Appalling lack of historical knowledge.
2. Rabid hatred of anyone with a differing viewpoint.
3. Blind embracement of identity politics.
4. Engaging in mindless tirades.
5. The belief that more than two genders exist in nature.
6. The belief that statues, cars, flags or other inanimate objects somehow have the ability to be racist.
7. The embracement and promotion of Marxist Socialism, without even knowing the definition of those words.

8. The belief that anyone that doesn't embrace ultra-left ideologies is a "Nazi."

9. The idea that wide open borders and a disarmed population somehow keeps a nation safer.

10. The belief that public schooling has anything to do with education.

11. The belief that heterosexual, Caucasian men are the cause of all the world's problems.

12. The belief in censorship to protect from being offended.

13. The promotion of political correctness.

14. Inability to form coherent arguments based on sound logic.

There are many more symptoms of this pervasive illness known as *Rectal-Cranial Inversion,* or in perhaps more layman terms, "Mental Libtardation." Now, if you've read this far, then you understand by now my view that both parties are controlled by the same behind-the-scenes manipulators, the same ruling oligarchs; therefore, I am neither liberal nor conservative. I refuse to be polarized and divided. I have no political affiliation whatsoever.

I see politics as nothing more than a divide and rule mind game, a perceptual illusion set in place to split the human herd into opposing camps and to convince people that they have a choice. As far as I'm concerned, both major parties are two sides of the same coin, different masks on the same ugly face, two wings on the same shit bird.

That being said, the left has really shown its hand since the last [s]election and I'd like to examine some of the lunacy that has been placed on open display for all to observe in this highly entertaining time within the Earth Game in the here and now. I also feel that injecting a bit of humor into the act of pointing out all the absurdities can lighten the load so to speak and can also be quite a lot of fun. If we couldn't have a good laugh occasionally, as we examine all this mindlessness, and if we took it all so damned seriously, we may very well go insane. Life in the Earth Game, and western culture in particular is a mental asylum, and the lunatics have taken over.

In the run up to the 2016 US presidential election, the mainstream media played a massive role in pushing the narrative that there was no chance that Trump could possibly win. Droves of unquestioning Democratic supporters bought into this narrative so comprehensively, that when Trump actually won, the absolute shock, dismay and disbelief that immediately followed was staggering, monumental, and very entertaining.

Grown adults were caught on film crying like children over the loss of their would-be political savior, as if the end of the world had been ushered in over Clinton's loss in the meaningless charade that is the US election process. In the eyes of the mentally libtarded, it's as if Hillary was the female Jesus, come to save the country, and Donald Trump was Satan himself. Numerous film clips exist showing the weeping and wailing adult crybabies displaying their childish and infantilized mentality, and I suppose it could be argued whether these films are sad and pathetic, or hysterically funny. Personally, I find them to be quite hilarious. One thing that characterizes those suffering from Rectal-Cranial Inversion is irrational and extreme mental instability on a massive scale, accompanied by unrestrained emotional outbursts.

I've never in my entire life as an American, witnessed so much hatred being spewed upon an incumbent president. Of course, there are always those that oppose whichever CEO happens to be occupying the oval office at the moment, but this time, the vitriol and venom is at a level I've never seen before. Some of the most draconian laws and legislation were passed under the Bush and Obama administrations, and there was not nearly this much anger and contempt directed towards the figurehead, sock puppet president. It really makes you wonder.

Trump was presented as the anti-establishment candidate, the one who would "drain the swamp" and yet, his administration is full of members of the Council on Foreign Relations and fellow neocon affiliates of the notorious Bilderberg group, two massive front organizations of the Consortium, the ones who hand select those who will become president and do the bidding of their globalist masters.

College campuses all over the country provided "safe spaces," comfort dogs and hot coco to their young adult students to ease their pain after the day that Trump won and the Earth stood still.[1] Many celebrities, such as Cher, Miley Cyrus and many others said they would leave the country if Trump won, but they're still here.

What a shame. The infantilized mentality and emotional instability that has taken hold of the mentally libtarded is truly astounding to observe.

A great example of this was the gathering of the mentally libtarded in large numbers, and on several occasions, as they took to the streets to shout loudly at the air to show their disapproval at the appointment of the new figurehead. Groups of people with their placards in hand, gathered to yell together and it was like observing petulant children throwing tantrums because they didn't get their fucking cookie. Grown adults shouting and stomping their feet like four-year-old children is a glaring example of how far the left has fallen and exhibits Rectal-Cranial Inversion on wide open display, in all its astonishing glory.

It appears that everywhere we look within today's climate of political correctness and censorship, we can readily observe the victim mentality on open display. The world is awash with this limiting and completely disempowering state of consciousness, and what makes this so appalling, is that so many are deliberately *choosing* to be victims, rather than searching for ways to step into a greater level of awareness and become the victor in their own life, to create *themselves*! Instead, they spit on the gift and cast blame, forever failing to see that for the most part, their plight is internal.

It seems as if people are searching for things to get offended about and then demanding that the world caters to their manufactured sensitivities. This has gotten way out of hand and

Our entire culture
has become degraded to the point of utter insanity.

Idiocy passes as intelligence,
tyranny passes as freedom,
superficiality passes as beauty,
corruption passes as virtue,
ignorance passes as knowledge
and
consumerism passes as success,
foolishness passes as wisdom
and
lies pass as truth.

This societal and cultural collapse is simply accepted

by the masses

DOUG MICHAEL
TRUTH

just appears to be getting worse as the days go by.

There appears to be this growing trend of being offended and then the demand for censorship as more and more groups and individuals play the victim card. We have an absolute epidemic of victimhood occurring, and interestingly, many groups or individuals that cry victim, seem to have no problem taking on the role of victimizer when it suits their agenda.

It's come to the point where comedians, people who tell jokes and make people laugh for a living, are censoring *themselves* out of fear of backlash by certain groups or individuals being offended, and once self-censorship takes hold in a society that is supposed to have freedom of speech as one of its foundational principles, well then, they've got you by the balls! Once the freedom of speech and expression is taken away, or willingly surrendered, you are on the cusp of complete enslavement, absolute subjugation. This is where we are, whether we like it or not, but it seems as if the general population is far more concerned and distracted with irrelevant nonsense, like this charade of political theater that's got everyone's attention, or the absolute enthrallment with social media. "Hey, let's create a platform, that we can use to gauge how stupid and ignorant people are, steal their data, and spy on them. They will willingly worship at our digital altar." Enter Facebook, Twitter and all the rest of it… Suckers!

One thing that really gets me, is how easily people are caving in to the demands for censorship just because some thin-skinned, juvenile minded victim complains about whatever it is that offends them. People demanded that a Christmas song from the 1940s be pulled from the rotation, and certain radio stations kowtowed to the whiny victims' demands. They've been *trained* to be so easily offended, like spineless jellyfish. They've been systematically conditioned to operate purely from their emotions; the intellect has been left out of the equation. It amazes me that people will take such offence to a harmless song or to a Charlie Brown cartoon but seem to be unphased at billions of dollars being funneled into the coffers of the war profiteers, or the growing numbers of homeless people or the massive corruption infesting the body politic. They seem to have no shame when it comes to advertising and displaying their ignorance, folly and abject idiocy.

I would go so far as to suggest that certain organizations

instigate this and that useful-idiot liberals are manipulated into promoting this agenda while ignoring matters of true importance. I think these wussy simpletons, these *wimpletons*, sit around with their unresolved anger and their cheap chardonnay, and try to *find* things to be offended about. It seems that being offended is what keeps these half-witted dullards going.

In 2017, I watched a video of an incident that occurred at a car show in Canada. For my readers that may not be familiar with what a car show is, they are very popular in many areas of North America. Basically, a bunch of people will get together at a specific location to show off their hotrods, have cookouts, gather etc. It's a gathering of motorheads and car lovers. In this video I saw, one of the participants displayed a car that was a replica of the General Lee, a 1969 Dodge Charger, which was a car that was featured in a television show that aired from 1979 to 1985 in America, called *The Dukes of Hazzard*.

The vehicle displays a painted, confederate flag on the roof, and the words "General Lee" are painted next to it. A woman at the car show flipped out at the owners, referring to their vehicle as a "racist car." She had an absolute meltdown which was an ugly yet colorful display of ignorance at its finest.[2] The woman claims that black people were murdered because of the battle flag of the confederacy. She screams and yammers about privilege in the video and demands that the car be removed from the show while making threats and generally making a jackass out of herself.

Slavery was an inherited institution and it was only the

wealthy, primarily plantation owners that possessed slaves. Most of the soldiers that fought in the confederate army during the Civil war were defending their right to secede, and they were also fighting against huge tariffs imposed by the union. Lincoln was not the great emancipator that official history has presented him as; in fact, he was a tyrant that was motivated by gaining as much power as he could, just like today's politicians. He was a power-hungry puppet of the bankers and he didn't give a shit about the slaves. He was the same as these modern-day sycophantic misleaders. I'm digressing a bit here, and there will be more on revisionist history a bit later in this writing.

Unfortunately, these emotionally unstable, mentally libtarded buffoons are everywhere these days. Do they not realize that black people were mistreated in the north? Slavery and segregation are absolutely disgusting in my eyes, but the point is that people seem to be looking for racism and are seeking to be offended, often when there is no reason to be. They are imprisoned by the victim consciousness, which of course is so openly encouraged these days.

The mass bombing of innocent civilians doesn't offend me but a "racist car" or a Rudolph the Red-nosed Reindeer cartoon has me outraged! Homeless people in the streets is no problem, but "Baby it's Cold Outside" is a moral outrage! To suggest that people's priorities are completely fucked is an understatement. Oops! I used the "F" word. If anyone is offended by that, well then good! They can just as easily choose to not be offended. This whole politically correct climate of "you can't say this; you can't say that" is absolutely ridiculous! It's an attack on free speech and free expression and is just one of many examples of Marxist subversion of our culture.

Some countries such as Canada, and a few nations in Europe, are jailing people simply for speaking out against their government's immigration policies. When it's come to the point that simply saying the wrong thing can have you imprisoned, perhaps it's time to begin seriously paying attention and reevaluating your situation? Unfortunately, far too many people simply ignore this unfolding scenario and choose distraction instead of acknowledging what is occurring. They will choose to ignore, believing that they will never be personally affected by it and in the eyes of the people behind this agenda, ignorance is consent. If someone chooses to remain ignorant, which is what it is, a choice, and if they willfully turn a blind eye, then they are nothing but a slave and they deserve to be. They deserve the chains that bind their heart and mind because they have chosen them! They have chosen them through their apathy, their tolerance of tyranny and their blasé' attitude.

Ultimately, what we see occurring across western culture is a massive homogenization. Homogenization is defined as:

1. "To form by blending unlike elements; make homogeneous."

2."To make uniform or similar, as in composition or function."[3]

This is what is occurring; it's a massive push for collectivism at the expense of individual freedom and expression. This is all part of the one world agenda. The powers behind this want one government, one currency, one religion, one race, one *gender*, and the further consolidation of wealth and power into the hands of the few. They want a collectivized and regimented herd. What makes this so sinister, is that this agenda seeks to completely destroy diversity, thereby denying experience.

There still seems to remain a high percentage of people that believe that government schools have anything at all to do with education. What the schools have become, are Marxist, indoctrination centers that twist and contort the children's minds, conditioning them with propaganda, to churn out a generation of dumbed-down automatons that cannot think critically. The Consortium, globalist Marxists, need to get the kids, and unfortunately, they've been very successful in their endeavors.

They are contorting the minds of children, and a good example of this, is the recent agenda to teach five and six-year-olds about sexuality and gender fluidity in the classrooms. The California Department of Education plans to make it mandatory to teach kindergarteners that there are *fifteen* different genders![4] Parents will not be able to opt out of this lunacy. Why 15? Why not 26, 8, or 39? No, that's just silly. In New York, some districts have welcomed transvestites into the classrooms, to teach about transgenderism to kindergarteners.[5] Now, I have nothing against gay people, or trans, or whatever, but small children have no business being taught sex when they should be going about the business of just being children. This is forced tolerance and it should not be accepted, but unfortunately, too many people remain asleep, so this agenda just keeps rolling on with very little complaint. Just trust the government, they will educate your kids and prepare them for the posthuman world.

This agenda of bringing "anything goes" sexuality into the classrooms, is the ultimate denial of experience, as it confuses kids and denies them the experience of simply being children! And far too many people are turning a blind eye to it. Some moronic and brain-dead parents are even permitting their children to have drugs or surgery to alter their physical bodies and there is a sinister agenda behind this. Boys are being feminized and girls are being masculinized in this attempt to contort and twist everything, including nature itself.

Regarding the transgender agenda, it is very much in line with the transhumanist ideology, which is why we are seeing so much attention being given to it. It's come to the point where every twisted, contorted, amoral, diseased and completely fucked up ideology has become normalized and accepted, as every depravity and insult to the spirit is paraded before the comatose masses, while they buy into every ready-made distraction, getting their panties twisted, being offended by irrelevant bullshit, turning a blind eye to what they ought to truly be offended by, the destruction of their freedom!

The race card is being played everywhere in this divide and rule shit show. Everything is racist: racist Christmas songs, racist cars, racist statues, racist flags, racist cartoons, racist everything! If the victim doesn't like something, they simply call it "racist," and demand censorship. The sad thing is that often, they get it! In early 2019, the *US National Academy of Sciences* published a paper claiming that air pollution is now racist.[6]

I no longer want to be referred to as a white man, that offends me. I want to be called "Caucasian American." That's another thing, all of these anti-white tirades that are going on. Apparently, the Caucasian, heterosexual male is the devil, the new enemy to cast aspersions on and the cause of all the evils in the world, as if to suggest that no African, Asian, Indian or any other race ever committed evil acts. In South Africa, mass genocide is occurring against peaceful, white farmers, but you don't hear much about this in the corporate controlled media.

If people could get past all this divisive bullshit and unite on common grounds, perhaps we might stand a chance at creating a better experience and change the direction in which we are headed. As it stands, we are marching headlong into a dystopian, posthuman world of surveillance and totalitarian control, and so few seem to care, as long as they have a few things to pacify and distract them.

If you want to get an idea of where this is headed, investigate

China's social credit system. Citizens' every move is tracked and monitored by cameras and smart devices and they are rewarded with points for good behavior or given demerits for non-compliance. Some people are even turning in fellow citizens to the government and are rewarded for it. Things like jaywalking could result in a reduction of points and can affect a person's buying options or their right to travel. Certain areas in Canada are implementing this system and with the rollout of the 5G system in America and elsewhere, this is the total, control grid system that we have to look forward to. An episode of a TV show called *Black Mirror*, eerily depicts what this system looks like. The episode is called *Nosedive*.[7]

Facial recognition, scanning technology is being implemented everywhere in this technetronic, digital, control grid system, and people think it's just wonderful! The vast majority have no idea of how far the technology has advanced and the threat that we face as we plummet into the world of artificial intelligence and total control and surveillance. They willingly accept this Orwellian nightmare with open arms, turning a blind eye to the threat that stares them in the face. Compliant slaves are always the easiest to control.

Rectal-Cranial Inversion infects much of humanity, but the radical left liberals seem to be the most affected by this growing affliction. The far left, neo-feminists are also quite a sight to behold. Third wave feminists, in recent years, have marched in "women's rights" protests demanding equal rights but often, the gatherings become little more than displays of open aggression against males, particularly, straight, white men. Often, many of the mental midgets that attend these gatherings will dress skimpily and wave placards that read "slut" or "slut pride" or "proud slut" or "I'm a hoe too" or "my pussy my choice."[8] These gatherings that have occurred in cites all over the world, have become known as "slut walks." The funny thing to me is that these 3rd wave feminists call this display of idiocy "liberation."

The thing that the neo-feminists, SJWs and the radical left do not understand, is that they are being used to promote cultural Marxism, to rip apart western culture from within, and it's an absolute tragedy watching this unfold.

All across western culture, we can readily observe the overt attacks against masculinity, the war against men, as if there is something wrong with existing within a male expression in the world at this time. The truly reprehensible and sadistic thing about this situation, is that they are targeting the children, the young boys, and we let them do it!

Everywhere you look, this is plainly visible, this absolute war on men! In television and advertising, in the schools, the media, everywhere! This neo-feminist bullshit, and this social justice warrior nonsense, has become a cancer upon this culture. No wonder movements such as MGTOW (Men Going Their Own Way) have grown so exponentially. Young men are growing tired of all the double standards and the demands to kowtow to the superiority stance that these feminists demand, that is merely *disguised* as equality. Men need to seriously wake up to this agenda and say no more! And you now what? They are!

Everything has been contorted and turned on its head as you are made to wallow in this imbalanced, cornucopia of lunacy, and woe to you if you don't just accept it without protest and swallow all the bullshit.

In this contorted mess of transgenderism, pangenderism, non-binary, transhumanism and all of the other nonsense being promoted for mass public consumption, boys will be girls and girls will be boys. Some parents will even allow their kids to receive drug treatments to slow puberty and alter the chemical makeup of their children because confused little Johnny, wants to become confused little Jill in the moment. This is nothing short of child abuse. This is happening all over the world, and we're talking about very young children. Parents will give their ten-year-old boy estrogen treatments to feminize him, and this is accepted! In New York, a law just passed that allows parents to choose X on the birth certificate, rather than being "gender specific."[9] What the hell is that?

In Illinois, the governor, J.B. Pritzker ordered the state's Medicaid program to pay for sexual reassignment surgery for transgender people that have been diagnosed with "gender dysphoria,"[10] which is defined as:

*"a distressed state arising from conflict between a person's **gender identity** and the sex the person has or was*

identified as having at birth,"[11]

Many amongst the mentally libtarded are demanding that the language be changed to accommodate their Rectal-Cranial Inversion. They want babies to be referred to as "they-bies."[12] Genital mutilation is called "reassignment surgery." These lunatics actually take all of this nonsense seriously and believe that a child can choose its own gender. Nature decides whether a child is male, or female based on either one or two X chromosomes present within the genes.

The entire feminist movement was a creation of the bankers. The Rockefeller Foundation, the Fabian Society, and the notorious Tavistock Institute, through their propaganda experts such as Edward Bernays, played a major role in orchestrating the feminist agenda. They did this for three main reasons:

1. To push women into the workforce so that the amount of taxation could be increased.

2. To break up the family unit, which is a necessary component for a functional society.

3. To create a war between the sexes, to divide and rule, which is the modus operandi of these globalist manipulators.

Observe the manipulation of the language, with words and phrases like: "toxic masculinity," "mansplaining" or a host of other language designed to undermine the male. Even the APA, the *American Psychological Association* has climbed aboard the pussification bandwagon, claiming that traditional masculinity can hurt boys.[13] All across western culture, boys and men are being emasculated and shamed simply for being males. Think deeply about what this does to a culture.

Roughly 25% of American children are being raised by single mothers.[14] Statistically speaking, children raised in fatherless homes are far more likely to commit crimes later in life. In fact, it's estimated that 85% of young incarcerated people come from fatherless homes.[15] Many young women will have multiple kids with multiple fathers and have no problem with the state taking care of them, which means working people's taxes provide for their poor judgements. Almost half of marriages in America end in divorce, most of which are initiated by women.[16]

What happens when the men become marginalized, emasculated and spineless? They will bow their heads in the face of tyranny and give their boys to the social engineering, mind doctors to be castrated and turned into impotent weaklings. It's an absolutely disgusting situation that is unfolding and for those that still want to put their children through the government schools and allow them to be indoctrinated into this climate of guilt, shame and twisted sexuality, while they turn a blind eye to this situation, you are not going to like the outcome! The system is churning out docile and emasculated boys and the result will be utter slavery.

In January 2019, Gillette ran an advertisement that was loaded with blatant anti-male propaganda, that outraged many men, and rightly so.[17] The company claims that the add takes on "toxic masculinity," using that buzzword again in this war against men. What about toxic feminism? It's good that so many men saw this add for what it is, but you need to really start paying attention because this kind of shit is everywhere now. Don't let these Marxist Socialists take your boys and twist their minds! I find it curious that Gillette would run an add like that being that their primary customer base is men, and I would bet that the Vegas odds are 1,000 to 1 that that commercial was written by a libtarded feminist, suffering with rectal-Cranial Inversion. It's a Crazy world we live in!

Everywhere we look in today's western culture, we can observe this attack against masculinity. The underlying theme seems to be prevalent: "men are stupid," men are pigs," "men are useless," and on it goes. All this nonsense is part of a dark agenda to break apart western culture, to instill victimhood, to create a false sense of entitlement and to divide and rule the masses.

Look around you with observational eyes. We have a nation that celebrates ignorance and embraces it willingly! The results are a growing police state and a surveillance grid system set up to monitor your every move and I think perhaps expanding to the point where it will monitor your every thought. So what? As long as I have my distractions, my video games, my TV, my microchipped credit cards, my gadgets and my bread and circuses, why would I want to be bothered with the rising tyranny in our midst? Just call those people who are aware of this and are speaking out about it, "conspiracy theorists" and go fetch some Pokémon. Shove some fast food slop down your gullet, click on the idiot tube and be a happy little slave! Your masters thank you for making it so easy.

In Pennsylvania, in 2017, there were anti Sharia law protests occurring. Sharia law is rule by oppressive religious ideology. Under Sharia, women are treated as subhuman and freedom is basically non-existent. Female genital mutilation, child brides, and all manner of barbarity and oppression are practiced and accepted under Sharia law. In places like Saudi Arabia, gay people are hung in the streets from cranes simply for being gay. Public beheadings occur on a regular basis and people accused of "blasphemy" are put to death by stoning. Sharia is an open display of oppression and tyranny. During these protests, the left was anti-protesting against the Sharia protesters. Many of these mentally libtarded were "women's rights activists," protesting in favor of Sharia law. It makes absolutely no sense, but then, those suffering from Rectal-Cranial Inversion are so far removed from reality, what else would we expect?

Many of the leftist, completely uneducated dullards claim to be women's rights activists and yet fight against those who do not want oppressive Sharia in their country. One lunatic stabbed a police horse with a flagpole![18] What the hell did the horse do?

131

Tolerant liberalism at its finest! The ironic thing is that the jackass that did this is a transgender woman but doesn't seem to have a problem with Sharia! In a country such as Saudi Arabia, this person would be hanged or publicly beheaded, simply because of her sexuality. What an idiot, and you can't make this stuff up!

In many areas of Europe, Sharia law courts that exist alongside established, western law are becoming all too common. Western ideals are not compatible with Sharia and this is being done deliberately, to divide and rule. The majority of the migrants flooding into Europe and America have no desire to assimilate into western culture; they want to establish their own way of life which is diametrically opposed to western culture and values. We see the results of this as many European nations are becoming completely decimated, such as Germany, France and Sweden. This is an engineered cultural and religious war and it is about to explode like a powder keg.

As I mentioned, I've heard many amongst the mentally libtarded claim that "America was built by immigrants." That's true, but what they don't consider is that many of the migrants that came to America returned to their respective homelands because they simply couldn't make it here. They worked very hard to establish themselves. Another thing the libtarded don't seem to be aware of, is that in the late 19th and early 20th centuries, there was no welfare state. The migrants (mostly European) that came to America in those days had to sacrifice a great deal, and they certainly weren't striving to establish Sharia law! They sweat and bled to make a better life for themselves, unlike today's migrants that expect everything to be handed to them for free.

These days, migrants cross the American border illegally and are handed everything, including housing, welfare, voting rights, medical care, etc. Health care for illegal immigrants costs American taxpayers roughly *$18.5 billion* annually![19] This is a massive, destabilization effort, and it's working. Meanwhile, growing numbers of American combat veterans or citizens cannot receive necessary assistance as the number of homeless people keeps rising. It doesn't seem to make sense, but from the point of view of the Consortium, it is perfectly logical because the idea is to destroy western culture. Of course, simply pointing out these facts is often met with the labeling of one as a "xenophobe," a "racist," a "conspiracy theorist," or any number of smear words designed to discredit the ones pointing out these things and spewed so thoughtlessly by those suffering from Rectal-Cranial Inversion.

The Consortium's plan to create a pan-European union was laid out in a book authored in the 1920s by the Freemason, Richard Coudenhove Kalergi, titled *Practical Idealism*. Apparently, Kalergi received support from Louis Nathaniel de Rothschild and the banker, Max Warburg to put the project into motion and became known as the "Kalergi Plan."[20] The idea was to destroy nation states and homogenize Europe through forced immigration, precisely what we see unfolding in Europe today. The idea is to destroy native Europeans and create massive destabilization through instigating an engineered cultural war. In *Practical*

Idealism, Kalergi wrote:

"The man of the future will be of mixed race. The races and classes of today will gradually disappear due to the elimination of space, time and prejudice. The Eurasian-Negroid race of the future, similar in appearance to the Ancient Egyptians, will replace the diversity of peoples with the diversity of individuals."[21]

In many areas of Europe, the mentally libtarded turned up in numbers, with placards in hand to welcome the refugees with open arms, embracing the destruction of their own nations. Much of Europe is in absolute chaos due to this forced, mass migration. It is divide and conquer on a massive scale.

Of course, the mainstream media has dutifully done its part in spreading Rectal-Cranial Inversion. Today's left-leaning, ultra-liberal media seems to do all that it can to create division and stoke the fires of hatred. Trump has been branded a "racist," and therefore, any white person that supports him is labeled a "white supremacist," or a "neo-Nazi." Trump is merely a tool for the Consortium's, pro-Israel Zionist chess pieces, but most of the herd will have no idea of this, or of what Zionism even is. They react solely from emotions and hate who they are told to hate.

The media is the propaganda apparatus the Consortium uses to shape and influence public opinion and masses of people are still deeply affected by this powerful form of mind control. Critical thinking and common sense have become all but extinct in today's climate of instant information and cognitive laziness. Watching people fall for scripted nonsense over and again, without engaging in any thinking of their own is intriguing to me. In recent times, the mainstream media has been shown to be little more than a propaganda machine, a lie factory, and yet people will still go on believing what they are told if it is what they *want to hear*. They still allow their opinions to be shaped and contorted by corporate controlled media and they are being misled like blind and babbling mentally libtarded sheeple on their way to the slaughterhouse.

In this age of information and instant communications, an age where the veil is lifting away to expose all that has remained hidden,

ignorance is nothing more than a personal choice.

DOUG MICHAEL
TRUTH

SEVEN

Manufactured Crises

One of the prime tactics that the Consortium uses to advance its agenda towards the totalitarian, New World Order is a technique known as the Hegelian Dialectic. Since they cannot openly introduce their system, it must be achieved in increments, step by step. The Consortium must chip away, little by little, piece by piece, and very carefully and methodically remove freedom in such a way that it goes unnoticed by the masses. However, in this day and age, they've really become brazen and sloppy because time is rapidly running out. The Masonic dictum, "ordo ab chao" or order out of chaos is precisely the technique that is utilized to achieve the ends of the Consortium. They create the chaos from which order is established, *their* order. The symbolic phoenix rising from the ashes is the new order of the Luciferian Consortium. How this is done is through a variety of engineered situations, such as:

- False flag terrorist attacks
- Economic collapse
- Heavy increase in violent crimes such as school shootings
- Acts of war
- Panic warnings
- Pandemics, real or imagined
- Assassinations

This list could go on, but you get the idea. The term "false flag" means that an attack is perpetrated by inside forces, and blamed on someone else, and governments have a long history of perpetrating false flag events. Another modern definition of false flag is:

"Covert operations conducted by governments, corporations or other organizations which are designed to appear as if they are being carried out by other entities."[1]

The best example of a modern false flag event is the attacks that occurred on September 11, 2001, and there are numerous examples throughout history. The official story of what happened on the morning of 9/11/2001 is absolute nonsense. There are many volumes and video documentaries that are in circulation that prove beyond a doubt that the official story of 9/11 is a steaming pile of crap from start to finish. None of the pieces of the official story fit together and in fact, the story of *Goldilocks and the Three Bears* is far more believable. The public has been sold countless lies about the 9/11 event, and many others, which I would like to touch upon in this section so as to explain the Hegelian Dialectic.

George Wilhelm Friedrich Hegel was a German philosopher whose dialectic triad is continuously employed by the Consortium. There is argument as to where the dialectic triad idea originated, but it is not important, nor is it important to discuss the ideas of Hegel for the purposes here. I only wish to explain what the dialectic triad is, and to explain how it is used by the Consortium and point out some modern examples of it, because it is one of the prime tools of the Consortium. The Hegelian Dialectic has three parts:

- Thesis
- Antithesis
- Synthesis

1. **Thesis/problem:** a problem is covertly created that will initiate a reaction from the public. Crucial to this stage is to make sure that a patsy is lined up to take the blame to keep all eyes off the true perpetrators. The problem could be any number of staged events, i.e. a bombing, an assassination etc.

2. **Antithesis/reaction:** The Consortium then waits for the reaction from the public, and also influences that reaction through their mainstream media outlets with spin,

disinformation and outright lies. In the event of a false flag attack, the reaction is fear, outrage, panic, anger etc. and what the Consortium wants the most, the demand from the public that something be done to combat the problem.

3. **Synthesis/solution:** next, the Consortium ushers in their solution, which they would not have been able to do otherwise. Using the example of 9/11, the Consortium needed the reaction from the American people in order to wage wars in the Middle East and to pass draconian legislation that dismantles freedom. The United States is very close to becoming a total police state, which would not be so without the horrific events of 9/11, or at least we would not be this close to it. Britain is also very close, which most likely would not have been possible without the London bombings of 7/7/05. The chaos is created, the reaction is evoked, and then the solution is ushered in, which ultimately brings us closer to the New World Order.

The Consortium creates a dichotomy, in which they control all sides and create a faux opposition. For instance, in the US, both the Democrat and Republican political parties are controlled by the same force. They appear to be in opposition but in actuality, they are one and the same. Out of all of the 2008 presidential candidates, twelve were members of the Council on Foreign Relations. Six of them were Republicans and six were Democrats. While they appear to be in opposition, the twelve CFR candidates actually serve the same force, so it doesn't matter if one of the CFR Democrats or one of the CFR Republicans wins the presidency; they still serve the CFR and the Round Table Network, even if they aren't fully aware of the agenda they are being selected to serve. The US is a plutocratic, one-party system disguised to appear as a democracy and freedom of choice is merely an illusion.

For the purposes of explaining how the Hegelian Dialectic is utilized by the Consortium, I will outline a few examples:

The Sinking of the Lusitania

Sometimes, the Consortium will use a bait & switch tactic, and the sinking of the British luxury liner, the Lusitania, is a good example. On May 7, 1915, an ocean liner loaded with passengers-most of them civilians-was torpedoed off the coast of Ireland by German U-boats. Even official history shows that the Lusitania was loaded with ammunition and that the ship was fitted for war and registered as an armed, auxiliary cruiser. The Germans apparently even warned Americans not to travel on such ships by printing newspaper articles but due to intervention by the state department, only one newspaper add was ever printed.[2]

Also, aboard the ship was British Prime Minister, David Alfred Thomas. The Lusitania sank in 18 minutes and 1,198 people died as a result of the attack. The problem was that a "passenger" ship was sunk. The reaction was outrage and anger. The solution was that the sinking of the Lusitania was the catalyzing event that garnered public opinion for American intervention in WW I, under the direction of Wilson (Edward Mandell House and the Round Table Network). The placement of ammunition (millions of rounds of rifle ammo and 76 mm shells) was a direct violation of American law, and should have never been placed on a ship carrying passengers, but it was done so on purpose, with foreknowledge that the Germans would sink it for the means of justifying American involvement in the war. Some historians and researchers claim that the ship was sunk by the British and blamed on the Germans, and I certainly wouldn't be surprised to find out that was the case since that is how the Consortium operates.

A similar incident happened on February 15, 1898, when the American battleship, the USS Maine was sunk off the coast of Cuba. Official reports of the time concluded that a naval mine had caused the explosion, but those reports were refuted by experts. This was the catalyzing event that won public approval for the Spanish-American War. Explosives experts investigating the explosion concluded that it was an accident but nevertheless, the sinking of the Maine was blamed on Spain and public support for war was high, even prompting the slogan: "remember the Maine, to hell with Spain!" As a result of the Spanish-American War, Spain lost its control over its remaining overseas empire, including Cuba, Guam, Puerto Rico and the Philippine Islands. Sometimes the Consortium does not have to stage an event; they can simply take advantage of an event and spin it the way they want people to perceive it, so as to get the necessary reaction to advance their agenda.

Operation Ajax

In 1953, the British and American governments conspired together to instigate a coup against the democratically elected Iranian President Mohammed Mosaddeq. The British government had asked President Harry Truman for assistance, but he refused, and in 1953, the Administration of Dwight D. Eisenhower agreed to assist in the overthrow of Mosaddeq.

Mosaddeq began the process of privatizing the vast Iranian oil fields, believing that the nation should profit directly, which would thereby deny the British the opportunity to monopolize the oil fields, which were controlled by the Anglo-Iranian oil company, which later changed its name to British Petroleum (BP). The British initiated a worldwide boycott of Iranian oil which plunged the country into financial turmoil.

The American Central Intelligence Agency (CIA) was directly involved in the coup and one of its top officials at the time, Kermit Roosevelt Jr. (grandson of Freemason Theodore Roosevelt) was heavily involved in the widespread bribery of Iranian government officials and news media. A safe haven was established in Southern Iran, from which CIA backed guerrilla forces and agents operated.

The CIA conducted covert operations including false flag attacks, propaganda campaigns, controlled media disinformation, bribery of government and military officials, acting as agent provocateurs in controlled protests and mob riots and arming opposition parties. Eventually, the Consortium was successful through their CIA coup d'état and Mosaddeq was ousted. The Shah was placed into power to act as a dictator that would be friendly to western interests. Eventually, the Islamic revolution in 1979 ousted the Shah and Ayatollah Khomeini took control after years of exile. This ended western control over the oil fields again, and now the Consortium have their sights set once again on Iran. Trump is following the neocon agenda of his predecessors. A US invasion of Iran would be disastrous, as the Iranians maintain a strong military, and are prepared to defend themselves. Iraq did not have near the military capacity that Iran does, and look at the mess in that country. There were no weapons of mass destruction and the entire pretext to the war in Iraq was a lie and has caused untold death and destruction.

Operation Northwoods

In 1962, the US Department of Defense (DoD) actually drafted a plan to stage false flag terror attacks against American citizens on US soil. The idea was to carry out attacks and blame them on Cuba to justify war. This is perhaps one of the most well documented examples of the Hegelian Dialectic triad that exists, due to its declassification. This insidious scheme was drafted and signed by the Joint Chiefs of Staff and part of the Northwoods agenda proposed the idea of hijacking jet airliners both within US and Cuban airspace.[3] Included in the Northwoods plan were proposals to:

- Stage mock attacks at Guantanamo Bay and blame them on the Cubans.
- Destroy a US ship in Guantanamo Bay and blame it on Cuban military forces. (Remember the Spanish Maine).
- Use aircraft disguised as Cuban Migs to destroy US aircraft.
- Destroy a US drone aircraft and claim that it was full of college students to promote outrage in the public mind.
- Destroy crops.
- Sink boats loaded with Cuban refugees.
- Murder civilians on American streets.
- Commit terrorist attacks in Washington DC and in other American cities and blame them on Cuba.

The truly disturbing thing about Operation Northwoods is that all of the Joint Chiefs of Staff supported and were willing to carry out this plan to initiate the reaction needed from the public to support war against Cuba. President Kennedy rejected the plan, and he also came between other schemes that the Consortium wished to carry out which is why he was murdered. JFK stepped on too many toes. It's interesting to me, that even though this information is declassified, Americans seem to think that the government would never wish to carry out similar false flag events such as the attacks of 9/11. But then, how many people have ever even heard of Operation Northwoods? It certainly isn't mentioned much in the mainstream press, if at all.

The Northwoods plan was linked to two other operations titled *Operation Mongoose* and *Operation Bingo*. Operation Bingo outlined a plan to:

"create an incident which has the appearance of an attack on U.S. facilities in Cuba, thus providing an excuse for use of U.S. military might to overthrow the current government of Cuba."[4]

Operation Bingo also apparently outlined a plan called *Operation Dirty Trick*, which would place the blame on Castro if the 1962 manned, Mercury space flight happened to crash or if it was sabotaged. A Pentagon report in relation to Operation Northwoods and Operation Mongoose stated:

"We could blow up a US ship in Guantanamo Bay and blame Cuba...Casualty lists in US newspapers would cause a helpful wave of national indignation."[5]

This is the Hegelian Dialectic in action; create a situation, then use the media to whip up public outrage, and then offer the solution which usually involves war and the removal of freedom. To his credit John F. Kennedy rejected the Northwoods plan and although it wasn't carried out, people should be familiar with this information and the fact that high level military leaders were perfectly willing to carry out these atrocities under the orders of their Consortium masters.

The Assassination of President John F. Kennedy

There are volumes of information in existence that clearly show that the official, government story of the assassination of JFK is completely ridiculous, so I will just touch on a few points here and be as brief as possible. President Kennedy's murder was a classic problem/reaction/solution scenario and most importantly to understand; it was a ritual sacrifice. Lee Harvey Oswald, the "crazy lone gunman" blamed for the assassination was the fall guy and he was also a CIA asset, as was Osama Bin Laden.

On November 22, 1963, President John F. Kennedy was shot to death while riding with his motorcade, in Dealey Plaza, in Dallas, Texas. The Plaza is named after George Bannerman Dealey, a high-level Freemason who was a publisher for *The Dallas Morning News*. Interestingly, Dealey Plaza was the location of the first Masonic temple in Dallas. The Warren Commission, which was the official organization set up to investigate (whitewash) the Kennedy assassination, was set up by CFR members. What a surprise huh?

The site Where Kennedy was murdered was chosen carefully by the Consortium and the ritualistic aspects of his murder are staggering. Dallas is located close to the 33rd parallel. The point where Kennedy was shot was at the apex of a pyramid with a missing capstone. The assassination of JFK was a professional hit, and there is no way that it was carried out by a lone gunman, as the famous Zapruda film clearly shows. He was shot at least three times and from different angles, and the fatal headshot came from the front as the film demonstrably shows. As Kennedy's car neared the point where he was shot, the vehicle slowed to a mere 7 MPH, which violated Secret Service protocol, and it wasn't until after the fatal headshot that the car finally accelerated. President Lyndon B. Johnson ordered an investigation which was headed by Freemason and Chief Justice, Earl Warren.

Hundreds of witnesses made statements that contradicted the official Warren Report, but their testimonies were swept under the rug, just as the many credible 9/11 witnesses that claimed to have heard multiple explosions coming from the sub-basement levels of the Twin Towers had their testimonies discounted. Many of the witnesses to the JFK assassination that have come forward, including FBI and CIA agents, receive death threats to this day. One hundred seventy-seven people involved in the case have died under mysterious circumstances, including several Dallas Policemen.[6]

The CIA was intimately involved in mind control experiments such as MK Ultra, in which people can be literally programmed to carry out horrible acts and not even remember their involvement in them. Just as with the secret society networks, the intelligence agencies operate in a compartmentalized, top-down, pyramidal structure, so that those within the lower levels will never know the true workings of the upper levels. The CIA and all intelligence agencies are creations of the Consortium and are intimately connected.

After the Kennedy assassination, witnesses were intimidated, discredited and murdered. Within hours, Oswald was blamed and demonized in the media, just as Bin Laden was taking the fall within hours after 9/11, and just like the 9/11 Commission Report, the Warren Commission Report was an absolute whitewash. Coincidentally, Oswald was murdered by Jack Ruby before he ever got to tell his story and the murder took place very close to where Kennedy was killed, within the pyramid at Dealey Plaza. Interestingly, the word Dealey means "goddess line." The city of Dallas is loaded with esoteric symbolism and the Consortium operates in such a ritualistic fashion, that the fact that the assassination was an inside job is a no-brainer to those that understand the ritualistic side of these types of incidences. The Consortium places their mark everywhere, and after the death of JFK, an obelisk was placed near the murder site in Dealey Plaza and the eternal flame was placed on Kennedy's grave

The obelisk and the eternal flame are both signatures of the Illuminati/Consortium. The obelisk is symbolic of the penis of the Egyptian god Osiris (male energy) and the eternal flame is the flame of Prometheus. Kennedy was shot in the exact locations that the allegorical, Freemasonic figure, Hiram Abiff was stabbed as the legend goes, in the back, throat and back of the head. This symbolizes the purging of the Templar Knights, according to research journalist Kentroversy.[7] Abiff was the legendary builder of Solomon's Temple and his murder is acted out in Freemasonic rituals.

Oswald also had connections with the FBI and the ONI (Office of Naval Intelligence) and operated out of an office which was shared by CIA agent Howard Hunt. The only person ever convicted in the murder of Kennedy was a man named Clay Shaw, who also had connections to the CIA.[8] After the assassination, evidence was removed and tampered with and documents were locked away under "national security" restrictions. Witnesses began to die including policemen that would testify to attorney Jim Garrison who was investigating the case to prove a conspiracy to commit the murder of President Kennedy. Garrison's investigation was obstructed and compromised by high level people within the intelligence community and he was thoroughly discredited in the media which is what happens when anyone dares to challenge the Consortium. Apparently, the Mafia was also involved in JFK's murder and was allied with the CIA, and at the top, both organizations are controlled by the Consortium.

Key information was simply discarded from the official Warren Report, just as crucial information was deliberately left out of the official 9/11 Commission Report; history repeats! The Consortium placed its people within the commissions to investigate itself so that key evidence would be ignored, and fabricated distortions could be presented as truth.

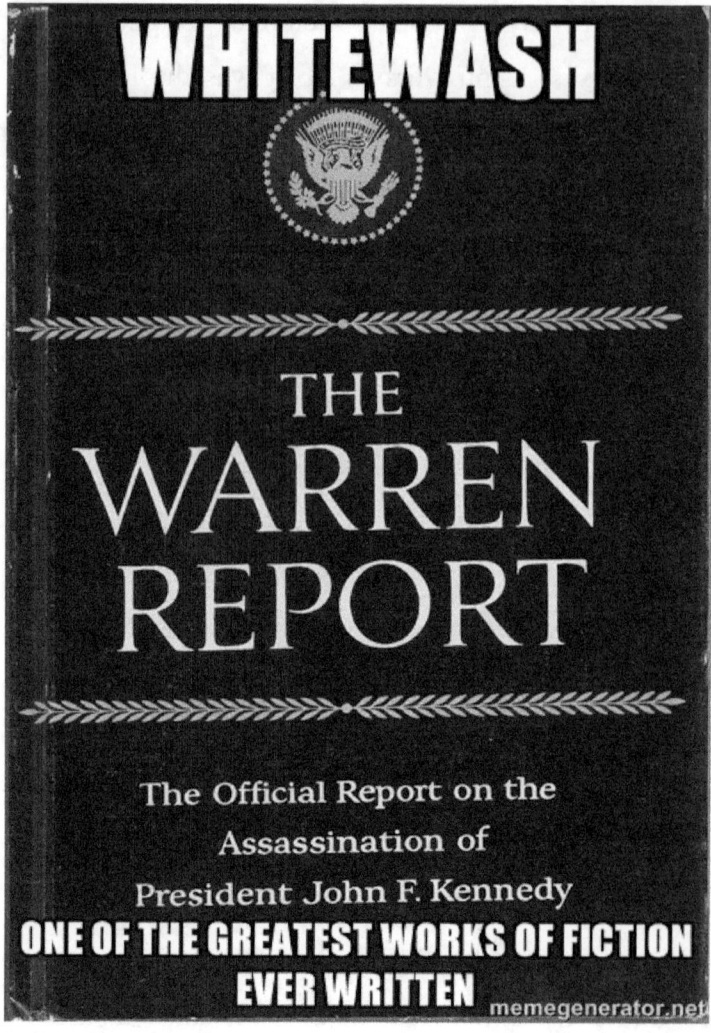

WHITEWASH

THE WARREN REPORT

The Official Report on the
Assassination of
President John F. Kennedy
**ONE OF THE GREATEST WORKS OF FICTION
EVER WRITTEN** memegenerator.net

The route that Kennedy's motorcade took was deliberately set
up to take his car into triangulation crossfire within the pyramid of
the street plan of Dealey Plaza. Kennedy was the only American,
Roman Catholic president, and former Naval intelligence officer,
William Cooper stated that the murder of JFK was revenge for the
Catholic Church's purging of the Templar Knights.[9] November 22,

the day that Kennedy was murdered, was the same day that the Catholic Church ordered the Templars to be tortured and burned by a papal bull issued by Pope Clement V.[10] Again, the ritualistic aspects of JFK's murder are numerous and there are also numerological "coincidences" as well, and I've barely scratched the surface here. After a while of studying the global elite, Consortium/Illuminati network, you begin to realize that there are *no* coincidences.

In 1978, the *United States House Select Committee on Assassinations* was set up to investigate the murders of JFK and Martin Luther King Jr. Even though the findings of the Committee were official conclusions, they were not completely in line with the findings of the Warren Commission Report and the FBI reports. The House Select Committee concluded that Oswald was the assassin, but I believe that if he fired any shots at all, that they were merely diversions, especially when you look at the Zapruda film which shows clearly that JFK was shot from behind, *and* from the front. New research suggests that the Zapruda film was doctored but even if that is true, Kennedy must have been shot from multiple angles due to the location of his wounds. The Committee concluded that there had to have been at least two shooters, and this conclusion was based on scientific, acoustic evidence.[11] The committee also concluded that Kennedy's murder was the result of a "conspiracy" and that Kennedy did not have adequate protection. Who has the power to issue orders that circumvent standard, Secret Service protocol? Those within the upper echelons of the Consortium and their enclaves of power do.

The question must then be asked; why did the Consortium want Kennedy killed? I believe he was murdered for a number of reasons, among them:

- During Kennedy's term, the CIA was active in Cuba. JFK ordered the CIA out of Cuba and sent FBI squads in to shut down CIA training camps. The CIA's job was to train Cuban soldiers to overthrow the Castro government in what was known as the Bay of Pigs invasion. It was a colossal failure.

- Kennedy wished to dismantle the CIA and was quoted as saying that he wanted to: *"splinter the CIA into a thousand pieces and scatter it into the winds."*[12] He tried to transfer the responsibility of covert operations directly to the Joint Chiefs of Staff.

- JFK signed a ban on nuclear testing.

- He ordered US troops to withdraw from Vietnam.

- Kennedy fired Allen Dulles (CFR) who was the director of the CIA at the time.

- Most crucially in my opinion is the fact that Kennedy began printing interest free currency that was independent of the international, Federal Reserve Consortium-controlled, Rothschild/Rockefeller banking network. On June 4, 1963, Kennedy signed Executive Order number 11110, which gave the government the power to issue its own, interest free currency. This took power away from the Consortium-controlled, Federal Reserve Bank, which loans money to the government, and which working citizens pay the interest of through their taxation. Kennedy gave power to the treasury to issue silver certificates backed by silver bullion, silver and silver dollars in the treasury, and his order brought nearly $4.3 *billion* of these silver notes into circulation. Federal Reserve notes are backed by nothing and are intrinsically worthless. Kennedy was trying to take away the Consortium's ability to lend money to the government through their central banks and their ability to screw the American taxpayer for the interest on those loans.

If enough of the silver backed certificates came into circulation, it would have eliminated the need for Federal Reserve notes and the Rothschild/Rockefeller banking establishment would have lost their financial grip on the United States. The government having the power to produce and issue its own interest-free currency would eliminate the staggering debt of the US, but the Consortium creates debt to keep the people enslaved economically. This is the same system that was developed by the Templar Knights and it's still in use because the same people are in control.

The problem was that an American president was publicly executed. The reaction was shock, outrage, disbelief, despair and fear. The solution was that Lyndon Baines Johnson (Freemason) became president and acted to reverse many of Kennedy's policies.

Johnson reversed JFK's order to withdraw troops from Vietnam, thereby permitting all of the horrors that came with that war. Johnson kept the CIA intact. The one thing he didn't change was the executive order granting the government the right to print its own currency. Apparently, that order is still in effect, but no president has dared to act upon it; for they would meet with the same fate as Kennedy if they did. The massive debt in the US would not be near as much if the power to print interest free currency were issued. Not that it really matters anymore, since the government is so thoroughly corrupted now and infested with agents that serve the Consortium and their Round Table Network. Debt equals control, and the Consortium certainly won't relinquish the stranglehold they have on the American economy and people.

There is so much to the Kennedy assassination and many books and documentary videos have been published that show conclusively that Oswald could not have acted alone. I recommend the book by Jim Marrs called: *Crossfire: The Plot That Killed Kennedy*,[13] which was the basis for the screenplay of the movie *JFK*,[14] by Oliver Stone, which I also recommend. Stone's film was attacked in the media before it was even released! It is a very well done and controversial film.

JFK's brother Robert, a US Senator and Democratic candidate, was also assassinated on June 5, 1968, in Los Angeles, California. A Palestinian man named Sirhan Sirhan was blamed for the murder, but an autopsy report of the time concluded that a second shooter must have been present. A cover-up ensued, photographs were confiscated, evidence was tampered with, and court files disappeared. Perhaps the Consortium was worried that Robert would gain sympathy from the American voters and eventually be elected president?

I'll end this segment with a couple of quotes. The first is from Sherman Cooley, a former Marine who served with Oswald and saw him shoot:

"If I had to pick one man in the whole United States to shoot me, I'd pick Oswald. I saw the man shoot. There's no way he could have ever learned to shoot well enough to do what they accused him of doing in Dallas."[15]

Before her death in 2002, Madeleine Duncan Brown, Lyndon Johnson's mistress, claimed that the night before the JFK assassination, L.B.J. claimed that:

"Those SOB's will never embarrass me again."[16]

The 1993 Bombing of the World Trade Center

When most people think of the World Trade Center, they think of the attacks of September 11, 2001. Very few are even aware that the WTC was bombed on February 26, 1993. At approximately 12:17 PM, a 1,200-pound car bomb that was placed in the underground parking garage in tower one, detonated. The intention was to knock tower one into tower two causing severe destruction and killing tens-of-thousands of people. Six people were killed and 1,040 were injured and the explosion caused a half-billion dollars in damages. Apparently, the van containing the explosives was not parked close enough to the concrete foundation to cause the tower to collapse.

The FBI had commissioned an informer to infiltrate a terrorist cell to gather information on the intention to bomb the WTC[17] and this is according to official reports. Emad Salem was a former Egyptian Army officer whose job it was to help a group of radicals build a bomb which was to be used to try to bring down the World Trade Center. The idea was that Salem was to help the group construct a bomb that consisted of harmless powder. An FBI supervisor called off the plan thus allowing the actual bombing to go forward. When Salem was issued the order to not construct a dummy bomb, he began audio taping his hundreds of hours of conversations with FBI officials.

The FBI had enough foreknowledge to thwart the attack but allowed it to happen on orders from the Consortium. Salem was in a position to thwart the attack by using a dummy bomb filled with harmless powder, but the FBI allowed the bombing to occur, killing six and wounding over 1,000. Does anyone honestly believe that they wouldn't allow it to happen again in 2001? The upper and corrupted levels of the intelligence agencies and the military industrial complex were intimately involved; 9/11 could not have happened any other way.

When people become familiar with schemes such as the

Northwoods operation, in which the government admitted to plotting to stage false flag events, one can begin to see the horrific events that unfold in a whole new light. When one begins to understand the ritualistic aspects to so many events that occur, it shifts the perspective even more and the events can truly be seen for what they are.

In 1993, the FBI had every opportunity to stop the bombing of the WTC and did nothing. They had prior knowledge and allowed the attack to occur. The problem was that a bombing occurred in New York City. The reaction was fear, panic, shock and outrage. The solution was that society was brought one step closer to the New World Order. Had the towers fallen in 1993, it is likely that by now, we would already be living in a complete, totalitarian, police state. We are getting closer to that by the day, but sometimes things do happen that hinder the Consortium's plans.

The Waco Massacre

Just two months after the Consortium-sponsored attacks on the WTC, another horrific event was engineered by the Consortium which claimed the lives of at least 74 men, women and children. On April 19, 1993, the Federal Bureau of Investigations was ordered to raid the Branch Davidian compound of David Koresh at Mt. Carmel near Waco in Texas, thereby ending a 51-day siege. It is no accident that the siege at Waco ended on April 19. That date is ritualistically significant to the Consortium and practicing Satanists. For dark occultists, April 19 commences 13 days of bloodletting that culminates on May 1, the beginning of the pagan, Beltane ritual and the founding day of the Bavarian Illuminati. The massacre at Waco was a ritual sacrifice, which occurred on the 50th anniversary of Hitler's burning of the Warsaw ghetto in Poland in which innocent people were incinerated in much the same way that Branch Davidians were. Koresh was 33 years old, and there are other numerological coincidences relating to the Waco event, and so many others. Again, *everything* is ritual and symbolism with the Consortium network.

The Branch Davidians were dissidents, but they were law abiding. The firearms they owned were legal and they were a religious community and of course Koresh and the Davidians were portrayed as cultists and militants in the Consortium-controlled media. I personally feel that they were misguided; however, the Davidians seemed to simply live their lives according to their particular beliefs, which is supposed to be the right of everyone in the US.

The siege by the ATF (Bureau of Alcohol Tobacco and Firearms) and FBI began only two days after the bombing of the World Trade Center, and many tragic events just so happen to occur on or near the 19th of April. The ATF was investigating firearms law violations, and several of the Branch Davidians were firearms dealers that made their money buying and selling firearms at gun shows. A documentary film titled: *Waco: The Rules of Engagement* shows the truer picture of what really happened at Mt. Carmel, including the circus sideshow that took place afterward at the court hearings.[18]

Koresh, upon hearing that he was being investigated by the ATF, invited them to the compound to investigate the allegations for themselves. If the authorities ever wanted to take Koresh into custody, they could have picked him up at any time, because he used to leave the compound frequently to go jogging. There was no reason for the ATF to issue a warrant, and the one that was issued was very sloppy and contained false claims.[19] The Consortium needed to make an example of what happens to people that try to be too independent of the system and also to conduct one of their horrific ritual sacrifices. The Waco massacre also allowed for anti-terrorism legislation to be railroaded through the Congress.

The media claimed, based on ATF reports, that the Branch Davidians opened fire first but that was a lie, as the *Rules of Engagement* clearly points out. Evidence disappeared which always seems to happen when events like this take place. The ATF apparently even murdered puppies that were penned off at the compound.[20] It's clear that the ATF used excessive force and that they began firing weapons at the Branch Davidians first.

A jury in San Antonio, Texas found that the four ATF agents that were killed in the standoff were shot in self-defense. The command was eventually turned over to the FBI and that's when things at Mt. Carmel got really ugly. Tanks were deployed and the FBI broadcasted the recorded, blood curdling screams of rabbits being slaughtered through a PA system. They shined bright spotlights on the compound at night to deliberately keep the

Davidians from sleeping. These tactics are essentially a form of psychological warfare. One of the survivors claimed that a tank proceeded to run over one of the graves of a buried Davidian, over and over again.[21]

Janet Reno (CFR) Attorney General under Bill Clinton (CFR) ordered the FBI to attack the compound of the Branch Davidians on April 19, 1993. Battle tanks rolled in and teargas comprised of the volatile CS chemical mixture was deployed into the compound, despite the fact that there were many children present. Such is the mentality of the Consortium and the underlings that blindly follow their orders. The siege began just after noon which is significant. JFK was murdered just after noon as well, when the sun is "most high." The Consortium-controlled, mainstream media simply parrots the official line it is fed by official sources, and so it is possible for agencies such as the FBI to massacre innocent civilians and for people to believe that such actions are justifiable.

During the Waco siege, women and children retreated to a concrete and steel reinforced area of the compound. A tank was sent through the side of the compound to deliberately reach the safe hold area and deploy the CS gas where the women and children were taking refuge. There was no ventilation in that area.[22] CS dust as well as fumes from kerosene tanks that were destroyed by armored vehicles filled the entire inside of the compound. In addition, the compound was ventilated from the destruction so that the conditions were perfect to cause a blazing inferno. Infra-red films examined by experts clearly show detonations within the compound at Waco, and survivors testified to experiencing massive flames engulfing the inside of the compound, and pyrotechnic projectiles were found within the compound. Specifically, 40 mm, military devices that were fired from a hand-held grenade launcher were found within the compound. Two of such devices were found and the FBI claimed that it did not use any devices which could start a fire, or in other words, they lied. Shortly after 12 PM, the Branch Davidian compound was set ablaze by the FBI in one of many of the Consortium's horrific, ritual sacrifices.

Infra-red film reveals that two individuals were firing automatic weapons into the flames near the dining room area of the compound, while retreating away from the inferno.[23] The FBI confiscated forensic, photographic evidence to prop up the official story and to basically cover their asses. The siege ended with dozens of people gassed to death and burned alive. Key information was omitted from official reports. The entire compound was utterly destroyed, and fire fighters were prevented from doing their jobs. The FBI claimed that they didn't want the firefighters subjected to gunfire, but in truth, the ritual needed to go on to its completion.

Utah Senator Orrin Hatch (CFR) claimed that there was no evidence of political corruption, and claimed that Koresh and the Davidians set fire to the compound themselves and committed suicide.[24] The Branch Davidians were murdered in a ritual sacrifice, which was televised for all to see, due in part to the subconscious effects such horrors would have on the collective mind. The Davidians were made an example of and the official agencies involved removed and destroyed evidence and the cover-up ensued. There is always more to the story when events such as the Waco massacre take place than what appears on the surface and is presented in the mainstream media. The fact that the siege ended on April 19 is absolutely no coincidence; it was purposely ordered to conclude on that ritualistically significant day.

The Oklahoma City Bombing

On April 19, 1995, an explosion shook downtown Oklahoma City, as the Alfred P. Murrah Federal Building was bombed, leaving 168 people dead and over 800 wounded. This was another event in which the official story of what happened could not stand up to scrutiny and serious investigation, quite simply, because the official findings were mostly lies.

The destruction to the Murrah Building was blamed on a fuel fertilizer bomb placed in a Ryder, rental truck by a lone nut named Timothy McVeigh. The Ryder, truck bomb was merely a diversion and others had to be involved due to the fact that multiple, unexploded bombs were found inside the building. Eyewitnesses close to the scene reported hearing multiple explosions as well. There were also multiple reports of McVeigh being spotted with another man (John Doe 2) but of course these reports all seemed to vanish from the official findings, because the story of a lone nut assassin needed to be propped up. This is the pattern that repeats when these horrific, Consortium engineered events take place. Twenty-four people reported to the FBI that they spotted McVeigh with an accomplice but of course those reports were swept under the rug. Official reports state that all of the eyewitnesses were mistaken, and they were never called into court to testify.[25]

A retired, career, military man (USAF) by the name of Brigadier General Benton K. Partin-an explosives and weapons expert-issued a report on July 30, 1995, which claimed that the damage caused to the Murrah Building could in no way be caused by an ammonia nitrate, fuel fertilizer bomb. Columns inside the building were so severely damaged that Partin claimed that the damage could only be caused by devices placed on the columns, not from a fuel-truck bomb a great distance away. Seven other experts agreed with Partin's assessment, including demolitionists, scientists and bomb specialists. Partin is referred to as "one of the world's premier explosives and ordnance authorities."

The mainstream media even reported, from official sources on the day of the bombing, that government agencies claimed that other unexploded bombs were removed from the building. Eyewitnesses close to the scene claimed to have heard multiple explosions and so did witnesses close to the WTC on the morning of September 11, 2001. Multiple news reports claimed that two other bombs were found on the east side of the building and that bomb squads were present at the scene to try to diffuse the remaining explosives.[26] One reporter claimed that whatever did the damage to the Murrah building was a: "tremendous, very sophisticated explosive device."[27]

KWTV in Oklahoma City reported that a third bomb had been found in the building,[28] and other news agencies claimed that the two unexploded bombs were even more powerful than the first that caused the damage. A reporter from KWTV stated:

"It has now been confirmed through federal authorities that a second bomb has been found inside that federal building in Oklahoma City. It was an explosion at 9:00 this morning that did that damage you're looking at right there blowing off the entire north face of that building. Again, you're looking at the north face. A second bomb was found on the east side of that building. A bomb squad is on the scene. That second bomb has not exploded. We don't know quite the status yet-if they have managed to defuse it-but it has been confirmed that a second bomb has been found on the east side."[29]

It's interesting that these official reports gradually vanished from the media as the story of lone nut McVeigh and a fuel truck bomb took their place. When false flag events occur it's always the same thing that happens. The official story changes as the days go by and the cover story is accepted as absolute truth. It's been demonstrated time and again by researchers that the face of the Murrah building was blown outwards.

Coincidentally, two years prior to the Oklahoma bombing, Martin Keating, brother of Oklahoma Governor, Frank Keating, authored a book titled: *The Final Jihad,*[30] a novel in which the "Oklahoma City Building" is bombed by a terrorist named Thomas McVeigh. Keating dedicated his prophetic book to a Masonic, secret society known as the *Knights of the Secret Circle.*

A company by the name of Controlled Demolition was hired to demolish the Murrah building and to remove the rubble. Explosives experts as well as McVeigh's defense lawyers were forbidden access to the rubble to conduct investigations. Why? Controlled Demolition is the same company that was hired to remove the rubble from the World Trade Center after the September 11 attacks of 2001. The remains of the Murrah Building were kept under guard by a company called Wackenhut, a private, Consortium owned company with heavy ties to the CIA and FBI.

Another "coincidence" concerning the bombing of the Murrah building, is that no ATF agents were in the building that morning, and the offices of the ATF were supposed to be the target according to the official fairy tale. Some ATF agents even told civilian witnesses at the scene that were asking questions that they were tipped off through their pagers not to show up to work that morning. Witnesses also reported seeing the bomb squad, in full gear in the vicinity of the Murrah Building, *before* the explosions took place!

What a stroke of good luck that they just so happened to be there, ready and waiting. Eventually, despite the FBI's lies, the Oklahoma Sheriff's Dept. was forced to admit that the bomb squad had been there prior to the explosions.

Just days prior to the explosions at the Murrah Building, a private pilot photographed a Ryder truck within a military compound near Camp Gruber-Braggs in Oklahoma.

The FBI has withheld 12 surveillance camera tapes and over 4,000 documents pertaining to the Oklahoma bombing. Although the alleged target was the ATF offices, the Ryder truck was parked on the opposite side of the building. Seismographic spikes were recorded in Norman Oklahoma at the time of the bombing and on 9/11 seismic spikes were also recorded at the exact times that both of the twin towers collapsed. The FBI claimed that it identified the Ryder agency where McVeigh rented the truck from the VIN (vehicle identification number) stamped on the rear axle. The trouble with this claim is that manufacturers do not imprint axles with VIN numbers nor does Ryder. This magic axle was somehow found amidst the wreckage and also three blocks away from the Murrah building, according to official statements. McVeigh, like Oswald, was the fall guy made to take the blame for the real perpetrators of the event. Having a patsy to blame is crucial in carrying out false flag attacks.

McVeigh claimed that he had been implanted with microchip technology. As the late researcher Jim Keith pointed out:

"Had McVeigh gone off the deep end in his belief about being implanted? Perhaps not. A significant detail about McVeigh's past that is never mentioned by the media is that, after his stint in the Army, McVeigh was employed as a guard with Burns International

Security Services at the Calspan facility in Buffalo, New York. Calspan is a division of the Fortune 500 company Arvin, which manufactures automobile parts, but the lower profile Calspan, according to the InvestText database, 'provides technological services to the United States government and various industries.' More precisely, according to industry sources, Calspan does research into aeronautics, electronic warfare, microwave technology, and electronic telemetric devices. Microchip implants are by definition electronic telemetric devices, and this technology is anything but science fiction."[31]

Agencies such as the CIA are intimately involved in mind control experimentation as with the secret projects such as Project Bluebird, Project Artichoke, Project Monarch, and the infamous and declassified, MK Ultra. Mind control through the use of drugs, hypnosis and technology is nothing new. Reporter Sally Barclay claimed that:

"Something strange happened to McVeigh after he was with a psychologist during a mysterious counseling testing-session, prior to his aborted attempt to enter Special Forces. McVeigh's Army associates noted 'He seemed quite a bit different than he'd been before...'He wasn't the same McVeigh, didn't have the same drive...' Phil Morawski, a friend of McVeigh's, states that he complained that he had a microchip implanted in his buttocks by the Army. McVeigh apparently thought that it had been implanted

in order to monitor his movements, although at least one source has stated that McVeigh believed he was being mind controlled through the use of the microchip."[32]

So many "lone" assassins, terrorists, bombers, killers etc. seem to have connections to military and/or intelligence agencies. How many of them are mind controlled? I would suggest that it's a very high percentage. Mind control technologies, projects and techniques is a major piece of the puzzle when it comes to understanding false flag events and Consortium-engineered chaos.

The official line was that McVeigh bombed the Murrah building in retaliation to the siege at Mt. Carmel in Waco. Actually, both events were ritual sacrifices conducted by the sick minds that make up the Consortium's inner core and let us not forget that both events took place on the ritualistically significant date of April 19.

Due to statements of experts such as General Partin, the official story changed to fit the "lone nut theory." The ATF and other agencies originally claimed that 1,200 pounds of ammonium nitrate fuel oil (ANFO) was used in the Ryder truck bomb, but when experts refuted such nonsense, claiming that in no way could that fuel truck bomb have caused such damage, the amount of ANFO miraculously increased in size. It became 4,000 pounds and increased to 4,800 pounds. Even research conducted by the US Air Force concluded that an ANFO bomb could not have even remotely caused the damage sustained to the Murrah Building.[33]

Concerning the damage sustained by the Murrah Building, Partin stated in an official report:

"The pattern of damage would have been technically impossible without supplementing demolition charges."[34]

The Air Force study was titled: "The Eglin Blast Effects Study," and in part concluded that:

"The damage to the Murrah Federal Building is consistent with damage resulting from mechanically coupled devices placed locally within the structure."

And further:

"It must be concluded that the damage at the Murrah Federal Building is not the result of the truck bomb itself, but rather due to other factors such as locally placed charges within the building itself...The procedures used to cause the damage to the Murrah Building are therefore more involved and complex than simply parking a truck and leaving."[35]

Of course, the findings and conclusions of the Air Force study and those of General Partin and other experts were simply dismissed while the official cover story was being propped up. The entire north face of the Murrah Building was blown outwards.

The problem was that a federal building was bombed and innocent people died, many of them children in the day care center of the Murrah Building. The reaction was panic, outrage, anguish, shock and disbelief. The solution was the railroading of anti-terrorism legislation through the Congress that curtailed civil liberties; the discrediting and demonization of militia groups in the US; President Clinton's call for the easing of restrictions on military involvement in domestic law enforcement; and essentially the push towards driving America one step closer to the New World Order. Once the Hegelian Dialectic triad/problem-reaction-solution technique is understood, it becomes clear that this method of creating false flag events occurs repeatedly throughout history.

The London Bombings

On July 7, 2005, a series of bombings occurred in London that killed 56 people and injured 700. The target was London's transportation system as the underground tube trains, and a public bus were attacked. Like so many other events, the London bombings show all the signs of a false flag operation. Tony Blair, Prime Minister of Britain at the time claimed that an open, public investigation into the bombings would be a "ludicrous diversion," and would take away valuable resources from the war on terror. The Blair government rejected independent inquiries into the attacks despite demand from the Muslim communities and from the families of the victims.[36] The Bush government did the same thing with the 9/11 attacks and it was only public demand of the victim's families that forced the 9/11 Commission investigation, which was an utter whitewash.

The London bombings and the events of 9/11 contain some eerie similarities; for instance, during both events, there were drills being conducted by the government of the exact same targets being hit at the exact times that they were attacked! The official stories pertaining to both events contain contradiction after contradiction, impossibilities, distortions of facts and outright absurdities.

A few hours after the London bombings, it was announced that the Al-Qaeda terrorist network confessed to the attacks, but there was one problem; the confession was traced to an internet server in Texas.[37]

Peter Power of a crisis management company called Visor Consultants, publicly admitted that his company was hired to run *drills* of simultaneous bombings occurring in London precisely at the time and locations in which they occurred.[38] The hidden perpetrators of false flag events do this to provide a cover for the real bombings and to confuse the authorities thereby preventing any action being taken to thwart the attacks. This pattern repeats again and again.

What always seems to happen following these horrific events, is that legislation is passed that curtails basic freedoms and increases surveillance. Military budgets increase exponentially, and certainly, after the events of 9/11 and 7/7, massive funding for the war on terror was increased dramatically. Defense contractors profit enormously on human misery directly as a result of these staged events. Massive fear is also generated in the public mind and that is the idea. A population full of fear is far easier to corral and control than one that is not.

At 8:50 AM, three explosive devices simultaneously detonated on three separate London subways. British authorities claimed for over an hour, that the disruptions in the subway system were due to a power outage, even though eyewitnesses were reporting multiple attacks. Almost an hour into the attacks, the London Police ordered the number 30 bus to be diverted from its normal route. The bus was diverted to Tavistock Square, home to one of the Consortium's major sociological, think tank organizations. Shortly after the bus was diverted, at around 9:47 AM, an explosion ripped the bus apart killing 13 people and wounding several others. British authorities admitted that the number 30 bus was the only one that morning that was diverted from its normal route.

It was reported that each of the bombers purchased round trip tickets. Why would suicide bombers bother to buy round trip tickets, knowing that they would not be coming back? British detectives claimed publicly that they felt that the bombers did not know that they had explosives in their backpacks and one eyewitness on the number 30 bus claimed that the alleged bomber began nervously fumbling through his backpack just prior to the explosion. Haroon Aswat, the man believed by British police to be the mastermind behind the attacks, was a British intelligence agent of the MI6 organization and this has been confirmed by both US and French intelligence agents.[39] MI6 is the British equivalent of the CIA, and all intelligence agencies are joined at the hip and controlled at the upper levels by the Consortium. Osama Bin Laden, the alleged mastermind behind the 9/11 attacks, was a CIA asset for years. The Al Qaeda terrorist network was funded and trained by the CIA to fight against the Soviets in Afghanistan throughout much of the 1980s and this is confirmed; it is an historical fact. The Consortium places their own people into positions to either carry out attacks or to take the fall for them. Aswat was protected by top authorities and this has also been confirmed, even in the mainstream media.

Official reports claimed that the four bombers met at the Lutton train station to board the 7:40 train to London. Interestingly, the 7:40 train was canceled that day. The alleged bombers also purchased a seven-day pass to park in the station parking facility. Why the hell would they do that if they knew they would be suicide bombing later that day? When it was pointed out that the alleged bombers would not have made it to London in time to carry out the attacks due to the cancellation of the 7:40 train, the official story changed as is what always happens once the absurdities of the official version of events are pointed out.

What a stroke of bad luck that the number 30 bus surveillance camera just so happened to not be working that day, even though the cameras are checked and maintained regularly. A few eyewitnesses claimed that the metal on the floor of one of the trains was pushed upwards, which would indicate that the bomb was placed underneath the train. An eyewitness on one of the tube trains named Bruce Lait stated:

"The policeman said, 'mind that hole, that's where the bomb was.' The metal was pushed upwards as if the bomb was underneath the train. They seem to think the bomb was left in a bag, but I don't remember anybody being where the bomb was or any bag."[40]

In order to secure bombs underneath the railway cars, the perpetrators would need access to the trains. It is claimed that all four of the bomber's identification documents were found amidst the rubble and aftermath of the explosions. How convenient. The same is claimed to have happened after 9/11, as the official story claims that somehow, one of the hijacker's passports miraculously survived an explosion of fuel and metal, only to be found at the scene, allowing the authorities to identify the hijacker! Trains, buses and planes are blown apart, steel frame skyscrapers melt, but a piece of paper magically survives unscathed? Are you fucking joking?

Regarding the London bombings, one of the alleged bombers ID cards was found at two separate locations, just as the axle of the Ryder truck McVeigh drove was mysteriously found in two different locations. The nonsense that the public is told to believe would be hysterical if it weren't so tragic. Obviously, the ID cards were planted at the scene to prop up the official fairy tale.

Former Israeli Prime minister, Benjamin Netanyahu, received

a warning to stay in his hotel the morning of the attacks. Netanyahu planned to attend an economic conference near the site where one of the blasts occurred. The Associated Press reported on 7/7:

"British police told the Israeli Embassy in London minutes before Thursday's explosions that they had received warnings of possible terror attacks in the city, a senior Israeli official said. Benjamin Netanyahu had planned to attend an economic conference in a hotel over the subway stop where one of the blasts occurred, and the warning prompted him to stay in his hotel room instead, government officials said...Just before the blasts, Scotland Yard called the security officer at the Israeli Embassy to say they had received warnings of possible attacks, the official said. He did not say whether British police made any link to the economic conference."[41]

Similar warnings occurred before 9/11 when high level officials were warned not to fly on the morning of 9/11. So why weren't civilians warned then? The answer is obvious; the attacks needed to be carried out to advance the agenda of the Consortium network.

Another interesting anomaly concerning both the London bombings and 9/11 is the fact that short selling of stocks occurred just days prior to both attacks. Ten days before the 7/7 attacks, short selling of the British pound occurred, and the value fell by

6% against the US dollar. Somebody reaped huge profits when the pound fell further after the attacks. Put options were placed on United and American Airlines stocks just days before the 9/11 attacks. A put option is basically a bet that stocks will take a dive. The put options of United and American Airlines stocks indicate prior knowledge, and an investigation into these mysterious transactions led to one of the executive directors of the CIA being involved.[42] The levels of put options purchased were six times higher than normal.

Put options were also placed on stocks for the companies Morgan Stanley Dean Witter & Co., and Merrill Lynch & Co. Both companies occupied 22 floors of the World Trade Center. It was reported on September 19, 2001, in a story published by *the Israeli Institute for Counterterrorism* that:

"Between September 6 and 7, the Chicago Board Options Exchange saw purchases of 4,744 put options on United Airlines, but only 396 call options. Although there was no news at that time to justify so much 'left-handed' trading, United Airlines stock fell 42 percent, from $30.82 per share to $17.50, when the market reopened after the attacks. Assuming that 4,000 of the options were bought by people with advance knowledge of the imminent attacks, these 'insiders' would have profited by almost $5 million."

And further:

"On September 10, 4,516 put options on American Airlines were bought on the Chicago exchange, compared to only 748 calls. Again, there was no news at that point to justify this imbalance; but American Airlines stock fell 39 percent, from $29.70 to $18.00 per share, when the market reopened. Again, assuming that 4,000 of these options trades represent 'insiders,' they would represent a gain of about $4 million."[43]

When researchers bring up these facts they are simply dismissed as "coincidence," but the coincidences regarding these false flag events are often so numerous that they simply cannot be coincidental. Too many pieces of the official stories simply do not fit together, and when real investigators get too close to the truth and attempt to expose the inconsistencies, anomalies and outright lies, they are usually dismissed as conspiracy theorists, whackos, nut cases etc. regardless of whether or not their information is accurate or true. Then when glaring contradictions are pointed out in the official version of events, the story just changes to fit the version that the Consortium wants the public to believe.

On July 22, 2005, British police viciously gunned down an innocent man in a tube train, who was claimed to be a suicide bomber. Jean Charles de Menezes was an electrician by trade. He was a Brazilian working in England. Police shot him at least eight times in the head at point blank range. The story changed repeatedly and low and behold; the authorities claimed that none of the surveillance cameras at the station where de Menezes was killed were working that day. Just another coincidence I'm sure. A company called Tube Lines, which provides maintenance services for the tube trains, stated:

"We are not aware of any faults on CCTV cameras at that station on that day. Nothing of that nature has been reported to us."[44]

Britain has the largest percentage of CCTV cameras per capita in the world. What a coincidence that on the day of Princess Diana's death, all the CCTV cameras on the route her car drove in France were also malfunctioning according to the official story. It's estimated that Britain contains one percent of the global population and 75% of the world's surveillance cameras yet, they always seem to malfunction when events such as the London bombings take place.

The police were caught in many lies concerning the murder of de Menezes. For example; it was claimed that de Menezes was wearing a bulky jacket with wires sticking out; when it was later confirmed that he was wearing a light denim jacket. It was also claimed that he vaulted the ticket barriers and ran suspiciously, but it was later confirmed that he was walking at a leisurely pace and did not jump the ticket barrier. Police did not retract their statements until the media picked up on the inconsistencies in the story.

A total of 11 shots were fired when de Menezes was murdered. Hollow point bullets were used, and it was reported by police that de Menezes's body was "unrecognizable." He was killed execution style by a special military unit. Is it possible that he simply knew too much, or witnessed something he wasn't supposed to?

Government officials and police were arrested and suspended simply for telling the truth concerning the shooting.[45] Witnesses claimed that they saw police squat over Mr. de Menesez and shoot him in the head. As researchers into this type of information always point out, it's very important to always ask ourselves when these events are carried out, *cui bono*, who benefits? Who stands to gain from the attacks?

The London bombings boosted Prime Minister, Tony Blair's falling approval ratings and also bolstered support for the war on terror. The Blair government, in the aftermath of the bombings, used it as an opportunity to pass legislation that removed freedoms, and set the stage for marshal law takeover through the *Civil Contingencies Act*. Recently, an officer involved admitted to deleting records contained in key documents concerning the de Menezes shooting.[46]

History is replete with numerous examples of the Hegelian Dialectic in action. The problem-reaction-solution game is played out over and over to advance the Consortium's agenda to create a global, totalitarian super state. As stated, after false flag events occur, legislation is pushed that removes basic freedoms, military budgets increase dramatically, a climate of fear is created, wars occur, surveillance increases, power is abused, and basically the noose tightens a little more each time an event is engineered.

It's also been shown that the bombs used in the 7/7 attacks were military grade explosives, contradicting the official claim that they were homemade bombs. Often the official story of these and many other events are literally demolished by serious, independent researchers and investigators. However; because the media determines the views that most will adopt, when evidence is presented that challenges the official story, the people presenting it are referred to as "lunatics" or some other unfair label, regardless of how credible the evidence may be, and this is another point that cannot be stressed enough. Even highly credible people will have their testimony discounted without investigation or their careers destroyed simply because their conclusions were not in line with what the public is meant to believe, and this happens time and again. When major events occur, the history of those events is concocted within the first 72 hours and becomes the publicly accepted version, regardless of how ridiculous the story may be.

Other examples of the Hegelian Dialectic:

- **The Gulf of Tonkin incident:** This event launched the US into the war in Vietnam. The official story claimed that an American ship on a routine patrol in the Gulf of Tonkin, was fired upon by North Vietnamese PT boats and that a deliberate attack on two US ships followed two days later. President Johnson (Freemason) went on national television on August 4, 1964 to announce airstrikes against North Vietnam as a retaliation to the torpedo strikes against US ships. There was one problem however; the torpedo strikes had never occurred, and this is now declassified. Of course, the media simply did what they always do; they engaged in no real investigation, and simply parroted the official, government story. James Stockdale, a Navy pilot who flew overhead the night of the alleged torpedo boat attacks claimed: "I had the best seat in the house to watch that event, and our destroyers were just shooting at phantom targets-there were no PT boats there... There was nothing there but black water and American fire power." In 1965, Johnson claimed: "for all I know, our navy was shooting at whales out there."[47] In this case, it wasn't a false flag event, but a completely fabricated one. Millions of lives were lost in that conflict all because of a lie. In 2001, the *LBJ Presidential Library and Museum* released taped, telephone conversations Between President Johnson and the then Secretary of Defense, Robert McNamara discussing how the phony Tonkin incident could be used to expand the war.

- **Operation Gladio:** On August 3, 1990, Italian Prime Minister of the time, Giulio Andreotti publicly admitted the existence of a secret army within the state, code named

Operation Gladio. The word Gladio comes from the Latin *Gladius* which means "sword." Gladio was an operation that was backed by western intelligence agencies like the CIA and by NATO (North American Treaty Organization) which many researchers suggest is a forerunner of the Consortium's planned, global army. Hundreds of false flag bombings occurred under Gladio around the world, including in Asia, Europe, Latin America and the Middle East. Gladio lasted almost forty years, from 1947 to 1981. High level officials admitted that Gladio targeted innocent civilians in false flag bombings with the intent of advancing political agendas. Trains, busses and schools were among some of the targets of this sick Consortium operation.

- **The Madrid bombings:** On March 11, 2004, exactly 911 days after the September 11 attacks of 2001, a series of bombs exploded aboard a commuter train in Madrid, Spain, leaving 191 people dead and wounding 1,755. In June of 2004, The London Times reported that the man accused of supplying dynamite that was used in the blasts, had connections to the Spanish security services. In fact, he had in his possession, the private phone number of the head of Spain's Civil Guard bomb squad.[48] Three men identified as culprits were known police informers.

- Currently, Israel and the US are preparing for conflict with

Iran and the war in Syria has escalated under the Trump administration, despite his rhetoric to the contrary. China and Russia both have vested economic interests in that country and the attempt at expansion in the Middle East could very well be the trigger that ignites the Consortium's well-planned WW III. Chinese Major General Zhang Zhaozhong commented that, "China will not hesitate to protect Iran even with a third world war."[49]

• Banks and lending institutions have been folding massively and in 2008, hundreds of billions of dollars were stolen to provide bailouts to some of the country's largest lenders and investment houses. When the financial system goes poof, masses of people will be in a panic and far easier to manipulate into accepting a microchip as a means of currency, and I would suggest that the microchip is a large part of the agenda to collapse the economy, as is the creation of the North American Union and the single currency to accompany it. The US Army War College issued a report in 2008, urging the use of the military to contain civil unrest in the event of economic collapse. The report states that the US military must prepare for a "violent domestic dislocation provoked by an economic collapse."[50] In other words, martial law. In 2012, the DHS (Department of Homeland Security) purchased some 1.2 *billion* rounds of ammunition and several thousand armored vehicles. Most likely, they are preparing for civil war that will follow an economic collapse. The Pentagon announced its plans to deploy 20,000 US troops within the US to "help state and local officials respond to a nuclear terrorist attack or other domestic catastrophe."[51] Unemployment is at staggering highs and we've witnessed economic unrest all over the globe, not least in Greece as the Consortium prepares for the engineered, global economic collapse.

- **Pearl Harbor:** The event that led to American involvement in WW II was the attack on Pearl Harbor, on December 7, 1941. In 1994, a document called the *McCollum Memo*[52] was declassified that detailed an eight-step plan to entice the Japanese into attacking the US. President Roosevelt (Freemason) implemented all eight of the recommendations on behalf of his masters. It's been established beyond doubt, that Roosevelt's administration had absolute foreknowledge of the impending attacks. Communications from the Japanese admiral, Yamamoto were intercepted and decoded, and showed clearly that the Japanese had every intention of attacking Pearl Harbor, but FDR's administration did nothing. The Consortium wanted to get the US involved in the war, but the majority of citizens were vehemently opposed, especially, since all of the horrors of WW I were still recent. Since there has been so much fantastic research done on this topic, I will only outline a few pertinent points here. What is important to understand, are the reasons why the Consortium wanted

184

American involvement in WW II. Crucial to understand is that the Rothschild banking dynasty was behind the funding of all sides in every major war of the 20th century, including the Bolshevik revolution, and both world wars. World War II was the most horrific problem-reaction-solution event of the 20th century, which claimed the lives of tens-of-millions of people. Part of the agenda behind this living horror show, was to establish the United Nations. After WW I, the League of Nations was established as the precursor for a global government. The league failed, but after WW II, the establishment of the United Nations was successful with heavy involvement of the Fabian Society. The very forces responsible for establishing the UN are the same forces that brought WW II, into existence. After two major wars and the horrors implanted in the collective mind, people wanted peace, and the inception of the UN was to promote peace, or at least that's how it was presented. The Japanese attack on Pearl Harbor, was also used in part to justify the atomic bombing of Hiroshima and Nagasaki, which was the Consortium's testing of appalling, nuclear weaponry on civilian populations.

- **The Underwear Bomber:** On Dec. 25[Th] 2009, Umar Farouk Abdulmutallab boarded Northwest Airlines flight 253 which was headed from Amsterdam to Detroit. He was allegedly caught on the flight trying to detonate explosives that he had in his shorts and he became known as the "underwear bomber." As usual when events like this occur, the whole damned story is fishy. This man was allowed onto the flight without a passport. He was aided by an unnamed intelligence agent. With the absolute crackdown since the inside attacks of 9/11/01, the idea that a passenger would be allowed onto a flight to America without a passport is just absurd. He was aided. This blatantly staged event was used to justify the rolling out of naked body scanners in the airports in America and the presence of the TSA (Transportation Security Administration). The TSA is a blatant example of what a police state looks like. The agency has molested children[53], groped seniors and disabled people, and there are many examples of the agency robbing people's personal belongings.[54] The scanners have been alleged to cause Cancer.[55] In 2012, a mainstream British newspaper called, *the Guardian*, reported that the underwear bomber was working as an undercover informer for the CIA and Saudi intelligence.[56]

- **Operation Fast and Furious:** In 2011, the US govt. Agency of the Bureau of Alcohol, Tobacco, Firearms and Explosives was caught red handed selling firearms to Mexican drug cartels. It even broke in the mainstream press that the ATF did this to make the case for gun regulations in America. Some of the weapons sold were used to kill border patrol agents. Some 30,000 firearms were sold to the cartels that traffic their poison into America. Can that not

be considered aiding and abetting the enemy? The Consortium has its hooks in America, and it uses the agencies it controls to advance its agenda and will stop at nothing to obtain its goal of manifesting a totalitarian super state. The fact that they're cracking down on the right to keep and bear arms is very telling. American citizens represent the largest armed camp on the planet. Crucial to the Consortium's agenda is to disarm the American population.

- **The Boston bombings:** The enacting of martial law occurred in Boston in the wake of the bombings on April 15th, 2013. House to house, warrantless searches were conducted, media blackouts were enacted, people were ordered to stay indoors, and the military, DHS and police deployed 9,000 armed units, heavily armed assault vehicles and sniper teams in a scene that resembled something straight out of Nazi Germany. The entire city was closed down and this relatively large city of 650,000 people looked like a ghost town. All of this, to search for one man. After the suspect was captured, many people gathered to cheer the police and military for protecting them and keeping them safe. Their basic human rights and freedoms were violated, and they gathered to cheer the oppressors! This was a successful psyop. I watched the media carefully every day and witnessed the story change numerous times in the days following the attacks. The same happened with the aforementioned events as well. Alternative, independent media was instrumental in demolishing the official story and exposing the mainstream media's nonsense. One thing that many of these events have in common is that there were drills being run at the exact locations and following the same scenario as the actual events. For instance, on the morning of 9/11, simultaneous drills were being run called, *Operation Vigilant Guardian* and *Global Guardian*. These joint exercises simulated hijackings of multiple aircraft being slammed into the exact targets that were hit. What a coincidence. These drills were designed to create confusion amongst the agencies that monitor US airspace i.e.

NORAD and the FAA. The same was occurring on the day of the Boston bombings. University of Mobile cross-country coach Alastair Stevenson stated to the media: *"At the starting line this morning, they had bomb sniffing dogs and the bomb squad out there. They kept announcing to runners not to be alarmed, that they were running a training exercise."*[57] This man's testimony disappeared from the mainstream media the next day. The official story always changes while the authorities are solidifying the version of events they want the public to believe. This happens over and again in the wake of these horrific events. Then there was the report of a captured Saudi national who was detained as a suspect. Apparently, the Saudi foreign minister met secretly with Obama and was immediately deported for reasons of national security. This report was also buried in the media. When secretary of Homeland Security, Janet Napolitano was questioned about this, she became defensive and denied it.[58] Then there were the photos of a private security firm at the scene sporting black backpacks, radiation detectors and other gear. This branch of the Seals calls themselves the Craft, which is interesting terminology as the word craft, refers to Masonry. Paul Joseph Watson posted these pictures in the independent media which prompted the FBI to publicly state that only the official pictures they released to the public should be looked at! Believe what you are told! Do not question authority. Go back to sleep!

Examples of the Hegelian Dialectic, problem-reaction-solution technique could fill entire volumes. The most blatant example in modern times would be the attacks that took place on the morning of September 11th, 2001. The official story of what transpired on that day is a fairy tale with about as much credibility as *Jack and the Beanstalk*. In fact, that story has a much higher probability of being real. The official story of 9/11 is a monumental pile of bullshit from start to finish. The event was staged and used as an excuse to invade Iraq, launch an open-ended war of terror, pass more draconian laws, remove more freedom and set the stage for the police state takeover. 9/11 was the catalyst to massively advance the Consortium's disgusting agenda, and that single event has been instrumental in bringing down the hammer of tyranny.

EIGHT

What Happened on 9/11?

On September 11, 2001, the worst attacks in American history occurred on US soil. Close to 3,000 Americans lost their lives in Manhattan as the twin towers of the World Trade Center complex collapsed into their own footprints, at near freefall speed. The people of the world were told that 19 Saudi hijackers armed only with boxcutters simultaneously took control of four passenger, jet airliners and successfully slammed them into three of their intended targets, over the most heavily monitored airspace in the entire world, the entire operation directed by a man in a cave, somewhere in the mountains of Afghanistan.

Of the 19 hijackers listed by the FBI, seven of them turned out to be alive. The public has been told a stream of lies by undoubtedly one of the most corrupted administrations to ever occupy the thrones of power in the United States, as the official story surrounding the events of that tragic morning were being solidified within the public mind.

What has unfolded in America as a direct result of the attacks has been nothing short of a draconian police state and an open ended war on terror with no ending in sight, all based on a thin veneer of lies, deceptions, impossibilities, and outright absurdities, which unfortunately has been believed by the non-thinking, non-questioning masses.

The official story of what happened on 9/11 is an absolute fairy tale, a monumental fraud from start to finish. We were told that somehow kerosene jet fuel burned over 1,000 degrees hotter than its maximum burning temperature and managed to melt 47, steel core columns in two skyscrapers, as they fell evenly into their own footprints. A third building, the Solomon Building, building seven in the WTC complex, also fell evenly into its own footprint, in what was quite obviously, a controlled demolition.

We were told that what was, on record, very small and contained office fires, brought down building seven, and the 9/11 Commission didn't even bother to acknowledge that building seven collapsed; they ignored it. Never in history have skyscrapers collapsed due to fire but on that day, the laws of physics were suspended as three skyscrapers were reduced to rubble, one of which, building seven, was not even hit by an aircraft.

The public was told that somehow a hijacked aircraft was able to penetrate the most heavily guarded airspace in the world at the Pentagon, pull off impossible maneuvers, and slam into the side of this military installation. When no wreckage, no bodies and no luggage were found, official sources claimed that a 100-ton, jet airliner vaporized on impact, again, defying the laws of physics. The vast majority blindly believe this nonsense and condemn the few brave people that dare to question the official, bullshit story.

We were told that one of the hijacker's passports was found neatly intact on the ground near the WTC complex. People actually believe that a piece of paper somehow survived the explosion that magically caused steel beams to melt. Unfortunately, the vast majority seems to have no problem being told what to think and believe, and the level of cognitive dissonance required to believe the official fairy tale, is absolutely staggering.

The flag waving statists came out in droves as they nodded their heads in approval of the open-ended wars that would soon follow and applauded the destruction of their freedom at the hands of mass murdering psychopaths.

So many otherwise intelligent people allow their entire worldview to be dictated by what they see, read or hear in the establishment, mainstream media. The media is not there to inform or educate; that is not its purpose. The media's job is to shape and influence public opinion. Goodness help those whose research differs from the official version of events; they are at once attacked, ridiculed and branded as lunatics, simply for offering different information, *even if the information they offer is true and provable*! But such is the awesome power and deep level of conditioning. Primarily, omission, and distortion are the media's tools to achieve this collective un-awareness.

Highly credible people have come forward offering data, testimony, eyewitness accounts and research that shows clearly that the public has not been told the truth concerning the most horrific attacks against America to date, including: pilots, firefighters, rescue workers, police, researchers/authors, former heads of state, flight school instructors, engineers, physics experts, and many others that show the official story to be nothing more than a fairy tale of enormous proportions.

The attacks perpetrated on New York and Washington DC were far more than a colossal intelligence failure, as many would have you believe. They were coldly calculated, vicious attacks that could have only been pulled off with help from within the highest levels of government, and compartmentalized intelligence agencies. The evidence that keeps coming forward to support that claim is simply too overwhelming for any thinking person to ignore.

In this segment, I just wanted to raise a few pertinent points to show that we have not been told the whole story concerning 9/11 and to further reiterate the Hegelian Dialectic triad. Mountains of information are available to anyone who cares to look at it.

9/11 Anomalies and Unanswered Questions:

- The public has been told that on the morning of Sept 11, 2001, 19 hijackers simultaneously took control of four commercial jets and slammed them into their targets. Of the list of 19 hijackers published by the FBI, why are at least five of them (hijackers) still alive?[1] And why has the FBI never amended the list?

- When a commercial aircraft turns off its transponder, and deviates from its flight plan, it is FAA standard operating procedure to scramble fighter jets immediately. Why did fighters stand down on the morning of 9/11? Who has the authority to order a stand down, bypassing ordinary procedure?

- NORAD (North American Aerospace Defense Command) is the institution in charge of monitoring all airspace in the US and Canada. Located deep within the Cheyenne Mountains, in Colorado, NORAD possesses the most advanced tracking technology on the planet. Why did NORAD stand down when four airliners deviated from their intended flight path? Again, who ordered no military action, despite standard operating procedure?

- How was a hijacked aircraft able to penetrate the most protected airspace and attack the most fortified military installation in the world, at the Pentagon?

- Why were there drills being conducted (Operation Vigilant Guardian among others) of hijacked aircraft being rammed into the exact targets that were hit on the very same morning of Sept. 11?[2] The Associated Press even reported on this.[3]

- The maximum burning temperature of any hydrocarbon fire is 1700 degrees Fahrenheit. Steel used in support columns of buildings does not even begin to reach its melting point until 2720 degrees Fahrenheit. Why then, did three buildings on 9/11 collapse due to fire? How does fuel burn at 1,020 degrees hotter than it normally would?

- Building seven-which was the furthest away from the towers, and which was not hit by any aircraft, and only very little debris-collapsed at about 5:30 PM on 9/11. What caused the building to collapse? Why has the 9/11 Commission ignored this pertinent fact? Building 7 is the greatest smoking gun of the whole event. The government and 9/11 commission have still not offered a logical explanation as to why this building collapsed. In fact, the 9/11 commission failed to even mention building 7 in their official whitewash, er, report.

- There were a few, very small, contained fires within building seven. The sprinkler systems in the building should have easily extinguished the fires. What caused the fires in building seven? Why has the Commission not told us what started the fires?

- Larry Silverstein, the lease holder for buildings 1, 2, and 7, said on a PBS documentary called *America Rebuilds*, that he and the NYC fire dept. made the decision to "pull" building seven. "Pull" is engineering jargon for demolish with explosives. It takes weeks of planning to plant the necessary explosives in a building to bring it down properly. How did the engineering crews set the explosives in building seven, amidst all of the chaos? Why have the media and the 9/11 Commission refused to address this?[4]

- Is it just coincidence that only the buildings for which Silverstein (who stood to gain billions of dollars) held the leases came down on 9/11? Silverstein invested *$150 million* to purchase the WTC complex, and raked in *$7 billion* after the attack. Quite a return wouldn't you say?

- Securecom[5] was the company in charge of security for the WTC. Is it coincidence that their contract was up on 9/11? Is it also merely coincidence that Marvin Bush, George W. Bush's brother was head of security? Moreover, is it only coincidence that Securecom also oversaw security at Dulles Airport?

- Why did Columbia University's seismographs show a 2.1 earthquake just prior to the time that the south tower began collapsing and a 2.3 seismic spike prior to the time that the north tower began collapsing? Another coincidence?

- Put options, are basically a bet that a particular stock will drop. Why, in just days before 9/11, were enormous put options (up to and exceeding ten times the daily average) placed on United and American airlines stocks? Why, when an investigation led to the highest levels within the CIA, was the investigation halted?[6] Why did the SEC (Security Exchange Commission) destroy the records?

- Why did the FBI claim that no black box transponders were found amidst the WTC rubble, while rescue workers claimed to have found three of them?[7]

- The FBI claimed that they found a passport of one of the hijackers amongst the rubble of the WTC.[8] I posed this question in the last chapter, but it bears repeating: how does a piece of paper survive an explosion of fuel and metal? How does a piece of paper survive temperatures so hot, that they melt steel frame support beams? The FBI also claims that a hijacker's passport was found amidst the rubble of the flight 93 crash in Pennsylvania. What are the odds of finding two separate passports amidst two separate crash sites? What are the odds that both passports would survive such explosions and be recognizable? Are Americans supposed to be that stupid, to believe such nonsense? Apparently so. By the way, the passport allegedly found amidst the flight 93 rubble, belongs to a person named Ziad Jarrah, who is still alive![9]

- Condoleezza Rice, who served as secretary of State under G.W. Bush, claimed that shortly after 9/11, the government would offer indisputable proof that Osama Bin Laden was responsible for the attacks. Why are we still waiting for it?

- How many among the general public are aware that Osama and the Taliban were trained, funded and installed into power by the CIA? The Taliban were trained to fight against the Soviets who invaded Afghanistan during the mid-1980s. Why has the mainstream media not acknowledged this fact?

- Why was George Bush Senior meeting with Osama's brother Shafig Bin Laden at the Ritz-Carlton hotel Washington on the morning of 9/11?[10]

- How many of the general public are aware that the Bush and Bin Laden families have enormous, long-standing connections through one of the world's largest defense contractors known as the Carlyle Group?[11]

- How was researcher William Cooper, in June of 2001, able to predict that a major event would occur, and that Bin Laden would be the scapegoat?[12]

- William Rodriguez was a maintenance employee working in one of the towers on the morning of 9/11. He has been recognized by the city of NY and the govt. for his heroic efforts to rescue people from the towers. Why has the media and 9/11 Commission ignored his testimony that he heard and felt explosions in the basement of the north tower? 14 people have backed his testimony and yet the media ignores it. Why?[13]

- Rodriguez pulled a badly burned man from the basement. How does a jet that hits the 90th floor, burn a man in the basement?

- Former New York City Mayor, Rudolph Giuliani claimed that he received prior warning that the towers were going to collapse. Who told him? Why didn't the firefighters and rescue workers get the same warning? Who could have known that the buildings would collapse? abc News reported on this.[14]

- Why was the rubble from the WTC carted away and not allowed to be examined by experts until recently?

- Why did the Bush administration block independent investigations into the 9/11 attacks?

- Why has the media ignored the fact that a Brigham Young University physics professor by the name of Steven Jones has found traces of thermate on some of the structural steel residue from the WTC? Thermate is used in controlled demolition.[15]

- Why was the British owned company, *Controlled Demolition* hired to remove the rubble from both the WTC and the Alfred P. Murrah building in Oklahoma City without it being investigated by experts? The ironic thing is that the name of the company actually tells what happened at the World Trade Center.[16] Often times the truth hides in plain sight.

- Bush claimed that he saw the first plane strike the tower on the morning of 9/11 on a television monitor, before entering the classroom at Booker Elementary school in Florida. How is this possible, when no such footage had been aired?

- Why did the Bush administration order investigations into Bin Laden to cease, soon after Bush took office?[17]

- How come the Windsor building, in Madrid, Spain, which burned for over 20 hours straight, did not suffer a similar fate as the WTC towers and building 7, even though its structural steel was weaker than that of the towers? I guess steel in Spain behaves differently. On April 3, 2013, the tallest building in Chechnya, the Grozny City skyscraper, a 40-story building, was engulfed in a raging inferno for about 29 hours. The entire building was destroyed but did not collapse. So how does a 110-story skyscraper collapse into its own footprint in under an hour, when most of the fuel exploded outside of the building? I think the answer is obvious. Fire cannot melt steel.

- Why was the Patriot Act, a reprehensible piece of legislation that destroys civil liberties, railroaded through Congress without the signatories even being allowed to read it, and solely as a result of the attacks?

- Why was San Francisco mayor, Willie Brown as well as other public officials warned on Sept. 10, 2001 not to fly on 9/11?[18]

- If the fires were so bad, that they somehow melted steel in three buildings, then why did NYC firefighters report prior to the first collapse, that the fires were minimal, and under control? Recordings exist that confirm this.[19]

- Why has the media and 9/11 Commission ignored the initial report of a NYC fire chief, who reported bombs in both the towers, and on the planes? NBC reported on this.[20]

201

[NOTE: As mentioned in the previous chapter, the same thing happened when the Oklahoma City bombing occurred on April 19, 1995. Initial mainstream media broadcasts reported eyewitnesses hearing multiple explosions and seeing bomb squad personnel remove unexploded devices from the Murrah building. Shortly thereafter, reports like these disappeared because they conflicted with the official story. I have the original abc news clips from the morning of 9/11. Peter Jennings claimed that the WTC collapses resembled a controlled demolition. After 9/11, no other anchor dared to make claims like that. The official version of events had become solidified, and the media repeated it unquestioningly. Journalism? Fair and balanced reporting? You must be joking!]

- On the weekend of 9/8, 9/9 2001, why was there a "power down" condition in the south tower for 36 hours, from the 50th floor and above? No power means no surveillance cameras, and no security locks. Just another coincidence I'm sure. Check this source for multiple news clips suggesting that explosives were used in the towers.[21]
- Why was credible witness testimony of engineers, as reported in *Chief Engineer Magazine* ignored by the media and Commission?[22]
- Why was a construction worker's testimony of an explosion in the basement ignored by the media and

Commission? So, an aircraft that hits the upper floors causes the wall in the subbasement to blow out?[23]

- There is a film clip of building 7 in which one can easily see charges going off in succession in the upper right-hand corner of the building. Why has this clip not been broadcast on Fox or CNN or any mainstream media outlet for that matter?

- Less than an hour before the WTC attacks, Donald Rumsfeld, former secretary of Defense under G.W. Bush, told a congressional delegation that a "shocking" event would occur soon. How did he know? Prior knowledge? No, of course not, that's crazy talk!

- The Department of Justice (DoJ) published a manual in 2000 titled: *Managing Weapons of Mass Destruction Incidents: an Executive Level Program for Sheriffs*. The cover of the manual depicts one of the twin towers in crosshairs. The Consortium often cryptically leaves clues as to what they are going to do.

- The people were told that a 757 passenger, jet aircraft hit the Pentagon. Why was there no wreckage from the crash? No luggage? No remains? Why was the lawn left unscathed? When questions arose, the media claimed that the aircraft disintegrated! How does a 220,000-pound aircraft just disintegrate?

- Why was there no response from Edward's Air base which is just down the road from the Pentagon? The Pentagon was not even hit until an hour-and-twenty minutes after the attacks began. Why weren't fighter jets patrolling the Nation's capital?

- We were told that flight 93, which crashed in PA. Was taken over by passengers and forced to the ground. Why then, was debris scattered over a seven-mile trail? Was flight 93 shot down?

- Why did the FBI confiscate surveillance footage from a gas station adjacent to the Pentagon and from several other businesses? This footage has never been released to the public. Why?

- Why did Christine Todd Whitman, head of the EPA (Environmental Protection Agency) at the time, claim that the air at around ground zero was completely safe?[24] Rescue workers and cleanup crews have been getting sick in droves due to the EPA's claims that the air was safe at ground zero. This is how we allow our heroes to be treated?

- The towers were designed to withstand hits by aircraft. 47 steel core columns existed within each of the towers. How could the south tower fall after burning for less than one hour? How could the north tower fall after burning for less than two hours? Most of the fuel burned up upon impact so again, how do fires melt steel?

- Cleanup crews reported molten metal being present within the wreckage of the towers weeks after the disaster. How could jet fuel, most of which exploded outside of the towers, have caused molten pools of metal in the rubble?[25]

- The BBC reported that Building Seven (Salomon Bros. Building) had collapsed over 20 minutes *before* the building actually came down. In a video clip that surfaced in 2007, one can clearly see the building still standing behind the reporter as she's reporting the collapse and official time stamps confirm the BBC's reporting of this event almost a half-hour before the building collapsed. When confronted, the BBC claimed to have lost the 9/11 tapes. I watched this unfold on live TV that day. It was around 5:20 PM that the building came down and yet the BBC reported the collapse at 4:54 PM. Are BBC reporters clairvoyant? Do they possess magic, crystal balls that can see into the future? Who knew the building would collapse and why did the BBC jump the gun so to speak? Many first responders are on record stating the building was coming down before it actually did. Is this why the commission simply ignored that building seven even existed? Sourced is a clip of the official news report in which you can see the building to the left of the reporter's head as she reports that the building has collapsed.[26] Who had foreknowledge of the collapse?

- On September 10th, 2001, Donald Rumsfeld announced that $2.3 *trillion* had gone missing from the Pentagon. Is it simply another coincidence that the budget accounting office at the Pentagon, that would have held the records, just so happened to be the area of the building that was targeted?

In 1997, a neo-conservative think tank group called the *Project for the New American Century* (PNAC) was created. The group consisted of members of the Bush administration and other neocons such as, Paul Wolfowitz, president of the world bank; Richard Pearle; John Bolton, US ambassador to the UN and current national security advisor under Trump; Richard Armitage, deputy secretary of state; Dick Cheney, vice president under Bush; Donald Rumsfeld, secretary of defense under Bush; Jeb Bush, governor of Florida; William Kristol, PNAC founder and former chief of staff to Dan Quayle, under the first Bush administration. Interesting, but not surprising, of the PNAC's 25 signatories to their mission statement, 17 are members of the CFR.

In September of 2000, a year before the 9/11 attacks, the PNAC published a document titled: *Rebuilding America's Defenses: Strategies, Forces and Resources for a New Century.* The document outlined the plan to dramatically expand military presence in the middle east, southeast Asia and Europe. The globalist neocons had plans to destabilize Iraq for years before the 9/11 attacks even occurred.

Shortly after the attacks, the Bush administration promoted their "axis of evil" campaign, demonizing Iraq, Iran and North Korea, and dutifully followed the script of the PNAC. The war on terror was born, which is really a war on freedom, conducted by the most ruthless, sycophantic henchmen the Consortium has to offer. The PNAC documents basically outlined a plan for US dominance and geopolitical restructuring in areas that are strategically significant and abundant in natural resources, particularly, oil.

The plan was always to completely dominate Iraq, which was already massively destabilized due to 13 years of economic sanctions placed on the country following the first Gulf war. In the run up to the second Iraq war which was launched in 2003, the Bush administration claimed that Saddam Hussein possessed weapons of mass destruction which he was intent upon using against his neighbors. That was a lie.

The Bush administration was shown to have lied, time and again, but we are supposed to believe these people when they tell us what happened on 9/11? The PNAC documents claim that: *"the process of transformation, even if it brings revolutionary change, is likely to be a long one, absent some catastrophic and catalyzing event-like a new Pearl Harbor."*[27]

The attacks of 9/11 gave the Bush administration the excuse to launch an open-ended war, to remove basic civil liberties, massively increase the surveillance society and to create a collective climate of fear which is what the globalist Consortium wants most. Basic freedom is destroyed under the guise of keeping people safe. A totalitarian police state has unfolded, and it is so blatantly obvious that one would need to be asleep or under a spell to not see it. Well, that is exactly the case.

The 9/11 attacks opened the door for endless wars, the removal of due process of law, indefinite detentions with no trial or due process, the removal of Posse Comitatus, economic devastation and the list goes on. The draconian policies continued under the Obama and Trump administrations.

The time has long passed for people to open their eyes and face the reality of the situation that surrounds them. Failure to see reality as it is will only ensure a tyrannical totalitarian state devoid of any semblance of freedom. Look beyond the distractions, the deceptions and the bread and circuses and educate yourself. For we are not in the final days, we are in the final moments.

NINE

Fabricated Reality

The point has arrived where to not have come to the conclusion that humanity has reached a serious crisis point, is to be completely lost within the illusion, mesmerized, brainwashed and oblivious to the reality of the situation that surrounds us. As we teeter on the brink of collapse and complete breakdown, as the system crumbles before our eyes and the matrix comes apart at the seams, there still appears to remain a high percentage of people who refuse to acknowledge what is there, in plain sight, right in front of their eyes.

Instead, they cling unwaveringly to denial, preconceived ideas, belief structures, false paradigms, ideologies, and archaic ideas about the nature of reality, life, and most importantly themselves. For all intents and purposes, they are under a spell. Their lives directed, not by the inner light of knowingness and intelligence, but by outer, manipulated, collectivized versions of a false reality, manufactured out of orchestrated fear and trauma.

There is currently underway-and has been for thousands of years-a psychological war upon the very consciousness of humanity.

The manipulating forces that operate behind the thrones of power in the world, seek at every turn, to distract, divide, dehumanize, subjugate, separate, coerce, control and manipulate and this is done through various means but ultimately, it is through the manipulation of human beings' understanding and ideas about what reality is and how they are experiencing it. It's a psychological mind game of immense proportions and the main tool used to keep human consciousness within the confines of the psychological prison cell, is through the constant exploitation and manipulation of the emotion of fear.

A traumatized mind is a highly suggestible mind and it is through the engineering of events that cause collective trauma that the controllers maintain their grip upon the consciousness of human beings. When people are faced with the reality of a situation that conflicts with their beliefs, emotions, ideas etc. often a situation arises that is known in psychology as cognitive dissonance.

Cognitive dissonance is loosely defined thusly:

"A distressing mental state that people feel when they find themselves doing things that don't fit with what they know or having opinions that do not fit with other opinions they hold. A key assumption is that people want their expectations to meet reality,

creating a sense of equilibrium. Likewise, another assumption is that a person will avoid situations or information sources that give rise to feelings of uneasiness, or dissonance."[1]

In other words, the mind will automatically resist something presented to it that conflicts with what it already *thinks* it knows as it seeks to reconcile two opposing views. Conditioned and indoctrinated people will react to new information on knee jerk response to avoid the uneasy feeling that arises when the comfortable belief systems are challenged. In this state, it is child's play to direct a person's consciousness or belief about a particular event or situation as the traumatized mind seeks to reconcile the dissonance to feel safe and comfortable again. Those pulling the reins of power are expert at manipulating this state of mind, to control the perception in the wake of orchestrated events be they bombings, economic crises, manipulated wars, or a myriad of other stage-managed events that cause shock and trauma to the collective consciousness. The ultimate goal is to keep people in a state of fear, so that they can be coerced into giving away their power, freedom and psychic sovereignty and beg for protection from what they've been manipulated to fear.

I've noticed also that in the wake of such events, people will be readily willing to embrace whatever explanation the authorities present through their unquestioning media, if it alleviates the fear and puts the cognitive dissonance at ease, no matter how ridiculous, inconsistent or absurd the official story happens to be.

The courageous few that do dare to question authority, or the official narrative are at once demonized, ridiculed discredited or otherwise attacked for asking questions or presenting alternative views that are not in line with the scripted, consensus made-for-TV version of events. It doesn't matter how credible the information they present may be or how nonsensical the mainstream, official story is, once the manufactured fear has been temporarily alleviated, most will outright reject anything that upsets their false sense of security and safety. People will willingly give up their freedoms and precious sovereignty in order to feel safe from what they've been manipulated to be afraid of. This scam is played out over and again and has been throughout history in order to keep human beings within a state of disempowerment and psychic disarray by the dark forces that skulk in the shadows like parasitic vampires and ravenous wolves. The Hegelian Dialectic technique of problem-reaction-solution has been so extremely effective at keeping humanity from standing in the light of their true magnificence and at separating us from the deeper understanding of who and what we are. This technique tricks people into giving away their freedoms in exchange for the illusion of safety. It's all a smoke and mirrors mind game, guided by the sorcerers that hide in the shadows.

Solutions to the manufactured crises are offered and in order to feel secure, people will willingly give away that which makes them human i.e. their freedom and autonomy, and even their own selfhood and right to think for themselves. They are inwardly so disordered and out of balance, that they will desperately cling to any solution that is offered that promises to restore that sense of balance, even if it is completely illusionary. People find solace in their illusions so how dare you come along and upset that false sense of comfort with little inconveniences, like the truth!

This is how massive droves of people deal with the uneasy feelings that arise when cognitive dissonance occurs; they adopt into their belief systems any idea that will ease the discordant feelings and inner anxieties in order to put those feelings to rest. This is very dangerous. It leads to absolute psychic enslavement as one abandons their right to think critically and instead adopts into their belief system any idea that coincides with what they've already been indoctrinated or conditioned to believe! People are trained to not trust their own inherent intelligence, lest they be labeled as "nut jobs" simply because their perspective does not fall in line with the generally accepted consensus. Do you see how this game is being played?

A culture of absolute fear has been created, which has convinced people that giving up their rights and freedom is a great idea in order to *feel* safe. In the wake of the Boston bombings, the Las Vegas shootings, and every other false flag event, expect more violations of basic rights, more military involvement in domestic law enforcement, more attempts to remove firearms from law abiding people, more surveillance, more tyranny, and less freedom as the totalitarian police state unfolds. There has been a long-standing agenda to turn America into a modern, technetronic version of Nazi Germany, and we are dangerously close to witnessing its full implementation. The good news is that the Consortium has become so brazenly open and sloppy, that it has caused a rumbling in the mass consciousness as more and more people are starting to see through the illusion. On the other hand, the majority still seems to be under the psychological spell and many of them will sleep to the very end as they allow and even applaud their own enslavement, ignoring the obvious and willfully embracing ignorance and abject denial. Willful ignorance and confirmation bias are two other aspects to this manipulation of consciousness. Remember, willful ignorance means denying anything that upsets the cognitive comfort zone, regardless of how factual the evidence may be. It is defending one's perceptual territory.

Confirmation bias is defined as:

"The tendency for people to only seek out information that conforms to their pre-existing viewpoints, and subsequently ignore information that goes against them".[2]

When people are faced with information that challenges their long standing beliefs, perceptions or ideas, cognitive dissonance occurs and in order to rectify the uncomfortable feelings, the psychological red flag if you like, the mind will immediately reject the cause of the discomfort (information) and willingly choose to

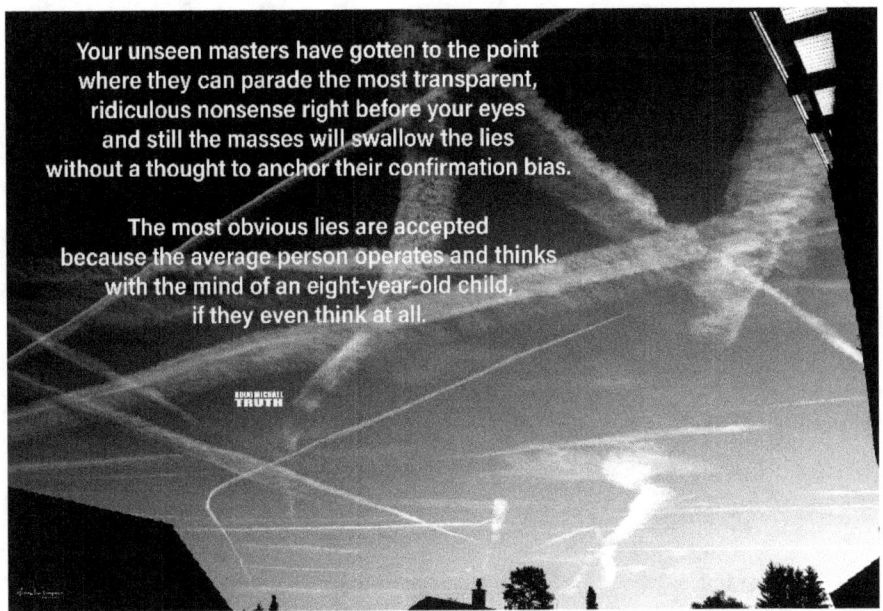

Your unseen masters have gotten to the point where they can parade the most transparent, ridiculous nonsense right before your eyes and still the masses will swallow the lies without a thought to anchor their confirmation bias.

The most obvious lies are accepted because the average person operates and thinks with the mind of an eight-year-old child, if they even think at all.

remain ignorant of painful truths. If I had a dollar for every time that I've witnessed this occur, I would be writing this from my private yacht right now off the coast of Maui!

Most of the sheeple don't even get to the stage of confirmation bias; they simply believe the pre-scripted, ready-made, official version of events, spewed by a media full of intellectual prostitutes and robotic repeaters. So called journalists within the mainstream media, are little more than spokespeople for the official version of events that the Consortium network *wants* the public to believe. If I had a dollar for every time I've witnessed someone click on a TV or pick up a newspaper and immediately, and with no investigation, adopt into their belief system what the headline or the broadcast is telling them to believe, I would be sipping Dom Perignon out of my solid gold champagne fountain!

It seems as if far too many have simply conceded their right to think critically, ask questions and trust their own inherent intelligence (if they have any) and instead mindlessly and blindly simply believe what they are told to from some outside authority. When did it become a criminal act to challenge authority? (Now it's a mental disorder)[3] The ones that do are immediately branded as dangerous, crazy or some other derogatory label because their daring to present information that flies in the face of the consensus, causes cognitive dissonance and they must be shut up at all costs to maintain the illusion. History is replete with examples of this.

The masses have been so comprehensively dumbed down, not least through chemical additives in the food and water, a miseducation system that promotes a hyper left-brained cognition, religious traditions that encourage believers to mindlessly follow, etc. that so many cannot even think critically anymore, and simply believe on reflex action whatever they are told to believe. They willingly embrace ignorance over truth. They shun rebellion for conformity. They willingly remain within the psychological prison cell out of fear of the consequences of thinking or being different. Many among the hypnotized will attack mercilessly anyone who dares to challenge the consensus or upset their carefully edited version of reality. If I had a dollar for every time I've seen this happen or been on the receiving end of such abuse, I'd be flying to Rio in my private jet.

In this age of information and instant communications, where so much information is freely available, it amazes me how many people will not ever bother to even try to educate themselves. Now with the advent of smart phones and I-phones with high speed internet access, many people essentially have the knowledge of mankind in their pockets. Why try to learn anything when you can watch videos of monkeys hurling feces at tourists? Why self-educate when you can go on social networking sites and post pictures of what you ate for lunch?

This is another thing I've noticed. Social networking sites such as Facebook are huge cyber communities. What could be an amazing tool for sharing information and exposing the consensus lie is instead used by the majority to advertise their own foolishness. So many, who may have been thought of as morons, simply update their social networking page and remove all doubt. I've seen people post pictures of their drug stashes, or other illegal things without a care in the world or the understanding that those sites are monitored by governmental agencies. I use it to promulgate information and to promote my musical projects and research, and there are a few out there that use it in the same manner, but the majority uses it to show the world how infantile they are. If you want to witness firsthand how incredibly moronic and dumbed down the majority have become, simply spend a day on Facebook.

The term "consensus trance" was coined by parapsychologist Charles Tart and is defined as:

"An automated state of consciousness; actually, the normal

Do not trust your own inherent intelligence or ability to seek knowledge and inform yourself!

There are people with expensive degrees and letters after their names that will happily do your thinking for you!

DOUG MICHAEL TRUTH

consciousness, based on the premise that people believe what they are told to be true as opposed to what they have themselves realized to be true."[4]

Despite the consensus trance that holds vast swathes of people under its spell, I do believe that we are in a unique time in history where the spell is breaking. This is what the elite fears the most, that the game will be exposed, and that people may actually come together and foil their plans. In fact, they are getting very desperate; they know their time is just about up. In the meanwhile, it's probably a good idea for those of us who have some insight into the machinations of this Consortium and their games, to keep exposing facets of it. In my view, it is very important to always remember and teach awakening people that first and foremost, this is a psychological coup d'état and the battlefield is the mind, the very consciousness of humankind.

Most people seem to display the attention span of a golf ball when it comes to mass media. They don't seem to ever notice how the story changes, the inconsistencies or the abject nonsense of the official reports. Instead, they blindly adopt into their belief system whatever the latest broadcast or news snippet is telling them to believe. They don't notice how what they are told to think today, is completely different from what they were told to believe yesterday. The story is solidified in the public mind, the history is written, and the public adopts the official version. It's a psychological mind game.

I could go on and on with this. Do your own homework and look at the inconsistencies for yourself. When we step back from the canvas, the movie screen, and reestablish our ability to think critically, an entirely different picture begins to emerge.

There exists another psychological phenomenon known as Stockholm Syndrome which is defined as:

"A psychological phenomenon in which hostages express empathy and sympathy and have positive feelings toward their captors, sometimes to the point of defending them. These feelings are generally considered irrational in light of the danger or risk

endured by the victims, who essentially mistake a lack of abuse from their captors for an act of kindness."[5]

We saw a blatant example of this in Boston as crowds gathered to cheer the cops and military after they locked down the city, conducted house to house searches without warrants and pulled innocent people out of their homes at gunpoint in a vulgar display of tyranny. This is what America has become and Boston was the testing ground for martial law. The fact that so many applauded their own enslavement is a glaring example of how successful this psy-op really was. Applaud your oppressor, worship your controller and love your servitude.

When the masses give up their minds and their rights in order to feel safe, what they get in return is a police state dictatorship. Always pay attention to what happens as a result of these events. The events that occurred in Boston will lead to more removal of basic freedoms. There will be checkpoints, increased TSA presence, and the enactment of a total police state. The Consortium is dangerously close to realizing its long-standing agenda of implementing a totalitarian, global super state. We seriously need to wake up! Unplug from the distractions, get educated and come together in unity and peaceful non-compliance. If we fail to do this, the result will be a George Orwell, dystopian nightmare where true freedom is nonexistent. What will you do without freedom? What kind of world will you bequeath to your children by allowing this to continue?

Is it possible that something within the psyche of man actually gives rise to the evils of the world? Has humanity been infected with a parasite of consciousness? Is what we understand as reality a projection of the collective and individual consciousness? Is it possible that all of the horrors we observe are the result of a traumatized and massively dissociated collective consciousness? Do we give rise to our own heavens and hells or are we merely passive, non-participants? This control system *wants* you to be a passive automaton. The greatest minds that have ever lived made a definitive connection between the collective unconscious mind and the outer world of manifested reality. Indigenous peoples and shamans, the great philosophers, psychologists and even modern-day quantum physicists have all understood this. Thought creates and our consciousness and the world that we perceive and experience are intimately connected. We are manipulated to perceive and identify with reality in a certain way; the way that benefits the hidden controllers. The outer world of manifested reality is a projection of the collective consciousness. Those that rule from the shadows are well aware of this and they are expert in manipulating human consciousness to collectively project the reality that they prefer, which is one of discord, imbalance and disharmony.

Does the outer reflect the inner? Do we unknowingly create the mirror for ourselves to observe as it reflects back to us all that needs healing? I would say, absolutely yes to both of those questions. Is it man's true purpose to act as co-creator or is it merely his plight to be dragged along for the ride? I suggest that the hidden persuaders are devoid of the creative, human element and therefore manipulate human consciousness to collectively project and create the reality that they prefer.

Television is perhaps the most powerful tool of psychological manipulation ever invented. TV literally shapes the opinions, indeed the very reality of frighteningly high numbers of people. In fact, according to Neilson, the average American watches four hours of television per day. If the average person lives to the age of 65, they would have spent roughly nine of those years watching TV!

The potential of television to manipulate consciousness was discovered as early as 1948. Simply observing today how comprehensively people are conditioned by what they see and hear on TV clearly demonstrates the control this medium has over the mass majority. The words television and "program" when used together spells it out all too clearly. Besides the mindless drivel that accounts for about 99.9% of broadcasting, TV is a sophisticated device capable of emitting [ELF] frequencies that interfere with a person's magnetic field and central nervous system, and this is frequency, or vibrational control. In addition, subliminal techniques are used constantly to create a literal hypnotic state on unsuspecting viewers.

US Patent and Trade Office, Patent #6,506,148, declares how it is possible to manipulate the nervous system of viewers by pulsing certain images or frequencies through TVs or computer monitors.[6]

I have witnessed on more occasions than I can count, people responding to a "news" item on TV, and simply reacting to it immediately with no thought, no questioning and no investigation whatsoever. If you can get the majority or even a certain percentage of people to react in this way, then I can't think of a more comprehensive, powerful and effective display of absolute mind control. It is this act of blind acceptance that creates the atmosphere necessary for societal degeneration to thrive. I've always been very curious observing the act of people simply accepting without question, whatever is told to them on the "news" as presented by the corporate, mainstream media. Who benefits from people simply believing what they are told without question? What are the main sources of the majority of mainstream information? Who owns the media outlets? Is the mainstream media truly a source of unbiased information or is it merely a tool for corporate advertising and the shaping and influencing of public opinion?

Television has been one of the main, modern tools for regimenting and controlling the masses, for creating a false reality and for effectively influencing public opinion. It is a powerful medium used to control the minds of programmed, conditioned and indoctrinated human beings. It has been extremely effective in aiding the controllers in maintaining unwavering belief in this manufactured, false reality.

All major media delivered through mainstream sources comes from one of two wire services. They are Reuters and the

Associated Press. Since AP is actually owned by Reuters, all mainstream, print and televised "news" comes from only *one* source. Reuters is owned by the Rothschild banking family, the financial force behind the funding of so many wars and atrocities. Who benefits from delivering news in such a way as to support war? Like everything else, the Consortium-controlled media operates within a hierarchical, compartmentalized, pyramidal structure, with one major force at the top trickling information it wants disseminated down to its subsidiaries. Those with the title "reporter" or "journalist" are nothing more than corporate voice pieces delivering slavishly what the AP or Reuters presents as news. The vast majority of them are news readers and nothing more.

The media and the entertainment industry create a reality bubble in which most people dwell. There is an infantile obsession with pop culture and celebrity status. With regards to what we laughingly refer to as "news," The general consensus appears to be: If it wasn't televised on the 5 O'clock news, then it didn't happen! Conversely, if it appeared on the 5 o'clock news, then it happened! Whether it actually did or not is irrelevant. Truth, logic and critical thinking must take a back seat while engaging in the shit show that is corporate media.

We witness the same media carnival over and again, after the death of some celebrity, or some pop icon scandal, or the latest propaganda claptrap or the demonization of the next country that's about to be bombed. We see this media, circus carnival occur all of the time, usually, when those in control of mass media wish to divert your attention away from events that really matter and bring your focus to irrelevant issues and TV does a wonderful job at it.

The false reality that TV presents, promotes crass commercialism, superficiality, worship of the physical and the acquisition of "stuff." The media is the corporate apparatus designed to control the free flow of information, influence public opinion, create a climate of fear, spread disinformation and government propaganda, and to keep consciousness in a low vibrational state of unawareness. Television also employs the use of subliminal messages, and a cursory understanding of the use of symbolism in advertising and corporate logos clearly demonstrates this fact. The idea is to put the viewer into a literal hypnotic state, in which the subconscious mind is suggestible, and then bombard the viewer with hidden messages, which very often contain heavy sexual connotations and occult themes.

In order to manipulate consciousness and maintain control, the free flow of information must be tightly regulated and what passes for entertainment must be molded with great precision as well. Alternative media has been a thorn in the flesh to the mainstream apparatus and has been gaining ground as more and more people awaken to the fact that they are being manipulated and lied to by the corporate run mainstream media. The internet has been the driving force behind the alternative movements and the only real place that the relatively few, courageous presenters of information contrary to the consensus, have a platform to present their views and findings to the general public. Of course, lately there has been a massive censorship crackdown across all social media platforms, and the alternative media has been infiltrated by disinformation agents. The dark sorcerers of the insidious, Consortium network are hard at work doing everything in their power to censor and regulate the internet. They are also implementing ways to impose and enforce internet taxation.

This technology has certainly moved us forward. Anyone with very rudimentary equipment can produce short films and distribute them online. Alternative blogs have sprung up all over and due to the explosion of unconventional views, major media networks have lost massively increasing viewership and newspaper sales have plummeted all over as more and more people become fed up with corporate media and its stranglehold on the airwaves and the flow of information.

But as stated, technology is a double-edged sword. With high speed internet connections readily available, bookstores available in so many major towns and cities, libraries with high speed internet, and the enormous amount of alternative media blogs and websites, you tube and so many other things available, Americans remain among the most uninformed (or misinformed) society on the planet! If not utilized to their fullest potential, all of these technological marvels seem to induce complacency, apathy and a passive, sedentary lifestyle. We are handed the tools of our own distraction and of our own destruction. Not many, it seems, will take advantage of what is right in front of them. To own a computer with internet access, is to have a library at your fingertips. But most people in the industrialized nations do not want education; we want *entertainment!* For so many, what could be an amazing tool for learning, education and the expansion of one's knowledge base, has instead become a device for relieving boredom, "social networking," mindless "entertainment," or a sophisticated porno machine. It seems as if so few will utilize the tools that are readily available to them and instead, embrace abject distraction.

Television frequencies (ELF waves) shut down higher brain functioning in the neo cortex, while activating lower brain activity in the limbic system. As stated, TV creates a hypnotic state on unsuspecting viewers, opening the lower mind to suggestion and this is why subliminal messages and symbolism are used so ubiquitously. When the mind is in a trance-like state, the subconscious mind does not filter; it just accepts whatever it is presented with (hypnotism) and people are bombarded constantly with images, flickering wave patterns, slogans and buzzwords, symbolism, and the list goes on. Add to all of this the fact that many news readers and politicians are absolutely proficient in the art of NLP (Neuro Linguistic Programming) and you have the perfect recipe for comprehensive, absolute mind control. The results are plainly obvious to any thinking person: a sleepwalking, misinformed, docile, intellectually lazy, mind-controlled populace with very little, if any ability to think critically.

If you can detach emotionally and psychologically, and simply observe, it becomes easy to see just how television works its sorcery. Just look at the average content. There is so much violence, sexual themes, fear, and general mindlessness within the three-ring circus of TV. Television presents ideas and images that appeal to the lower drives, the baser instincts. Its primary functions appear to be dehumanization, desensitizing and thought control. Television and entertainment set the norms in our societies and promotes a deep sickness which pervades the consciousness of the average person. Its ubiquitous bullshit seems to dominate the consciousness of the vast majority of minds.

Just listen to the average conversation of most people. What's being discussed around the water cooler? Is it topics that really matter or most often simple discussion concerning what programs were viewed the night before? "Hey, did you see the Walking Dead last night? I wonder who's going to die next. Hey, did you see Desperate Housewives? I wonder if so-and-so is going to fuck what's her name." Sadly, this is the level of conversation within far too many. So few even seem to have the ability to discuss ideas anymore or engage in any kind of even remotely intelligent conversation. The art of conversation is dead.

A rudimentary examination of the content and the advertising suggests that TV is geared towards the lowest level of intelligence. What an astounding invention and tool for the hidden rulers of the Consortium network! The controllers have found a way to program the minds of the average person, while providing all of the bread and circuses they will ever need! Even many basic cable packages offer over 100 channels of pure, Grade A, unadulterated, mindless shit to choose from.

If you simply observe an average media presentation, you can see clearly that what is happening is that a news reader tells you how to interpret the images that you are seeing. A video clip running on a feedback loop is interpreted for you by the good-looking news presenter with the two-thousand-dollar haircut and the overpriced wardrobe. Look at what they do when a guest that offers alternative views is in the spotlight. Usually it just becomes a mudslinging fiasco. TV and especially mass media, creates and maintains a false reality while simultaneously discrediting anything outside of the consensus it promotes. The fact that staggeringly high numbers of people adopt that consensus lock, stock and barrel, exemplifies the grip that this medium has on the mass consciousness.

A great example of TV and media control over the herd mentality was the May 1, 2011 announcement by Obama that US forces killed Bin Laden, of course without offering any evidence whatsoever, photographic or otherwise. The official story came apart immediately but that didn't stop the drunken hoards from shouting in the streets and waving their flags. It's gotten to the point where the most inane, ridiculous, absurd and outrageous nonsense is presented as news and it is simply accepted without question. Most people are completely content with being told exactly what to think. And the majority of those people probably don't even know what a book is anymore.

Here's a great example of what I'm talking about: at the time that the Obama administration announced that troops had killed Bin Laden (the CIA asset) I was working in the food service industry. Newspapers were sold there, and of course, when the government announced that they killed their former ally, the story was blasted all over mainstream media, on every front page and every news network. No evidence was presented to the public but of course, this didn't matter. The "news" was broadcast on every TV network and printed in every major newspaper so it must be true.

I watched a man walk over to the newspaper rack, pick up a copy of the propaganda rag, and claim with glee: "we got him! We got the son of a bitch!" No investigation, no critical thought, hell, he didn't even read the article! The front-page headline was enough to convince him, and this is exactly what I'm talking about.

My experience has shown me that there are two kinds of education, our formal education (indoctrination) that we get from the establishment, and one that we give to ourselves. Which do you think is more valuable? And if one's education or idea of reality comes solely from the TV, their mind is most likely on the level of an eight-year-old, and that's being generous! Reading is the basis of how we learn and expand our knowledge base in this five-sense reality.

With the hypnotic state that TV creates, the mindless drivel, newsreaders trained in NLP, and the constant drip-feeding of abject crap into the culture, it is nothing less than sorcery. This would explain why so many accept what they are presented with in media reports, regardless of whether or not it makes sense. Time and again, major events are portrayed in the media which seem to immediately become reality for the majority. When independent researchers/investigators offer a different version of events, regardless of how factual, true or comprehensive the results of their efforts are, they are immediately attacked from all sides and discredited without consideration. This happens again and again and quite frankly; it's getting rather old and boring. There are countless examples of actual journalists engaging in real investigation, having their findings shot down immediately by the mainstream, simply because their conclusions do not prop up the official nonsense. So many people cannot differentiate between logical, factual information and the psychobabble they are adopting into their belief systems through the tube.

Endless billions are spent each year on corporate advertising. In the first nine months of 2010, US advertising reached a total of $94.6 *billion!* In 2016, it was over $190 *billion!*[7] That is a staggering amount of money. What could be used to improve the lives of every single human being, is instead used to mind control you. Highly trained and specialized people are employed to carefully craft even a 30-second commercial or even the most seemingly innocuous magazine advertisement. A single, 30-second spot on prime-time TV can run well into the millions to produce and air. There is a reason why so much is spent on advertising. It is done in such a way so as to influence the subconscious mind and this is taken to extreme lengths. The subconscious does not filter; it just accepts what it takes in. Advertisers are well aware of this and they will be meticulous down to the finest detail, including lighting, placement of actors, use of symbolism etc. There are countless examples of this subconscious programming at work, it is truly ubiquitous. Advertising penetrates everywhere within the culture, it is all around us, permeating the cities and towns.

In 2010, global advertising reached an astounding $503 *billion!* Again, advertising is huge business and it is about more than merely raking in enormous profits. Beyond dictating to people what they need, how they should look, what the latest "in" fads or fashions are, etc. advertising is about molding the consciousness into creating a consumerist, trinket based, plunder-produce-discard culture. It has served its masters and done its job astoundingly well. The consumerist mindset is so anti human, that people are willing to trample other people almost to death in order to save a few bucks on some trinket, as they did in Buffalo, New York on Black Friday, in 2010, and no doubt countless other places.[8]

In 2009, a temporary employee at Wal Mart, in Long Island, New York was stomped to death by the hordes of animals fighting to be one of the lucky few to get a bargain Blu-ray player or a discounted video game system.[9]

I would suggest that advertising, with its hidden persuasion and subliminal manipulation of consciousness, has a lot to do with why people would behave in such ways. The marketers and owners of corporations that produce the trinkets must be ecstatic that people are willing to kill for their crappy products. They dance around the board rooms clanking their glasses and having a laugh at how stupid the mindless hordes of consumers are and how easily manipulated.

Top leaders in media and advertising are often affiliated with the Consortium's Round Table Network. The Council on Foreign Relations has many members in key positions, not only in media and advertising, but also big business, politics and all the rest. Membership in the Bilderberg organization also includes high level media moguls.

Through the [mis]education system, the entertainment industry, television and the mass media in general, the hidden persuaders of the Consortium have effectively restructured human consciousness. That so many are completely unaware of how they are being manipulated is disturbing to say the least. Any outsider that thinks outside of the consensus box in which we are encouraged to imprison ourselves within, is at once shot down, discredited, outcasted or shunned. The consensus that TV and entertainment has created reflects the sickness of culture right back in our faces. That so many buy into the lies and manipulations is a prime example of people acting like human cattle, unwittingly thinking and acting in ways that please their unknown, hidden global masters. But who is to blame? We can point the finger at these machinations but ultimately, who is responsible for what we think and how we act? Is anyone *forced* to buy into the ideologies, consumerism, or thought-stopping mediocrity that TV and its

Consortium gophers present them with? They can try to sell you any kind of shit or false reality they want to, but you don't *have* to buy it!

Unfortunately, so many do buy into the twisted reality that TV and the entertainment industry presents. I have a challenge for anyone that watches TV on a regular basis: turn it off for 90 days. Every time you get the urge to watch TV, instead read a book for the same amount of time you would've watched your favorite shows. There is one catch: it must be a non-fiction book; one in which you can actually learn something you did not know before. I guarantee that after those 90 days, you will feel and be smarter and you will feel a sense of accomplishment. You will probably also feel a greater sense of peace after not having your limbic system bombarded for three months. I have not actively watched TV in well over a decade and I have learned (and more importantly, un-learned) more in those last several years than in my whole life prior. Like it or not, reading is the basis of how we learn. Mark Twain once remarked that one who will not read is no better than one who cannot read.

I have a fairly large library of many diverse and interesting works. So few that have visited me over the years ever show even the slightest interest whatsoever in these books. Again, most of us could care less about knowledge and learning; we want to be entertained. We have become a nation of passive and intellectually lazy thinkers and TV has done quite an excellent job at promoting that dissociated mindset. If psychological energy and the outer reality are intimately connected (they are) then what reality do you wish to create? Do you want to live in the false and twisted reality of the mainstream consensus that TV and entertainment perpetuates and wants you to buy into?

What the mainstream media specializes in is disinformation. They will pepper the truth with misleading statements or outright lies. We can gather pieces of the truth from the mainstream, but we have to sift through all of the nonsense. This is why I examine both mainstream and alternative news and try to gather as much information as possible.

Enjoy life! Go outside! Be with your children! Plant a garden! Learn to play a musical instrument! For Goodness sake read! Paint a picture! Build a computer! Write some poetry! Raise a puppy! Do anything creative or constructive. And most importantly…**Kill your television!**

I believe it's very possible that we are on the verge of a civil war, which will follow an engineered economic collapse or some other contrived catastrophe. Whether we choose to give our minds to enslavement or unite and create something new is up to us and I cannot stress enough that this begins on an individual level, with a committed and conscious effort to break the psychological spell. It's difficult for many to examine their beliefs and deprogram but the alternative will not be pretty. We can create a heaven on Earth or a prison, control grid system. The Consortium advances its agenda because through willful ignorance the people allow it to occur. The time is now to take your power back and that begins with cognitive sovereignty. You must think for yourself and never concede your right to question authority and formulate your own opinions. Break the trance! Think for yourself! A word of caution: once you begin to awaken, there are those who will move against you to try and keep you within the collective trance. People will ridicule you and often become belligerent because you dare to step outside of the mental prison cell. I view this as a test to determine if one is ready to stand in the light outside of the consensus trance. Humanity in effect polices itself by attacking the daring ones who venture too far from the prison cell or who present a different perspective than the concocted, mainstream version of reality. Have you noticed that simply having a different perspective to the consensus automatically becomes synonymous with insanity? Evidence doesn't matter to the thought police; if you think differently you are crazy, end of story!

Always remember that despite the outward manifestations that we can easily identify, to confirm that we are living within an insane system, that first and foremost it is a psychological mind game that is occurring. It's like what was portrayed in the Matrix movie, a prison for your mind. I suggest taking the red pill. It's not easy to come to the realization that almost everything you've ever been told is a lie, but it is necessary to entertain that possibility if one is to come to a greater understanding of the situation that surrounds us and to contemplate solutions.

I put it like this:

"Give your allegiance to the mind doctors, the media manipulators, the servants of falsehood and Mammon. Be one of the gormless crowd; for that is easier and far more comfortable. Think for oneself? Why? That would require effort and invite ridicule. Who the hell wants that? Conform, believe what you are told, fit in, follow, bow down and lick the boots of your enslavers. They will promise you security at the expense of your selfhood, safety at the expense of your freedom and protection from the very crises that they have created. There is no more middle ground! The time is now to rise up and reclaim your psychic sovereignty."

TEN

The Fall of Civilization

American and European civilization appears to be in its final death throes. The once thriving, viable middle class is rapidly disappearing as jobs diminish and homelessness skyrockets at an ever-increasing and alarming pace. Meanwhile, liberal politicians, media mouthpieces, virtue signaling Hollywood celebrities, and even college professors and students cry for socialism, as if that is the solution to the engineered problems. You cannot solve the problems with the same level of consciousness that created them! In the minds of those suffering with Rectal-Cranial Inversion, Socialism, which has always failed, will somehow lead to some sort of utopian paradise where everyone is "equal" and receives free shit form the government.

I live in an area of the country that exemplifies the broken dreams of days long past, a once thriving city that has long ago died and moved on. Once upon a time, places like this gave hope to Americans that just wanted a better life for their children, for

238

This is an all too common sight in many areas of America where industry and manufacturing once thrived. This is an abandoned mall in Utica, NY, and the immediate area is filled with similar remnants of days long past. The broken-down buildings still remain as a reminder of how cities like this once prospered. Cities like this are canaries in the coal mine.

people that just wanted an opportunity to do better for themselves and produce something to leave their progeny, in hopes that their lives would be better. I'm sorry to tell you the bad news, but those dreams of a brighter future have been stolen from us. They've been crushed beneath the waves of greed and willful ignorance. I live in the ghetto, in the hood. I refer to the place where I live as "Detroit Junior." It's just another one on the list of amazing cities that have been gutted in this country, stealing the most from those whose blood and sweat built it. Compared to other places in America, it's not that bad; however, some of the most amazing cities, in Europe and America, have fallen and resemble the most poverty stricken third world countries.

The reason I mention the place where I live, is because it's a city that was once alive and thriving with industry, culture and manufacturing. It has long since died and moved on, and to me, living where I do, in the trenches, you can observe what happens when a country that was once the icon of the world, a bastion of innovation and ingenuity, begins to become a third-world hellhole. It tends to sink in and put things into the framework of a broader perspective.

We've allowed the glory that we could become to be stolen from our children, to be cast asunder, to be raked through the mud and spat upon. We may as well go to the cemetery and piss or deliberately vomit on the gravestones of our forefathers, the ones who slaved in the factories or died in the fields of battle. We can photograph it and call it modern art!

In the immediate area where I live, at the time of this writing, in the inner city of Utica, New York, people from multiple cultures and backgrounds live together and exist peacefully, well, for the most part. Many of the immigrants here just want to run their shops and businesses, raise their families and be left alone. In one square block, you've got businesses run by Italians, Asians, Pakistanis, Bosnians, Lebanese, and others. In the surrounding areas, there is crime, and I've heard gunshots pop off before. Sometimes, on the 4th of July, I like to play a game called: "gunshots or fireworks." I live in perhaps one of the most

Abandoned buildings like this appear all over this city. Many of the old buildings are filled with asbestos making their removal very costly. This is an all too common sight and a sad reminder of how this city once thrived with industry and manufacturing but has long ago died and moved on.

multicultural areas in the entire state, and for the most part, there is peace. The majority of people, just want to live their lives, raise their kids and be left alone, as any normal human being would. The riffraff is still present however, just as it is anywhere else. Some people even jokingly refer to this city as "Shootica."

There are also many refugees, within the same radius and in the 3 ½ years that I've lived here, I've never been hassled. It seems as if most people want to simply live their lives and be left alone. Well, imagine that! There was this one time, a few years back, when I was assaulted by a random druggie, uptown, in a nicer area of the city but that's another story.

I saw something so sad one 4th of July that broke my heart into pieces. I live in an area of the country that has a high migrant population. I'm in an inner city and this place brings in a *lot* of refugees. They bring them into the ghetto, into economically depressed areas in cities that cannot assimilate them. They occupy large two or three-family houses and they have LOTS of kids. I was walking up to the corner bodega to get some beer and it was nightfall, so the fireworks were starting. On Independence Day, fireworks go off all over this city. As I was walking back from the store, the booms were loud, and I watched a group of little children scream in horror as an adult man tried to corral them and bring them into the house. It was sickening. These people are from Somalia and were relocated from war-torn regions and they don't understand our holiday customs. These children were scared shitless and I was utterly stunned observing this; in fact, it made me want to vomit. These children lived through the horrors of having their villages bombed and perhaps witnessed members of their family or their neighbors getting blown to bits and naturally assumed that it was happening again due to the loud, booming explosions. The screams of horror and panic from these kids was intense and fortunately, they've adjusted to our celebrations and now they understand that the fireworks aren't bombs and they aren't frightened anymore. What does a four or five-year-old, newly resettled child know about 4th of July celebrations? The loud booms remind them of when their villages were bombed, and the crackling of fireworks sounds like gunshots and it was just

242

completely fucked up to observe this. It was another of many reminders of how humanity has allowed their world to be turned into a sewer.

I find it just so bizarre and disturbing that we live in an abundant and beautiful world in which plentiful and immense beauty surrounds us and yet we allow it to be destroyed at the hands of criminally insane psychopaths, creatures that plunder mercilessly for their own gain. When will we ever learn?

The number of homeless people seems to keep increasing here and in many areas across the country. In 2017, a good friend of mine, who is an Army veteran and commander of one of the local American Legion posts, found a Vietnam veteran living under a bridge. He was turned away several times from one of the local veteran outreach centers, which has been implicated in questionable activities, including embezzlement. We worked together to get this man off the street (something the outreach center failed to do for so many veterans) and we filled his apartment with furniture and necessities. Around the same time, I met a homeless man named Liam at the bodega I often frequent. He was camping out on the concrete with nothing more than the clothes on his back. After I emerged from the bodega and walked past him, I had a very strong urge to stop in my tracks as a very powerful impulse, a voice in my head if you will, urged me to: "go talk to that man." So, I did.

I sat next to Liam on the curb, introduced myself and offered him a beer. After a little while I asked if he was a veteran. He was not, but if he had been, I would have been able to help him more due to my friend's connection to the legion and his support of veterans. After a few beers, I gently asked him how he wound up on the streets. He proceeded to tell me his heart wrenching story of how he had lost his family in a house fire, had a breakdown and just started walking until he arrived in this city. He was from a city that is almost 150 miles away!

This man was not a drug addict; he was simply a person who suffered a breakdown due to a tragic event in his life. He collected cans and bottles, and some of the local businesses would pay him a few dollars to do odd jobs. Liam was trying to earn enough money for a bus ticket to get back home. The streets here are unforgiving, especially during the harsh winter months. I would bring him home-cooked meals, and I gave him a bunch of clothing, and I could tell that simply treating him like a human being made a big difference.

Winter was fast approaching, which meant that Liam would have a hard time being homeless once the colder months set in. It is not unusual during the winter here, to receive two or three feet of snow, or more, in one single storm. Being homeless on the streets here during the winter is extremely difficult.

On one particular evening, I prepared a plate of food to bring to Liam and when I got there, I noticed that he and all of the belongings he had accumulated over the few months since I met him, were gone. I went into the bodega to inquire if the owner knew what had happened. He told me that Liam was able to get his

This is a portion of the building where I found Liam. He was sleeping here with nothing except the clothes he was wearing. This is not a very nice area of the city.

bus ticket and headed home. I was relieved to find this out. I don't share this story to prop up my ego, but to point out that this can happen to anyone, that not all homeless people are lazy, or addicted to drugs. Many of them are, but many others have fallen upon hard times for one reason or another and wound up in the streets. Currently, over 500,000 people in America are homeless,[1] and over 35,000 of them are military veterans.[2] The US has over half-a-million homeless and yet has spent close to *$650 billion* on military expenditures in 2018 alone.[3] Since the "War on Terror," launched solely as a result of the 9/11 attacks, the US government has spent close to *$6 trillion* on war[4], which has seen close to

500,000 people killed, while the infrastructure in the US crumbles.

There are many homeless in this dead city, this underbelly of the ashes of broken dreams. Many of them are veterans, the poor kids who were sent to kill and die on behalf of the rich and elite that sent them to the killing fields for their own selfish interests. The bravest amongst us are sent to die in bogus wars of attrition.

The architecture in this city is exquisite; there are many Victorian and Colonial homes, many of which are subdivided and filled with poverty-stricken people. Well, it's a heroin infested hellhole but damn, the architecture is wonderful! To be fair, there are still nice places in this city and many wonderful people, in fact; some of the most amazing people I've ever met in my entire life are from right here and I am honored to know them. On the other hand, this is written from the perspective of the economically depressed areas, where the streets tell the awful and bitter truth.

Oh yes, Heroin. Heroin and pills. When I was a kid it was: "hey mister, can you buy us a six pack?" Or: "you got any weed?" Now, the young ones inject the venom or snort the powered death of the OxyContin or Vicodin they scored on the streets and flush their meaningless lives away into the misery that their existence has become. As much as it breaks my heart, I can't say that I blame them, having to cope in this world of shit they've inherited. What really gets me, is that for a while, the opiate pain medications were openly prescribed and readily available. Then, just as the laws changed, to make them virtually impossible to obtain, suddenly the streets are flooded with Heroin. Hmmm. Kind of makes you wonder huh? You want to destroy a nation? Then get the children! Get the kids hooked on gadgets and dope and you've got them by the balls! Well over 60,000 people died from drug overdoses in America in 2018.[5] The majority of those deaths were from opioids. Now, Heroin laced with Fentanyl, a synthetic opioid with a potency almost 100 times greater than Morphine,[6] has hit the streets and is killing people in droves. Now, synthetic Oxycodone pills laced with Fentanyl are hitting the streets.

You can plainly see the results within the eyes of the walking dead that surround you, the ocean of sullen and empty vessels adrift on the seas of despair. The sewer is backing up and the toilet is overflowing. Metaphorically speaking, you should grab a mop and bucket, because you're about to be inundated with shit! Roll up the sleeves! Put those rubber boots on and get ready!

Speaking of toilets, San Francisco has become a cesspool of filth, crime and decadence. The homeless population in San Francisco is around 7,500.[7] You can view films that show tent cities lining the streets in downtown San Francisco,[8] and this is occurring in what was always one of the wealthiest cities, in the wealthiest state, in the wealthiest country. The decline is readily apparent. What was once a beautiful city now resembles a third world country, and this is occurring in once thriving cities all over America. Collapse is imminent, and the signs are right out in the open, and yet, so few seem to be aware or they look to the politicians to fix the problems, which of course, is not going to happen. They *are* the problem! The Consortium's agenda is to bring America down, reducing the nation to third world status, and unfortunately, they are succeeding.

Many of the homeless population in SF are addicted to intravenous drugs and shoot up right out in the open, afterwards, discarding their used hypodermic needles all over the streets, and this has become a growing and widespread problem in the city. Tens-of-thousands of discarded needles pollute the city streets. In 2018, the city employed special cleanup crews to collect used needles from the streets and they retrieved 90,879 syringes in its first six months![9] The city enacted a needle exchange program, and in 2017, the city handed out *5.3 million* syringes but collected only 3.3 million.[10] In 2018, the program distributed 5.8 million syringes.[11] San Francisco Board of Supervisors expects a seven year extension of the program which could cost taxpayers *$26 million*.[12] It is estimated that there are 24,500 IV drug addicts amongst the population in SF.[13] In 2018, there were 9,659 complaints of needles scattered throughout the city.[14] Again, this is happening in one of the wealthiest cities, and it's highly likely, that over time, San Francisco may resemble cities like Detroit or Baltimore, which have fallen into utter ruin.

This is a massive health epidemic, but it's not the only problem plaguing San Francisco and other major cities. Many people defecate and urinate right in the streets and on the sidewalks. Since 2011, there were over 118,000 reports of human feces in the streets.[15] In 2018, there were over 28,000![16] The Department of Public Works hired a small team to clean the feces from the streets and they pay them each $184,000![17] I suppose they are so highly paid because they deal with a lot of shit. Since they are city employees, and since the needle exchange program is sponsored by the city, that means that taxpayers pay for drug addicts to receive syringes and the removal of their human waste from the streets. San Francisco has become a literal shit hole.

Another major problem in SF is crime. To support their habits, drug addicts will commit robbery and the cases of property crimes is skyrocketing. Each year, there are more than 6,000 property crimes per 100,000 residents.[18] Many people living in the city place notes on their car windows asking burglars not to break their windows stating that there are no valuables inside. On average, there are currently 51 car break-ins per day.[19]

The situation is just as bad (or worse) in Los Angeles. It's estimated that in L.A. County alone, there are upwards of 41,000 people living in the streets.[20] In 2018, the *L.A. Times* reported that homelessness had increased by 75% in only six years.[21] Homeless encampments line Venice Boulevard and crime has increased dramatically. This is a massive humanitarian crisis and it's in plain sight in many major cities. In 1987, I was living in Mar Vista, on Venice Boulevard, just three miles east of Venice Beach. It was very nice in those days, but now it is overrun with homelessness, drugs and crime. People are afraid to walk barefoot on Venice Beach for fear of stepping on used syringes. Los Angeles is being overrun with rats due to the filthy conditions. Another major problem in L.A. is huge piles of trash that are attracting large numbers of rats. Los Angeles has been dealing with an outbreak of Typhus due to the rats carrying fleas, which spreads the disease to humans. The city has no plans on how to deal with the rat problem.[22] Because of the massive rat infestation, there is a very real risk of triggering an outbreak of Bubonic Plague. Although in 2018, LA spent $620 million in tax dollars to deal with the problem, the city saw a 16% increase in homelessness.[23]

Seattle is another city that is falling into ruin. The homeless population in Seattle ranks third, with around 12,000 people living in shelters or on the streets.[24] Only New York and Los Angles have a higher population of homeless. Just as in San Francisco and Los Angeles, tent encampments line many of the city streets. A very good documentary called: *Seattle is Dying* shows the dire situation this city is facing.[25] The film received over three million views in just one month.

These dying cities are merely a microcosm of a dying world. In 2019, the *Intergovernmental Science-Policy Platform on Biodiversity and Ecosystem Services* (IPBES) released an alarming report, the most comprehensive assessment of its kind, it claims, that details the massive decline of nature and the extinction events that we are currently facing. The report claims that currently, *1,000,000* species are threatened with extinction.[26] IPBES chair, Sir Robert Watson claimed that ecosystems on which all life depends are "deteriorating more rapidly than ever."[27] In part the report points out:

- 66% of the oceans have been altered by human activity[28] [pollution overfishing, oil spills, etc.]
- 60 billion tons of resources are extracted globally each year.[29]
- Approximately *$577 billion* in annual global crops are at risk.[30]
- Between *300-400 million tons* of industrial waste are dumped into the world's waters each year![31]
- Over 400 ocean "dead zones" exist due to fertilizers contaminating eco systems.[32]

There's much more in the report which basically outlines the fact that humanity is committing suicide at an alarming pace. The IPBES report also claims that it is not too late to prevent complete catastrophe from occurring. The technology already exists to create far more sustainable systems and methods of doing things. Corporate greed, and the treatment of the Earth as nothing more than a resource, to be used and plundered, as opposed to a living entity, in which we share a symbiotic relationship, has driven humanity to the edge of our very extinction. As the legendary comedian, George Carlin once said: "pack your shit folks, we're going away." If an intelligent, extraterrestrial race were observing mankind from afar, it's probably a safe bet that they would conclude that humans are suicidal and ecocidal maniacs. Ecocide is defined as:

"the destruction of large areas of the natural environment as a consequence of human activity."[33]

The greed-driven corporations operate under a system that I refer to as: *plunder-produce-discard.*

1. **Plunder:** The Earth is mercilessly raped of its natural resources, at a fast-paced an unsustainable rate, causing massive environmental destruction in the process.

2. **Produce:** cheap goods are mass produced and the markets are flooded with unnecessary crap to keep the beast of consumerism well fed. Products are manufactured with built in obsolescence, deliberately made to not last so that this destructive cycle can continue as the corporations grow fat on the destruction of the planet and its creatures. Countries such as Taiwan or China, where labor laws are virtually nonexistent, produce goods in the sweatshops, where people work in horrendous, slave labor conditions.

3. **Discard:** all of the trinkets and poorly made goods are thrown away, turning the world into a garbage dump, increasing the size and toxicity of landfills, polluting the oceans and waterways, filling the air with noxious poisons, and destroying the Earth so that the cycle can repeat for the sake of profits. It's pure and utter insanity.

On March 11, 2011, a massive earthquake which measured a

9.0 magnitude, struck off the coast of Japan, triggering a massive tsunami which left parts of the country in shambles. This was considered one of the most powerful earthquakes ever recorded. Official reports claimed that over 15,000 people lost their lives, over 6,000 were injured, and 2,584 were missing. The earthquake was so powerful that it shifted Honshu, the main island of Japan by an estimated eight feet![34]

Roughly 30% of Japan's electricity is generated by nuclear reactors.[35] Most of the reactors are situated right along the coast in one of the most seismically active locations on the planet. The tsunami caused destruction of three of the six nuclear reactors at the Fukushima Daiichi facility, causing meltdowns of the reactor's cores which occurred within the first three days. In November of 2011, the Japanese Science Ministry reported that radioactive cesium contaminated 11,580 square miles of the land surface of Japan.[36] Since the devastating tsunami struck, the failed reactors have been dumping hundreds of tons of radioactive waste into the Pacific Ocean every single day, for the past eight years! Radioactive cesium (an alkali metal) rapidly contaminates an ecosystem and poisons the entire food chain, and this toxic waste has been detected in Japanese food over a 200-mile radius of the Daiichi facility.[37]

Cesium and other radioactive waste products are bioaccumulative, meaning that they accumulate in an organism at a rate faster than the organism can eliminate it. Of course, the Japanese government and TEPCO (Tokyo Electric Power

Company) have blatantly lied about the amount of radioactive waste that has been leaking into the Pacific, however, the devastating results have been impossible to ignore.

I've wondered since the beginning of this disaster-which has already shown to be far worse that the Chernobyl nuclear disaster in the Ukraine, in 1986-why the world's top, leading scientists have not come together to figure out how to stop the leaking radiation. The reason is because no one knows how to deal with this catastrophe.

In March of 2015, it was reported in the *Times of London,* that Akira Ono, the chief of the Fukushima power station admitted that the technology needed to decommission three melted-down reactors does not exist, and he has no idea how it will be developed.[38] Ono also claimed that decommissioning the plant by 2051 may be impossible without huge leaps in technological advancement. It's also been estimated that plutonium fallout has been 70,000 times greater than atomic bomb fallout in Japan!

Japan has also seen a skyrocketing of childhood Cancer rates, particularly, thyroid Cancer.[39] As of August, 2013, TEPCO admitted that between "20 trillion to 40 trillion becquerels[40] of radioactive tritium may have leaked into the sea since the disaster.[41] Since it's been shown over and again, that TEPCO repeatedly lied and covered up the true extent of the disaster, that number is most likely far greater.

While official sources keep claiming that there is no danger from the leaking radiation, sea life all along the west coast of the

US has been dying in alarming numbers, and many fish and sea creatures tested off the west coast have shown extremely high amounts of radioactivity, that far exceeds safe limits.

The *Japan Times* reported on Feb 25th, 2015, that cesium and other radioactive waste was pouring from the reactor one site, directly into the ocean.[42] There has been a massive die-off of marine life along the west coast of the US, which has scientists "baffled." Do you mean to tell me that scientists studying this death of the Pacific haven't taken into account the possibility that it could be caused by the hundreds of tons of nuclear waste that has been pouring into the Pacific for the last eight years? So few dare to admit the extent of damage caused by this disaster or the fact that it is forcing us to face the possibility of our own extinction. What happens when the planet's largest body of water is rendered lifeless on a planet made up mostly of water? What happens when the radiation accumulates in the atmosphere and is spread throughout the world by the jet stream?

In 2013, the *Huffington Post* reported that massive amounts of krill washed up along the west coast in a 250 mile stretch from Oregon to California.[43] Krill is an essential part of the ocean's food chain. When marine life on the low end of the food chain dies off, the larger animals that feed on that marine life starve to death. Carcasses of dead sea lions and seals that were examined revealed high doses of radiation,[44] and yet, mainstream scientists remain baffled.

The feeble efforts of TEPCO and the Japanese government to

stop the radioactive leaks, with ice walls, dams, and other paltry, makeshift remedies have been in vain. Nobody knows how to contain the radioactive leaks, so the Japanese govt. and TEPCO do the next best thing; they lie about it and downplay the dangers. Business as usual!

In March of 2019, scientists reported that radiation from the disaster has been found as far north as waters off a remote Alaskan island in the Bering Strait.[45] The head of the *National Cancer Research Center* in Japan, reported in Feb, 2015, that Cancer rates have skyrocketed by 6,000% and that it was being "swept under the rug."[46] In Jan, 2015, Japan's nuclear regulator approved TEPCO's ingenious plan to simply drain wastewater into the ocean.[47]

On April 20, 2010, the largest oil spill in history occurred off the coast of Louisiana in the Gulf of Mexico. An offshore oil drilling rig named *Deepwater Horizon*, operated by a company called Transocean, and leased by BP (British Petroleum) exploded due to core fractures that ignited the rig. Eleven workers were killed and 17 were injured. Two days later, the rig collapsed into the gulf and began spewing oil into the sea. Up to 60,000 barrels per day began pouring into the gulf according to US government officials.[48] Efforts were made to cap the drill site, but by July, it was estimated by a team of scientists that approximately *4.9 million* barrels of oil had already poured into the Gulf of Mexico.[49] It is estimated that over *200 million* gallons of oil spilled into the gulf.[50]

A highly toxic dispersant called *Corexit* was used in an attempt to deal with this massive spill. When combined with crude oil, the mixture of oil and dispersant becomes even more toxic. The concentrated toxins are known to cause Cancer.[51] The effects on wildlife have been devastating. In 2012, oceanographers were finding sea life with terrible deformities, including shrimp with no eyes, crabs without eyes or claws, and other sea life with lesions.[52] The chemicals caused a massive die off of microscopic organisms at the bottom of the food chain. Many gulf residents have gotten sick and some have reported bleeding from the eyes, ears nose and mouth. Marine life has been found that contained toxic hydrocarbons 3,000 times higher than what is estimated to be safe for human consumption.[53] Many people that live in gulf coastal states rely on the fishing industry which has been devastated in the region. The tourism industry in the region was also negatively affected. Over one thousand miles of shoreline were polluted which affected Florida, Alabama, Mississippi, Louisiana and Texas.[54] The cleanup and recovery operations cost BP an estimated *$40 billion*. Thousands of birds, mammals and sea turtles were found that were covered in crude oil.[55] Around 1,400 stranded dolphins and whales were reported, roughly half of which were shown to have lung and adrenal disorders linked to oil exposure.[56] The disaster is estimated to have killed some 800,000 birds.[57] Tens-of-thousands of turtles have also died.

The Deepwater Horizon spill was not the only one that has polluted and negatively impacted the Gulf of Mexico. In 2004,

Hurricane Ivan pounded the gulf coast region and destroyed an oil platform operated by a company called Taylor Energy. Twelve miles off the coast of Louisiana, oil began leaking into the gulf. Officials from Taylor Energy lied and covered up the extent of the leak which was discovered by the US Coast Guard and Greenpeace to be 20 times greater than what was reported.[58] Between 250 and 700 barrels of oil are leaking into the gulf every day since the collapse of the oil platform.[59]

On March 24, 1989, the *Exxon Valdez*, an oil tanker owned by the Exxon shipping company, struck a reef in the Prince William Sound, off the coast of Alaska, and spilled 11 million gallons of crude oil into the sound.[60] 1,300 miles of coastline were polluted and hundreds-of-thousands of birds, sea otters, whales and seals were killed.[61] This was the worst spill in US history until the Deepwater Horizon disaster. It was discovered that the captain of the vessel, Joseph Hazelwood, had been consuming alcohol and allowed an unlicensed crew member to steer the ship.[62] Good job Joe! Hazelwood was cleared of felony charges. It's estimated that the spill caused an economic loss of *$2.8 billion*.[63] The spill devastated wildlife in the region and many fishermen lost their livelihoods and went bankrupt.

Between Hawaii and California, lies a massive area of accumulated plastic, which has been dubbed the *Great Pacific Garbage Patch*. This massive patch of debris is estimated to cover an area of 1.6 million square kilometers,[64] an area that is twice the size of Texas and three times the size of France.[65] It is also estimated that between 1.15 to 2.41 million metric tons pollute the oceans each year.[66] When the area was examined by scientists, it was estimated to contain 1.8 *trillion* pieces of plastic.[67] The patch consists of mostly non-biodegradable plastic which photodegrades due to sunlight exposure, but does not completely break down. Unfortunately, marine life often mistakes the tiny plastic particles for food and consumes the plastic. A high percentage of the plastic contains toxins that the marine life consumes. Almost half of the debris in the garbage patch consists of discarded fishing nets. Many marine animals get caught in the nets and die. Chemicals contained in the plastic bioaccumulate and can be transferred to humans that consume seafood.

Perhaps the most alarming and major threat is to the coral reefs, which are the most biodiverse ecosystems on the planet, and have been dying at unprecedented rates. The planet has lost half of its coral in just the past 50 years.[68] Over 500,000,000 people depend on the reefs for food and jobs. Most of the world's oxygen comes from the reefs, and much comes from the rain forests, which are also being destroyed at an alarming rate. Unsustainable fishing practices and pollution are two of the main reasons the reefs are disappearing. Some scientists and oceanographers have estimated that by the year 2050, all of the remaining coral reefs could be gone, so when I suggest that humanity is staring its extinction in the face, I mean it quite literally.

Another major and potential catastrophe waiting to happen is the massive deforestation of the world's rain forests. The rain forests and coral reefs are diverse ecosystems that supply oxygen to the planet, and the Amazon rain forest alone provides the planet with 20% of the world's oxygen. Forests cover roughly 30% of the Earth's surface and their destruction continues at an ever increasing and unprecedented rate. Most deforestation occurs to provide for agriculture and every single second, 1 ½ acres of forest are cut down.[69] Areas of forests the size of 20 football fields are destroyed every minute. Some estimates predict that there will be no forests left in less than a century.[70] In just the next 25 years, it's estimated that upwards of 28,000 species may become extinct due to deforestation.[71] Already, about half of the world's tropical forests have been slashed, burned and cleared.

It's amazing that humanity simply keeps on plundering and yet paradoxically somehow remains convinced that it can continue unabated indefinitely, but in the end, the piper will have to be paid.

The widespread cultivation and use of industrial Hemp could seriously curtail the destruction of the forests and create an enormous economic boom, but that is not on the Consortium's agenda. Their plan is to make things so bad so that people will accept their solution of global governance.

For literally millennia, Cannabis Sativa was the companion plant of humanity and its use in woven fabrics dates back to as early as 8,000 BC.[72] From 1,000 BC, all the way up to 1883, Hemp was the world's largest agricultural crop and was used to produce *thousands* of products, most significantly, in my opinion, the oils were extracted for the high protein content for humans and animals alike. Cannabis is unquestioningly the most versatile crop on the face of the Earth. So why does this extremely beneficial plant remain illegal in so many places? A renewable plant, that can eliminate the need for the massive deforestation that is occurring, greatly diminish the need for the use of fossil fuels, create building materials, fabrics, paper and textile products, dietary supplements and highly effective medications, among many other uses, remains outlawed. How did the use of this gift of nature that stretches back into antiquity, come to be regarded as a useless, even dangerous substance? Why is it insisted that there is no medicinal value in the use of Cannabis, when mountains of evidence suggest otherwise? There are many uses of industrial hemp and the outright propaganda that stretches back over a century has demonized this amazingly versatile plant, primarily to eliminate competition of huge, corporate interests.

Cannabis is a very advanced plant that can grow in virtually any condition on Earth. It has a quick growing cycle and remains perhaps the planet's most important, renewable, natural resource. Hemp fiber is durable and so much of the world's textiles were made of Hemp fiber for centuries. Sailors' riggings, sails, fishing nets, clothing, maps etc. were all produced from Hemp. Clothing produced from Hemp is more rugged, warmer, softer and more absorbent than clothing produced from cotton. The Declaration of Independence was written on Hemp paper and in fact, many of the founders maintained Hemp farms and grew and cultivated this crop. Thomas Jefferson claimed:

"Hemp is of first necessity to the wealth & protection of the country."[73]

One acre of Hemp is equivalent to approximately four acres of trees. It needs no pesticides and grows very easily with little maintenance required to cultivate it. The uses are virtually endless and perhaps one of the greatest potentialities of this widely misunderstood crop would be in the use of biomass fuels. Through processes called charcoalizing or biochemical composting, Cannabis could replace or seriously diminish our reliance on fossil fuels. This would also reduce the risk of oil spills and the destruction of water and farmland through the gas mining practice known as hydrofracking. Hemp is more renewable and sustainable than other plants used for biomass such as corn, sugarcane, trees etc. Biomass fuels are non-polluting because the $Co2$ released into the environment is offset by atmospheric $Co2$, through photosynthesis.

I knew that Hemp had many fantastic uses, but I had no idea just how long that list is until I really started looking into the matter. This plant could literally save the planet by ending deforestation, diminishing the use of fossil fuels, seriously lessening the reliance on dangerous and destructive pharmaceutical medications, stimulating massive economic growth and ending wars fought for lands rich in natural resources. So, the question remains. Why is this amazingly versatile crop illegal? Think of how the widespread cultivation and production of Hemp into useful goods could seriously undermine the oil industry, the hydrofracking industry, the pharmaceutical industry, the timber industry, and other huge conglomerates and you will have your answer. Greed. While America teeters on the brink of economic collapse, the solution lies right before us, in an easily cultivated weed that has been mankind's companion plant since the beginning of recorded history and beyond.

America's once strong manufacturing base is all but completely gone and the introduction of Hemp farms and industry designed to create products made from hemp could absolutely stimulate economic growth and recovery, create wealth and abundance, and usher in a whole new era of productivity creating entirely new industries based on sane, environmentally friendly and practical uses of this amazing plant. The only way this new paradigm can manifest is if enough people become aware and simply stop complying with an insane system that mercilessly plunders the environment and places profits before people. To me, education and unity are the two driving forces that will turn the tide on this issue.

This extremely beneficial plant has so many positive uses. Huge corporate interests have fought incessantly to keep it banned and outlawed in the US. Like it or not, the global environment hangs on the precipice of total collapse and if humanity does not start to do things differently, the planet may not be able to sustain life for much more than a few generations, and I think that's being optimistic. Among the many incredible uses of hemp are:

- Hemp seeds can be ingested either raw or in teas, hemp milk, protein powders and many other consumable products. The seeds and leaves are very high in omega 3 and omega 6 fatty acids, protein (almost as high a concentration as meat, eggs and milk), amino acids, and roughly 80% essential fatty acids.

- Fiber: throughout history, Hemp was used to produce rope, canvas, linen, fabric, clothing, and many other textiles.

- Paper produced from hemp is much cheaper, environmentally friendly, more durable and longer lasting than paper produced from timber. Its use dates back thousands of years.

- Hemp can be used to purify soil and water and is actually being used to clean contaminants in the environment left over from the Chernobyl nuclear accident site.[74]

- Biofuels can be created from Hemp seed oil.

- Hemp can be used to produce cordage and rope that is far stronger than synthetic, nylon rope.

- Hemp fiber mixed with fiberglass, flax and kenaf is used to produce composite materials, which many automobile manufacturers are now using as panels on their cars. It is durable and rugged.

- Hemp and lime are utilized to produce a building material known as hempcrete. Hemp can also be used to produce fiber board, insulation, and many other building materials.

One misconception maintained by many people is that Hemp and Cannabis are the same plant; they are not. Although they are in the same plant genus, they're more like distant cousins. Hemp has many positive uses, particularly in industry, but also in medicine, as the plant contains high levels of a cannabinoid known as Canibidiol, or CBD. Cannabinoids are defined thusly:

"Organic substances present in Cannabis sativa, having a variety of pharmacologic properties."[75]

It has been discovered that the human body contains what is called the endocannabinoid system. The human body contains receptors that welcome cannabinoids which have been scientifically shown to provide homeostasis to the body, which means that they help to regulate balance within the body. Humans have evolved to be highly receptive to these compounds contained within the Cannabis and Hemp plants:

"The endogenous cannabinoid system, named after the plant that led to its discovery, is perhaps the most important physiologic system involved in establishing and maintaining human health.

Endocannabinoids and their receptors are found throughout the body: in the brain, organs, connective tissues, glands, and immune cells. In each tissue, the cannabinoid system performs different tasks, but the goal is always the same: homeostasis, the maintenance of a stable internal environment despite fluctuations in the external environment."[76]

Both Harvard and UCLA Universities have published scientific reports demonstrating how THC (the psychoactive ingredient contained within the Cannabis plant) causes Cancer cells to self-destruct.[77] There have been numerous testimonials of patients who have been able to completely eliminate Cancer with the use of medicinal Cannabis.

The reason that Hemp and Cannabis remain illegal for the most part is that they threaten the profits of big industry and big medicine. There is no profit in the cure, and under the current paradigm; it's profits before people. The US government has maintained the patent on Cannabis as a medicine for a long time:

"Cannabinoids including THC and Canabibiol, promote the re-emergence of apoptosis so that tumors will stop dividing and die." - US patent # 20130059018

There have been numerous reports from people who have healed many varying ailments due to the use of medicinal Cannabis. Many people have put Cancer into complete remission due to the use of Cannabis, and the bottom line is that the compounds found in this plant contain many healing properties and massive medicinal value.

In 1937, Cannabis was criminalized and demonized as a dangerous drug. William Randolph Hearst and the Du Pont Corporation stood to lose vast fortunes by Hemp coming into widespread use. Hearst owned a chain of newspapers and began a propaganda campaign to categorize this most useful plant as a dangerous "narcotic."

Perhaps the silliest anti-cannabis, propaganda stunt, was the production of a 1936 film called *Refer Madness*. This rather funny film depicts Marijuana as a dangerous drug that drives people crazy. The propaganda of the early to mid-20th century was enormously effective as many of the misconceptions concerning this useful plant are still believed by many. The AMA (American Medical Association) jumped right on board the propaganda bandwagon, and I can remember as a kid in school, being sold all of the lies in "health" class about how dangerous a drug this plant was alleged to be.

Cannabis was mankind's companion plant for millennia. It is long past the time to take the medicinal and the industrial potential of these plants seriously and to stop buying into all the lies of big government and big industry. Many people have had amazing success treating serious illnesses with the use of Cannabis, including but not limited to:

- Multiple Sclerosis
- Cancer
- Seizure disorders
- Diabetes
- ALS
- Fibromyalgia
- PTSD

This list could go on and on. Unfortunately, under the current paradigm, it's profits before people and lies before truth. There is no profit in the cure! The information is readily available so I would recommend that people do some homework and get educated as to the many useful benefits of these extraordinary plants. What if everyone just started growing these plants and demanded to bring production into widespread use? It would be impossible to stop an overwhelming outcry from the people, but then, far too many are still stuck in the lies and nonsense concerning these beneficial plants, and humanity remains divided.

The paradigm is shifting as more and more is discovered in this age of unveiling. In my mind, a crucial beginning step is to understand that we have been lied to for our entire lives. Ask yourself: in whose interest is it to continue the lie that Cannabis is a dangerous substance and that Hemp has no industrial value? Big government, big industry and big pharma! Why should we tolerate for one more moment, these plants which could benefit humanity in so many ways, being outlawed? The answer is that we shouldn't!

Look at culture; look at the world. I mean really look at it, with an unjaundiced eye and tell me what you see. If you are truly honest with yourself, you will see something so beautiful, something with so much potential that has been turned into a sewer. If you are even more honest, you may discover that *you* have a part in the projection of toxicity onto the stage of life; we contribute our shit to the mess by failing to cleanse our own energetic poison. We don't deal with it, we *project* it, and when billions do it collectively, a singularly beautiful planet, an oasis in the desert, becomes a surreal, toxic, wasteland, a garbage dump. It does *not* have to be this way nor should it because this ego-generated world is an affront to balance, an affront to beauty, an affront to life and an affront to the human experience. It's like taking a beautiful work of art and smearing it with excrement.

Everything that could mean *anything* at all is cheapened in this world, reduced to meaningless dribble, made worthless, corrupted, destroyed; and what *does* have value is twisted, contorted and sold back to you, and with a smile, the fallen will happily embrace and pay for their own enslavement and their tasty little bowl of shit stew. Freedom scares the living hell out of them because *never* have they known what it means to be *truly* free and never they shall if they are unwilling to face their own inner tyrant. The only "freedom" they have ever known is an illusion and a cheap facsimile.

ELEVEN

Technology and Transhumanism

Technological advancement is rapid and so few realize how far along it truly is. Much of the technology that is available, or being developed, particularly in military programs is astounding and like something right out of the wildest science fiction films. The ultimate agenda is to merge man with machine, to join silicon and carbon and to create a digital, global, hive-mind matrix. In addition to this, a massive, surveillance grid network is to be erected and we can clearly see this emerging by the day.

"Smart" technology is emerging onto the markets massively, even to the point that toilets, washing machines, refrigerators, televisions, dishwashers, even condoms and tampons are now endowed with smart technology and the massive push for all of this is not for convenience, but to monitor to the point that every intimate detail about people's lives will be known, tracked and

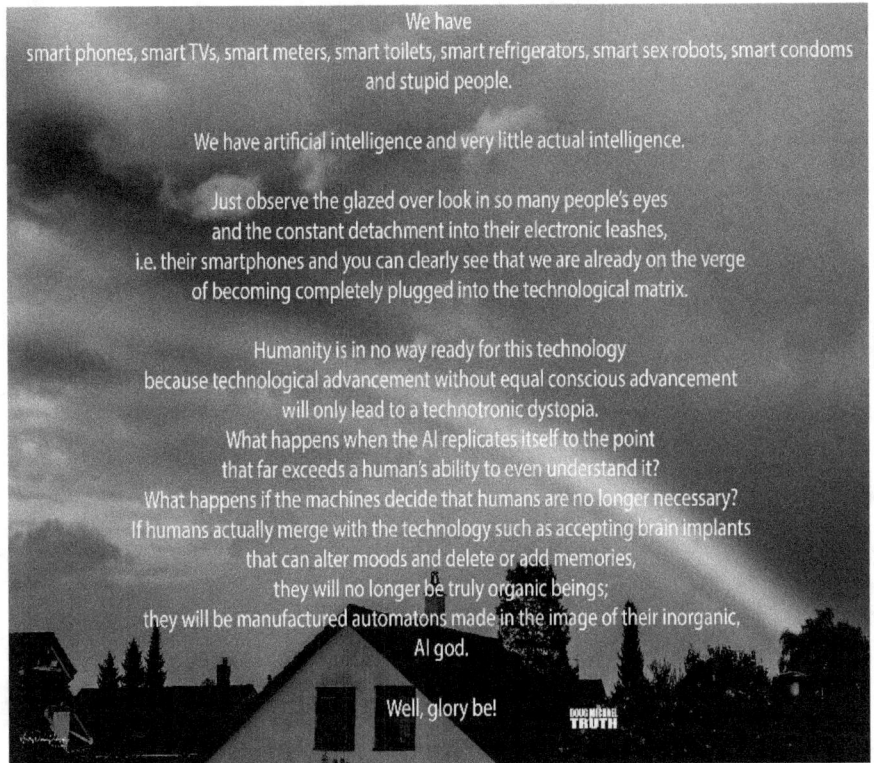

We have
smart phones, smart TVs, smart meters, smart toilets, smart refrigerators, smart sex robots, smart condoms
and stupid people.

We have artificial intelligence and very little actual intelligence.

Just observe the glazed over look in so many people's eyes
and the constant detachment into their electronic leashes,
i.e. their smartphones and you can clearly see that we are already on the verge
of becoming completely plugged into the technological matrix.

Humanity is in no way ready for this technology
because technological advancement without equal conscious advancement
will only lead to a technotronic dystopia.
What happens when the AI replicates itself to the point
that far exceeds a human's ability to even understand it?
What happens if the machines decide that humans are no longer necessary?
If humans actually merge with the technology such as accepting brain implants
that can alter moods and delete or add memories,
they will no longer be truly organic beings;
they will be manufactured automatons made in the image of their inorganic,
AI god.

Well, glory be!

monitored. In other words, total control.

Transhuman means "transcending human limitations," and of course, that is how the technology is being presented, but as, always, we must look deeper to discover the true intentions and agenda behind this push for super high-tech systems to be put in place, and the transhuman agenda is one of complete and total subjugation of the human mind. The idea is to eventually connect humans to "the cloud" via brain interface technology, which is currently in development and again, it's much further along than most people realize.

The military, as well as many private sector companies are

developing brain interface technology. Of course, this technology is being sold and promoted as the next step in human advancement, but there is a hidden agenda here that is anything but benevolent. Much of the technology that has been presented for the sake of convenience, has an underlying purpose of control, surveillance and the absolute subjugation of the human mind. With the rapid advancement of artificial intelligence and the rollout of 5G technology, a very eerie and sinister picture begins to emerge.

We've witnessed an explosion of advanced technology and I contend that humanity is not ready for this because rapid technological advancement without equal psychological or conscious advancement is not a good combination. The potential for abuse of this technology is enormous and difficult to contemplate. All the smart devices and high-tech gadgets that have exploded onto the market are primitive in comparison to what is in development in the military sector and behind closed doors within the Silicon Valley tech companies. What the public sees is light years behind what is already in development behind the scenes.

So many people are already "plugged in" to the digital matrix through their devices such as smart phones and tablets and the next step in this agenda is to plug people physically into the cloud as we emerge into the posthuman dystopia. Doesn't that sound just wonderful? We are currently in the transhuman phase, the transitional phase into posthumanism where humans will be merged with machines and artificial intelligence, and not quite human anymore. Leaders in the technology industry are of course heralding this as the next great leap in human evolution, and there is even a church in the Silicon Valley region that worships artificial intelligence as "the godhead." It's called *The Way of the Future Church* and they claim in their mission statement to support a "peaceful transition into the world of artificial intelligence."[1] People who are so readily accepting of this rapid unfolding of massive technological advancement (at least those who are aware of how far along it actually is) don't seem to question the potential for abuse or who it is that has their finger on the button so to speak. If human minds are plugged into the cloud, who is programming the technology? The potential for complete enslavement of human consciousness is monumental, and that is the idea.

What we are facing now is the rollout of the fifth generation, or 5G technology which is a cause for great concern. Based on the way that 5G technology works, there is enormous potential for great harm to our health and to the health of the environment. The amount of radiation that we are already swimming within, will massively increase and it is my firm contention that this technology is a weapons system.

In 2017, over 180 scientists and health professionals from 35 countries, came together to recommend a moratorium on the rollout of 5G so that potential health hazards could be investigated. The findings of this group are alarming, but of course, the telecom industry is set to create a multi-trillion-dollar generation of profits and it's always profits before people but there is far more to this than simply creating trillions in profits; the massive financial revenues are just a side benefit, the true agenda is the technological, electromagnetic enslavement of humanity. EMF (electro magnetic frequencies) have already been proven to be extremely dangerous and the 5G system will massively increase the exposure to intense radiation. Thousands of peer reviewed publications exist detailing the dangers of EMF technology. Scientists have already shown that the effects of EMF exposure include:

- Cancer risk
- Cellular stress
- Increase in free radicals in the body
- Genetic damage
- Reproductive harm
- Neurological disorders[2]

The exposure to electromagnetic radiation will increase massively due to the way that 5G transmits frequencies. 5G systems operate in the millimeter bandwidth range. Millimeter waves cannot travel very far and cannot penetrate buildings or trees very easily, so small cell towers, or waystations need to be erected in very close proximity to reassemble the data. The towers need to be positioned every few hundred feet from each other to successfully transmit the millimeter waves. Interestingly, 5G operates with the same frequencies that are utilized in crowd dispersion weaponry used by the military. We've seen a massive increase in neurological disorders, brain tumors, Alzheimer's Disease and many other ailments that may very well have a connection to the EMF soup we are swimming in. There has also been a massive, worldwide decrease in sperm counts.[3] Scientists have also observed changes in insects and wildlife, and there has been a massive, worldwide decline of many insect species.[4] Technology if used correctly, and in a balanced way, could assist humanity and the world, instead, it's used to destroy and enslave it.

The idea is to connect all smart devices into a cloud, called the "internet of things," or IoT. Eventually, the plan is to evolve the technology into human implantable, interface technology (which is already in development) and connect human brains to the cloud. It is suggested that the IoT will support over *100 billion* devices.

Elon Musk is the CEO for companies such as: *Tesla Motors*; *SpaceX*; *Solar City*; and *OpenAI*, among others. One other company Musk owns is called *Neuralink* which develops brain interface technology. On their website, the company claims:

"Neuralink is developing ultra-high bandwidth brain-machine interfaces to connect humans and computers."[5]

One of the products developed by this company is called *Neuralace*, and promotes its use in medical applications, and certainly, technology could have many positive benefits, but we must ask if there is a deeper agenda in having human brains connected to an internet of things. I would suggest that there is and that the idea is to create a hive mind and to basically turn man into a biological computer. Sounds great eh? The total enslavement of human consciousness sounds like a wonderful idea, doesn't it? To the Consortium, this technology is the ultimate control mechanism as they seek to create literal, remote controlled human beings. Interestingly, Musk has claimed that AI may be one of humanity's greatest existential threats, and that with AI we are "summoning the demon," but let's just go right on developing it anyway. Musk recently revealed that his company developed threads smaller than a human hair, which can be implanted in the brain to detect neuronal activity.[6] He also claimed that they were able to have a monkey control a computer by use of this interface technology.[7]

So many people are already operating on autopilot, so to speak, based on a lifetime of perceptual and psychological manipulation, and this technology would seal the deal of complete enslavement as the human race becomes one collectivized hive mind.

It seems as though for many decades, we have been subconsciously conditioned to the acceptance of this technology through television and the motion picture industry, through a process of "predictive programming." In other words, the public has been prepared for the acceptance of this super high-tech explosion into the world, and that goes for the acceptance of UFOs as well, but a bit more on that later.

Think of the science fiction movies and TV shows over the course of your life. I grew up on Star Trek and Star Wars and if we examine many of the films and television shows stretching back, we can clearly see the promotion of a technological world that we see emerging now. Movies such as: *I Robot; The Matrix; Total Recall; Ready Player One; AI; Singularity; X-Files,* and so many others exemplify this; the list is endless. Hollywood has always been a platform for mass indoctrination, and it is my contention that we have been prepared for the acceptance of this rapidly emerging post human world through the motion picture industry, television video games and mass media.

In 2017, two extraordinary events occurred. In October of that year, an artificially intelligent robot was granted citizenship in Saudi Arabia. The robot is named Sophia which itself has occult connotations, and it's interesting that a country that treats its women like 2nd class citizens would grant a robot citizenship. The damned robot is treated with more respect than actual women, but what else would we expect from this lunatic asylum of the Earth Game? In the Greek language, Sophia means "wisdom." The robot which was developed by a Chinese company called Hanson Robotics, uses voice and facial recognition technology, cameras and algorithms which allow it to "see." AI robots are becoming more and more lifelike and it's just creepy watching this thing give its presentations.

In December of 2017, right around the Christmas holiday season, the Unites States government, through Mainstream media such as the *New York Times*, and the British *Independent*,[8] newspaper, among others, announced that UFOs are real, and that specialized organizations exist to study aerial phenomenon to determine whether or not they pose a threat. Since then, there has been a slow trickle of information leaked out to the public, such as images and films from Navy pilots that show disc craft performing astounding maneuvers.[9] It's interesting, that for decades, legitimate UFO researchers and investigators were systematically vilified, marginalized and labeled as "kooks" or "whackos" and now the US government has come forward claiming that the presence of these objects is real. How many of the objects spotted in the skies are secret, military craft? The vast and sleeping masses are about to be blindsided in ways that defy the imagination.

Studies have shown that when pregnant cows graze near cell phone towers, calves are born with increased incidences of cataracts.[10] Studies have also revealed that pulsed waves, such as those emitted from smart meters are far more dangerous than continuous wave radiation.[11] It was reported that hundreds of birds fell from the sky during a 5G test in the Netherlands.[12]

It's expected that roughly *20,000* satellites will be launched by various companies to put the 5G system in place and this will bathe the world with microwave radiation. In March of 2018, the FCC granted approval to SpaceX, one of Musk's companies, to launch 4,425 low orbital satellites, and the company eventually plans to launch 12,000.[13] Every corner of the world will be covered and there will be nowhere to go to escape the radiation. Other companies that are expected to launch an array of satellites include:

- OneWeb: 4,560
- Boeing: 2,956
- Spire Global: 972[14]

Ground based 5G systems are already being rolled out in many major cities right now. The system is being switched on in Chicago, Minneapolis, Los Angeles, Nashville, Austin, San Francisco, San Jose, Orlando, Atlanta, Dallas, Kansas City and San Diego.[15] Despite warnings from many scientists and health professionals, the telecom companies are rolling out this untested technology and constructing the electromagnetic grid as the Consortium places the Earth into vibrational lockdown.

Dr. Moran Cerf, a neuroscientist working with Northwestern University, claims to be developing brain implant technology that could be implemented in as little as five years that could "increase intelligence."[16] Brain computer interfaces (BCIs) are rapidly emerging, and Columbia university is developing AI technology that can translate a person's thoughts into speech.[17] What could possibly go wrong? What concerns me is not only the ability to read thoughts, but the potential to *control* them. Social media giant Facebook is also working to develop this type of technology. Well, isn't that just great? Now they'll be able to mine data right from your brain.

As I stated, very few people are even remotely aware of how far the technology has evolved in this rapidly emerging technetronic dystopia. Distractions of all types occupy the consciousness of the vast majority, while the digital prison is erected all around them. Some scientists are even working to teach AI how to replicate by sharing its source code with other robots. They call this process, "high-tech Darwinism." While most people would discount this information as the wild imaginings of someone who watches too many science fiction TV shows, it is very real, and this is only what has been revealed to the public. What type of technology is in development behind closed doors, particularly in military development, black budget projects?

Donald Trump has publicly stated his full support for the 5G rollout and has even stated that he would like to see 6G technology be developed. Trump is on the puppet strings of Israel, his Zionist masters, and his administration is filled with Zionists and neoconservative "Israel first" operatives. He is a con man like all the rest of them. Although 5G technology was developed in Israel, the Israeli government has forbidden its use in that country.[18]

The current 4G system in place operates in the frequency range of 1 to 5 gigahertz. 5G will substantially increase radiation as it operates between 24 to 90 gigahertz. With regards to RF (radio frequency) radiation, the higher the range, the more potential there is for damage to living organisms. The 2.4 gigahertz range, which the current system operates within, is the same frequency range that microwave ovens use to cook food. Numerous studies have shown that rats placed in an environment of 2.45 GHz showed a marked decline in sperm counts.[19] How will the 5G system, operating in a much higher range of frequency affect fertility? The answer is unknown because the technology has not been tested and yet it is being rolled out anyway. Human beings are the guinea pig test subjects, with Americans on the front line.

To illustrate just how much advanced technology has slipped out of the realm of science fiction and into reality, I'd like to briefly mention something that is in development and has gotten the interest of organizations such as DARPA (Defense Advanced Research Projects Agency) which develops technology for the US military. The technology is called programmable matter, which is defined as:

"Programmable matter is matter which has the ability to change its physical properties (shape, density, moduli, conductivity, optical properties, etc.) in a programmable fashion, based upon user input or autonomous sensing. Programmable matter is thus linked to the concept of a material which inherently has the ability to perform information processing."[20]

Developers of this technology say that it can merge digital and physical reality. What could possibly go wrong? Imagine being able to shapeshift a table into a sofa, or a gun.

There are many different approaches to this technology including: shape changing molecules that can change shape or other properties based on external stimuli such as:

electropermanent magnets that can create self-building structures and claytronics, which utilize reconfigurable, nanoscale robots called "claytronic atoms," or "catoms," which are essentially tiny computers that can respond to user input and form different shapes. You can read about this technology in any number of mainstream tech journals; it is in development by many agencies and universities and no longer simply within the realm of science fiction.

In late 1999, I began writing and speaking about the coming emergence of implantable microchips, that would eventually be implanted under the skin of human beings. Of course, this was met with enormous ridicule and highly intelligent, well thought out comments such as: "you're crazy," "conspiracy theorist," "dude, you watch too many X-files shows," and a whole host of other remarks from those whose minds remain mired within cognitive fortresses and whose perceptions are about as narrow as you can get. Of course, now the technology has far surpassed mere microchip implants and many of those people still cannot see what is right in front of their noses.

The FDA (Food and Drug Administration) has approved the use of microchips in human beings,[21] and a company called VeriChip, a subsidiary of Applied Digital Solutions has been mass marketing them for years. Many cattle and domestic animals alike have been implanted for tracking purposes and although microchip technology is presented for use in medical applications, the deeper agenda is to tag and track human beings in the same way that animals are tracked. Just as the brain interface technology that is currently in development, the microchips are transceivers, which means that they can both send and *receive* signals. Ponder that for a moment. The genius inventor Nikola Tesla once claimed:

"Alpha waves in the human brain are between 6 and 8 hertz. The wave frequency of the human cavity resonates between 6 and 8 hertz. All biological systems operate in the same frequency range. The human brain's alpha waves function in this range and the electrical resonance of the earth is between 6 and 8 hertz. Thus, our entire biological system-the brain and the earth itself-work on the same frequencies. If we can control that resonate system electronically, we can directly control the entire mental system of humankind."

As I mentioned in my book *Simulacrum: Exposing and Transcending the Perceptual Control Paradigm,* it is my firm contention that this is the exact purpose of this technology, despite the fact that it could certainly have many positive uses, but again, that is not what the Consortium has in mind, the name of their game is **control!**

In Sweden and elsewhere, people are voluntarily being implanted with tiny microchips to replace credit cards and cash.[22] People can simply swipe their hands to pay for goods or services. Well isn't that neat? Trade your privacy for convenience, you know it makes sense. Already, over 4,000 Swedes have been implanted and the number keeps growing. Sweden is leading the way into a cashless society which is what the Consortium wants for the rest of the world. The fact that people are willing to trade their freedom and privacy for convenience is truly astounding and another thing to consider is the potential for hackers to steal information from unsuspecting implanted people. How vulnerable are the chips? Well, no one's really sure but as hackers grow more creative, I suppose we'll find out.

A Wisconsin company called Three Square Market, which manufactures vending machines, offered to implant its employees so that they no longer needed to use their ID cards to access different areas of the facility. Many of their employees jumped at the opportunity.[23] The chips replace credit cards, passwords and ID badges and people think it's just wonderful. The chips are about the size of a grain of rice and are inserted into the hand between the thumb and index finger. It's amazing to me that so many people have no problem inserting chips in their hands, and eventually, this will be made mandatory, most likely following an economic collapse as the Consortium ushers in its cashless system. This is where we are headed, and it is not somewhere off into the distant future; it is here now.

I'm not one to quote the Bible very often, but I do find this passage from Revelations very interesting when taking into consideration brain implants and microchips:

"And he causeth all, both small and great, rich and poor, free

284

and bond, to receive a mark in their right hand, or in their foreheads: And that no man might buy or sell, save he that had the mark, or the name of the beast, or the number of his name."

Perhaps the "beast" is the AI and 5G systems? Many researchers contend that the elite Consortium uses the Bible as a blueprint for their unfolding agenda. It certainly is a possibility.

In a cashless society, with digital credits attached to microchips as the method of financial transaction, people would not be able to shop for groceries, travel or pay bills without their slave tags firmly inserted into their brains or hands. This is the world that is rapidly unfolding by the moment and humanity has a serious decision to make.

In China, a social credit system is being implemented which tracks citizens every move and rewards them points for obedience and demerits for disobedience. The government rates people on their behavior and their "citizen score" effects them and follows them everywhere; there is no escape from oversight. Citizens are rewarded with things like faster internet speed if they behave but if they do something that the government disapproves of, such as questioning the official state narrative, they are punished in some way such as having their right to travel restricted. The government examines huge amounts of data from social networking sites and checks online shopping records to create huge profiles on citizens. It's estimated that there are 176 *million* surveillance cameras in China and that number is expected to increase to *450 million* by

2020.[24] People can even be rewarded for snitching on their neighbors that do not comply. I don't think Orwell in his wildest imaginings could have foreseen the level of this intrusive spying mechanism. Of course, other governments want to implement systems like this, and I believe that the 5G system is a huge part of that.

Currently, DARPA is working on brain interface technology that would allow soldiers to control weapons with their thoughts.[25] They call this lovely technology *Next Generation Nonsurgical neurotechnology* or N3. The companies working with DARPA claim that this interface technology could be used to control unmanned vehicles or control defense systems, and of course DARPA touts all of the positive uses of interface technology but this agency is at the cutting edge of creating weapons of death and destruction. They develop high technology for the US military, so surely, they are an agency that you can trust. The technology will be able to read and write to multiple points in the brain simultaneously.[26] Developers say that soldiers could fly drones intuitively by thought. Well glory be! Tens-of-millions of dollars were awarded to companies to develop this high-tech nightmare. DARPA is also involved with developing "super soldiers" through the use of advanced robotics technology. They've also invested billions in exoskeleton suits for soldiers, which increases their physical strength.[27]

The Russian military already has robots that can fire weapons and drive jeeps. The robots carry two automatic pistols and when you see the films of these things in action, it looks like something right out of the *Terminator* movies.[28] The Israeli military also employs similar technology and uses unmanned reconnaissance and remote controlled weapons systems to bring death and mayhem, particularly, to the Gaza strip.[29] It seems as though humanity's greatest technological achievements have been in the development of weapons of death and destruction and perfecting ways in which to annihilate one another. This is the immediate future we can look forward to as the Consortium and its overlords spread their sickness across the world and tighten their grip on a sleeping humanity.

Scientists are predicting that within the next decade, babies will be able to be grown in artificial wombs. This process is called "Ectogenisis" which creates an artificial pregnancy, outside the physical body.[30] We are rapidly heading towards an artificial, inorganic, dystopian world of high-tech slavery.

Something that I think may very well be connected to the coming 5G system is what has become known as the "chemtrail" phenomenon. All over the world, jet aircraft have been spraying plumes which fan out and encompass the entire sky on many occasions. I began noticing the trails around 1997 and have watched them increase over the years. I speak to people from many different places around the world, people from Switzerland, Virginia, the United Kingdom, California and elsewhere. They have all reported witnessing the aerosol spray operations on many occasions and I've received many images from various parts of the world clearly showing that something is not right. These are not simply condensation trails, as debunkers and media servants would have you believe. Normal condensation trails or contrails dissipate very quickly, and the atmospheric conditions have to be just right for them to appear.

Over the years, many ground samples have been taken of chemtrail fallout and tests conducted have shown the samples to contain heavy metals such as barium, aluminum and strontium. The researcher Clifford Carnicom has even found dried, red blood cells in some samples.[31] Many researchers suggest that the phenomenon is part of a massive geoengineering operation to manipulate the weather, and I think that is a huge part of it, but I think there is even more going on than that. I believe that it is a multi-faceted operation with very sinister implications. I think that it's very possible, even likely that the Earth is being sprayed with nanotechnology contained within the trails.

Nanotechnology and nanobots are so tiny, they can even exist on a microscopic level. Again, the hidden technology that the public has no idea exists is far ahead of what the public knows about. Nanotech could certainly be injected through vaccines, or ingested through food and who would know? We may very well be infested with this technology and if that is the case, I'm very concerned about how it may interact with the frequencies of the 5G system.

The skies have been supercharged with heavy metals for at least two decades which means that they have become conductive.

Aerosol spray operations over Switzerland. When the spraying occurs, the plumes fan out and encompass the entire sky. These are not normal jet aircraft emissions. Photo by Yardley Pearson.

Could holograms be projected into the sky to make it appear as if some religious figure, or fleets of UFOs are appearing? It's something to consider, and I think that now more than ever, people need to be paying attention to what's going on behind all of the minutia, the political freakshow, and all of the other nonsensical distractions that are so abundant these days. I've witnessed countless spray events over the years and many times they will

Chemtrails over Utica, NY photographed in August 2018. There are no natural clouds here, and I've noticed that many times, the spraying will occur the day before a storm front moves in.

occur the day before a storm front moves in. This is not normal. Many researchers have speculated that the chemtrails may be part of a program that works in conjunction with H.A.A.R.P. (High Frequency Active Auroral Research Program) which fires pulsed, electromagnetic, direct energy beams into the ionosphere.[32] This is a military project involving the US Navy, Air Force and DARPA, so I'm sure it's just used for benign scientific study, as the project

Chemtrails over Switzerland. Photo by Yardley Pearson.

claims. Is this an electromagnetic weapons system? It's officially claimed that this system is not being used for military purposes or weather control, but if you take a look at the patent, it certainly does have ominous implications for military purposes.[33] Weather control experiments have been going on for decades so it is possible that this technology could be used to intensify storms and weaponize the weather as many researchers have speculated. How does pulsing electromagnetic energy and gigawatts of power into

This was another clear and cloudless day turned overcast from the spraying in Utica, NY.

This ominous shot was taken over Switzerland. Many people have seen and photographed huge grid patterns. Photo by Yardley Pearson

the ionosphere interact with the heavy metal particulates sprayed from aircraft into the atmosphere? What is this doing to the environment and what is its true purpose? Dr. Bernard Eastlund was a physicist associated with the project. A patent was issued to him in 1987 titled: *"Method and apparatus for altering a region in the earth's atmosphere, ionosphere, and/or magnetosphere."* The patent claims that the temperature of the ionosphere has been raised by hundreds of degrees due to this project. It also claims that

293

This was a completely clear day in Utica, NY until the spraying occurred.

interference to communications systems can occur over large areas of the Earth. The patent also claims in part:

- The technology could be employed to disrupt land, air and sea-based communications systems.
- The system can be used to create a communication network, even if the normal grid were disabled.
- It could be used for eavesdropping.
- It produces huge amounts of power.
- The system can be used for weather modification.
- The Earth's magnetic field could be modified, and this system can be used as an EMP (Electromagnetic Pulse) weapon.[34]

You can view images of the H.A.A.R.P. facility online and it looks like a massive array of antennas. It is located near Gakona, Alaska. Of course, the facility claims that the technology is used simply to study the ionosphere, but I remain highly skeptical and feel strongly, that with all of the inferences mentioned in the patent, that it is being used for far more than that. Is the planet being geoengineered? Can storms be steered, strengthened and redirected towards particular targets? The military has long been involved in the development of technology for electromagnetic warfare, and H.A.A.R.P. certainly fits the bill for being a possible weapons system.

In a secret project code named *Project Seal*, during WW II, the US and New Zealand governments worked jointly to develop a "tsunami bomb," a tectonic weapon that could create devastating tidal waves. Official sources claim that the testing never fully developed but during the course of development, 3,700 bombs were exploded during testing.[35] What sort of technology might be available today that the public has no idea exists?

Another eerie and disturbing thing that some researchers have claimed to be in some way connected to the chemtrail phenomenon is a very bizarre illness known as Morgellons Disease. Those suffering with this nasty affliction often suffer with painful and itchy skin lesions, fatigue, brain fog, changes in vision, and a whole host of other debilitating symptoms. The most bizarre symptom is the presence of fibers that protrude from the skin, and that appear to grow on their own or self-replicate. Many have been photographed and examined under microscope.[36] Could this be nanotechnology from chemtrail fallout? Could those suffering with Morgellons be sensitive to the tech and thus their bodies are rejecting it? It's worth pondering.

What really gets me, is that when people suffering with Morgellons seek treatment, many times they are diagnosed with "Delusional Parasitosis," and told they are imagining it. Even though the sores are readily visible, and the symptoms are apparent, many patients are told that they are simply imagining their condition. Can you imagine suffering like that and merely being discounted as delusional? Many images can be viewed online, and they are disturbing.[37] Just viewing the pictures of the fibers is enough to make your skin crawl. It's just creepy and weird. Has the Consortium found a way to infuse AI technology into the human body through the dispersion of aerosol sprayed from aircraft? Are human beings being reengineered? One thing is certain, something very strange is going on and as disturbing as it is, human beings need to become aware of the magnitude of the situation, cast aside all of our differences and come together as one species, or not; the choice is ours.

As I mentioned earlier, the US government has been slowly leaking UFO information out to the public since 2017, including films of unusual objects. Here is another area where we need to be extremely cautious. As I mentioned in other writings and in podcasts, the UFO disclosure phenomenon could be presented in a couple of ways.

The program allegedly set up to examine whether these objects pose a threat is called the AATIP (Advanced Aerial Threat Identification Program). Louis Elizondo, the alleged former Pentagon official who headed the project, publicly claimed that the existence of UFOs exhibiting superior technology has been proved "beyond reasonable doubt."[38] He also claimed that nations now had to be conscious of a potential threat. What if various world governments were to come forward claiming that UFOs are real, and that they are hostile? They could easily call for the creation of a world government under the banner of keeping us safe from the alien threat. On the other hand, they could present them as benevolent space brothers, that have come to save humanity, but only if we came together under a new world order, something the Consortium stooges have been clamoring to initiate for a long time now.

I remember when I was a kid in high school, seeing president Ronald Regan give a speech to the UN, in which he asked people to imagine an alien threat from outside this world.[39] Perhaps this agenda has been in the making for a long time.

US Navy pilots have come forward claiming that between 2014 and 2015, they experienced encounters with fleets of UFOs.[40] The pilots claimed that their equipment detected unidentified craft performing at hypersonic speeds and that the craft had no visible means of propulsion.[41] The sightings were encountered during flying missions along the east coast of the US, between Virginia and Florida. One pilot claimed that fleets of UFOs followed his strike group up and down the east coast for months.[42] Could this have been an ongoing test of secret technology that the Navy pilots did not know existed? In 2015, Navy personnel were issued guidelines on how to go about reporting UFO sightings.

We certainly live in strange and extraordinary times. As I stated, I think that humanity may be headed for a massive, collective, psychological shock, or mind fuck if you will, and that masses of people's entire perceptual reality might just come crashing down all around them. I think it's a good idea to stay centered and to prepare oneself for what may come. The Consortium appears to be getting ready to pull the rug out from under humanity as they usher in their global super-state.

TWELVE

Game Over

It may not be the end of the world, but it certainly is the end of the world *as we've known it*. Either way, the situation is changing, whether humanity plunges into a dystopian world of inorganic, mechanized nothingness, or stands up as one to create something different, that lifts us out of the depths of the hell we have allowed to rise in our midst, and to engulf our experience of what it means to live and express as a human being. It's as if consciousness itself is infected with some sort of mind virus.

The most ruthless amongst us skulk in the shadows, like ravenous, vampiric parasites, and they place their sycophantic henchmen before you, to mislead you into distraction so that their masters can go undetected and advance their agenda beyond the light of public scrutiny. People actually go and vote for these sideshow freaks. The absolute worst and most sadistic that humanity has to offer, rise to positions of power in this lunatic asylum. Humanity can continue on being pushed to-and-fro, or perhaps instead, facilitate our own conscious evolution to propel ourselves into a new paradigm, an entire new experience of what it means to experience as a human being.

If you are well adjusted to the sick and depraved lunatic asylum that we courageously and laughingly call culture, then you may be suffering from severe mental health problems. As the moments go by it seems, the more the insanity is on full display for all to see, that is for those who have lifted their consciousness from the muck and the mire and aren't afraid to face it. Although there appears to be a stirring within the consciousness, I think that it's an appallingly few that can really put the pieces together and push forward in their perceptual and conscious advancement within this cacophony of bullshit.

These days, the absurdities and the madness is right out in the open, plainly visible, no longer in the shadows and yet, the more that the curtain lifts away to reveal it, it seems the more that people will fall deeper into the trance to avoid facing it. It's a strange quirk that has always intrigued me and I think it has to do with the avoidance of facing oneself.

Facing the challenges to me is a crucial step in the process of self-realization and self-actualization. I'm not suggesting dwelling on them, but simply to acknowledge them with courage and then willfully shifting our consciousness towards solutions. It's important to understand what we are faced with and the mechanics of the game so that we may be better equipped to deal with it.

The overall collective consciousness has been dumbed down so comprehensively that it defies belief. Facebook is a great way to observe how infantilized the average adult mind has become. It's astounding! The number of grown adults that display the mentality of a child is unbelievable. People seem to have no problem sharing their intimate, personal information on public platforms and show not even the slightest concern about being completely monitored. Intrusions into their personal lives do not bother them in the slightest and they have no problem airing their dirty laundry to the world or engaging within their silly cyber drama. A very childlike mentality has gripped the mass consciousness and it's been all according to a specific strategy that's been wildly successful. This is what happens when people refuse to educate themselves and instead use the tools available simply for distraction and entertainment.

The Consortium elites have everything they could ever want but it's never enough. They seek total control over the consciousness of the entire planet, and they are getting very close to achieving it. Just observe how comprehensively dumbed down the average person truly is and now imagine combining that infantilized mentality with brain implants, AI, neural networking, and all the rest of it and realize that the end game is absolute technetronic enslavement. We need to ask ourselves where it is that we individually stand within all of this. These technocratic elites are trying to set the natural world on its head and create an

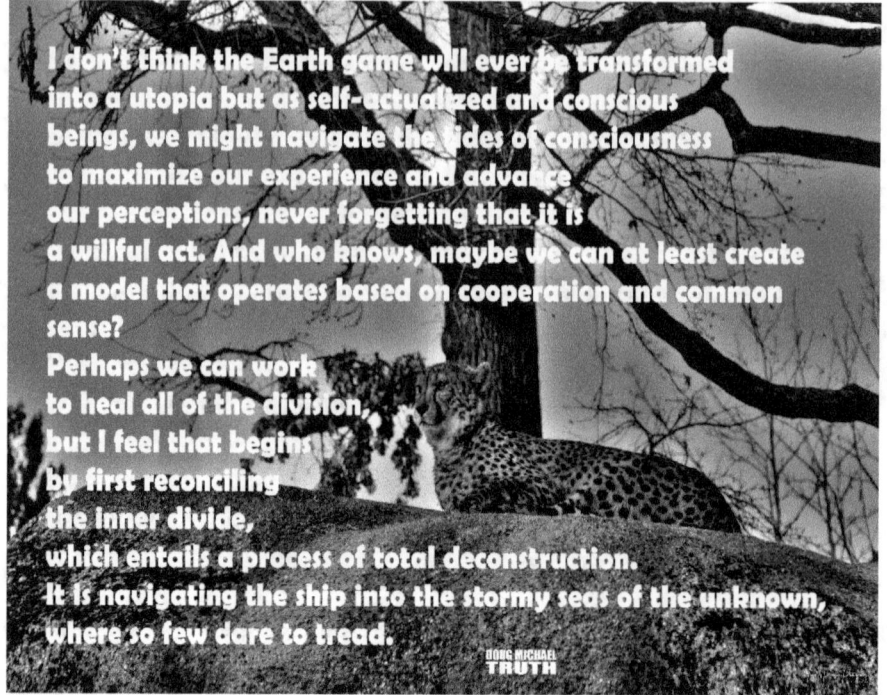

I don't think the Earth game will ever be transformed into a utopia but as self-actualized and conscious beings, we might navigate the tides of consciousness to maximize our experience and advance our perceptions, never forgetting that it is a willful act. And who knows, maybe we can at least create a model that operates based on cooperation and common sense?
Perhaps we can work to heal all of the division, but I feel that begins by first reconciling the inner divide, which entails a process of total deconstruction. It is navigating the ship into the stormy seas of the unknown, where so few dare to tread.

DONG MICHAEL TRUTH

artificial digital world, a global hive mind controlled by inorganic intelligences. Quite an arrogant undertaking wouldn't you say? It's as if they want to become the gods of their own digitally created, alternate reality. This AI technology will be sold as beneficial for mankind, but we always need to look behind the curtain to see what the true agenda is. The average good and decent person simply cannot comprehend the level of evil and insidiousness we're dealing with.

Humanity is being guided into a singular, hive consciousness by the hands of extremely malevolent creatures. People have come forward and claimed that scientists working at CERN, the large hadron collider, are actually working to rip a hole in the fabric of space-time to enter into alternate dimensions. Again, remember, science fiction is now science fact!

We've been consuming foods and products for decades that alter the DNA. There's a genetic component to this as well. Eugenicists have been working for years to isolate and alter the human genome. Many scientists have warned that the 5G system has the potential to cause strand breaks in the DNA of humans and animals. We're already genetically altered so how will the high-tech systems coming online affect this? The average person cannot even begin to wrap their mind around this so use caution when telling this information to friends and family. Get ready to be labeled a lunatic, a kook, a whacko, a conspiracy theorist or any other of a number of generic terms that people will throw at you on knee jerk reaction like the programmed robots they've become. It's amazing, it requires a shift in perception to see this stuff even though it is right out in the open on full display. So comprehensively has the human mind been programmed and locked down within cognitive conditioning.

For those very few who are aware of the position we are in, I think that it's imperative to consciously withdraw our consent from all of this insanity. To divorce our minds from all of the irrelevant distractions and to willingly evolve our perceptual awareness and cognitive expansion. It's important to be aware of the dangers and to withdraw any agreement with this agenda.

It's difficult for many walking this journey towards truth and understanding of the situation, to not get completely engulfed within fear. I think it's crucial to not react this way because it's very disempowering. The Consortium uses fear as one of its primary weapons. I would suggest, that if it starts to get to you, to walk away and do something creative or something that brings you enjoyment. The following passage is from a profound book called *Becoming*:

"The time of bringing the belief system into harmony with the actual physical reality situation in order to avoid the doom of destruction that is now awaiting the majority of earth's population is now. The important focus is not to dwell on the doom: it is the pivotal point that is now available to humanity that must be used as the impetus of change. Shocking as the facts are regarding the primrose path that humanity has been blindly following, these must be accepted and then the focus turned away from the deceptions toward creating a new reality. What is this new reality? How can it be created if there is no knowledge of what it is that should or could replace the present situation? It would appear that this reality as it is created would be nothing but a hodge-podge of each one's desires based on the programming that is already present within each. Who would have the ability to release what is known and envision new concepts that would not be tainted with dreams of the past?" [1]

When I mention divorcing one's consciousness from the lunacy, we need to replace our programming with a different consciousness, so to speak. I've always felt that the solution lies within each of us. It is in the discovery of what we truly are, beyond the veil of the ego. It is that discovery that is the greatest threat to the Consortium. If 7.6 billion human beings, operated within their potential and willfully worked to evolve their cognition and to support each other, and actually united for a common good, we would be impossible to control. This monumental feat needs to be accomplished but it's starting to look like it never will be. I think that the push to get the technological control grid in place is to thwart any chance of this shift in consciousness from occurring. Remember however, that ultimately, it is an *individual* act, a willful decision!

I think that maybe a beginning to the solution is in simply walking away from their game. If we refuse to play, there is no game! It's important to remember also, that many will simply never see through the veil. If 7 billion came together and transcended our differences, and walked away together, it would be over in a flash but unfortunately, so many are completely locked within the current paradigm to even see what is occurring. Again, from Becoming we read:

"The pivotal point at which this change takes place is not a shift from negative to positive. It is rather an uplifting to a new point in the spiral of experience that allows for a greater understanding and ability to utilize the positive/negative energies that are part and parcel of the outflow of creative energies in the

individual and collective foci that result in the larger matrix or design of the whole pattern of a galaxy. It is easier to grasp the larger picture of this description than to define it at the level of each individual awareness. Each being comes to the point of their own realization in unique ways and by unique combinations of experience and wisdom. The point is often approached and rejected many times before the actual crossover acceptance happens. It requires a great deal of courage to crossover to a new and different perspective of the life experience. It requires releasing well-learned lessons and entering into a completely new consciousness of what reality truly is. For those who are on the planet Earth now, the deceptions are of such magnitude and the truth of what each being is, so well hidden, that the acceptance of the truth by the masses is such a gigantic leap in consciousness that it appears to be impossible that it could possibly happen. Yet, happen it must if this segment of the human race and this jewel of a planet are to survive. "[2]

I feel that a powerful first step in reclaiming one's own power is the decision to define oneself not from anything external but from an inner knowingness that we are far greater than what we've been programmed, manipulated, conditioned, indoctrinated and encouraged to see ourselves as. It seems that the world of the simulacrum and all of its guardians are designed to discourage anyone from stepping into their own potential, unless of course it benefits the system of enslavement in some way.

The ego, overlaid consciousness seems to be chained to the future, while at the same time remaining a prisoner of the past. In this state of [un]consciousness the present moment is neglected in favor of worrying about a non-existent future, rather than working to create one that is desired. Simultaneously, the consciousness remains mired within the past, constantly reliving experiences that cannot be changed, burdening the mind and again, robbing one of the present moment.

Creation takes place in the here and now, not in our past or in a future that is yet to be. I would suggest that an effective warrior must first conquer their own inner tyrant and if anyone is suggesting that this is an easy undertaking, they're either lying or trying to sell you something. It isn't easy, nor is it meant to be! It is the most difficult battle but the rewards that come from dealing with all of the inner shit and reaching a point of cognitive liberation are immeasurable. It can be very, very lonely at times because you are trying to break through the cognitive fortresses to a more expansive level of consciousness in a world that is working overtime to keep you trapped within the constraints that you have *allowed* to define you.

I have been feeling for a long time that humanity as a species has arrived at a fork in the road in its earthly sojourn, but that feeling has been amplified as of late. This entire sick, tyrannical world is about to implode upon itself. I would suggest that when it does, those mired too deeply within their cognitive fortresses who refuse to budge will have a hefty price to pay for their position.

Our entire history is one of tyranny, manifesting repeatedly as if on some kind of historical feedback loop. Why? Why is this so? I think it's because humanity steadfastly refuses to deal with its own inner tyranny and thus the mirror of life reflects it back upon us.

We are mired within a war that so few can recognize or even remotely comprehend, and I think it would do us well to get our minds around that truth. The war is upon consciousness and the battlefield is the internal, inner landscape of your own mind! The temple is haunted! It's a war for the control of your perceptions, thus the reality that you experience. If one will not even go to the front line and do battle with their own inner tyrant, then what chance is there that they will affect any challenge to the outer tyranny? None!

The outer is a reflection of the inner. The world will never change unless *we* change. This is a process that must be initiated by the individual and the agents of the simulacrum will stop at nothing to prevent individuals from undertaking this journey of perceptual, conscious advancement and willing spiritual evolution. The first step is to set aside all that we have allowed to shape our cognitive fortresses and ensnare us within the confines of its superimposed consciousness.

Digging through the dumpster of our repressed memories is not easy but it is necessary if we are to move forward. We certainly don't need to dwell within the repression but simply to acknowledge it and deal with it. We must do this in a way that is gentle and forgiving to ourselves. We must bury the past where it belongs and stop allowing it to navigate our futures into oblivion. Before one can face their innermost light, they must face their innermost darkness.

This entire paradigm exists entirely to crush your essence, to snuff your flame, to diminish the light and the spark of all that you are. You are taught for your whole life to conform to it, to bend and compromise your perceptions and allow your mind to be contorted, and woe to you if you even dare to question the insanity. If you do, then you are the crazy one; you are the lunatic. There will be no mercy if you stand within truth and spiritual empowerment and **you will be a target.**

Once you begin to break the chains of the perceptual control paradigm, the entire system will move against you. It can break you. It can destroy you if you let it; it can completely fuck you up! This is the initiation. Are you truly a pioneer of consciousness, a creator of a new paradigm, or are you simply willing to take the easy way out and remain as a cognitive slave? It's entirely up to you, and it is nothing more than a change in attitude, beliefs and opinions. It's a psychological shift, a cognitive rebirth, a shedding of the skin if you will.

You need to learn to write your own story, to sing your own song, to create *yourself.* To hell with authority! For you are the author of you! Don't let anyone else write the script, for if you do, the play will end as a tragedy. Imagine a world of fully conscious, self-actualized human beings; what would that look like? What would it be to experience that? No one knows because we've never

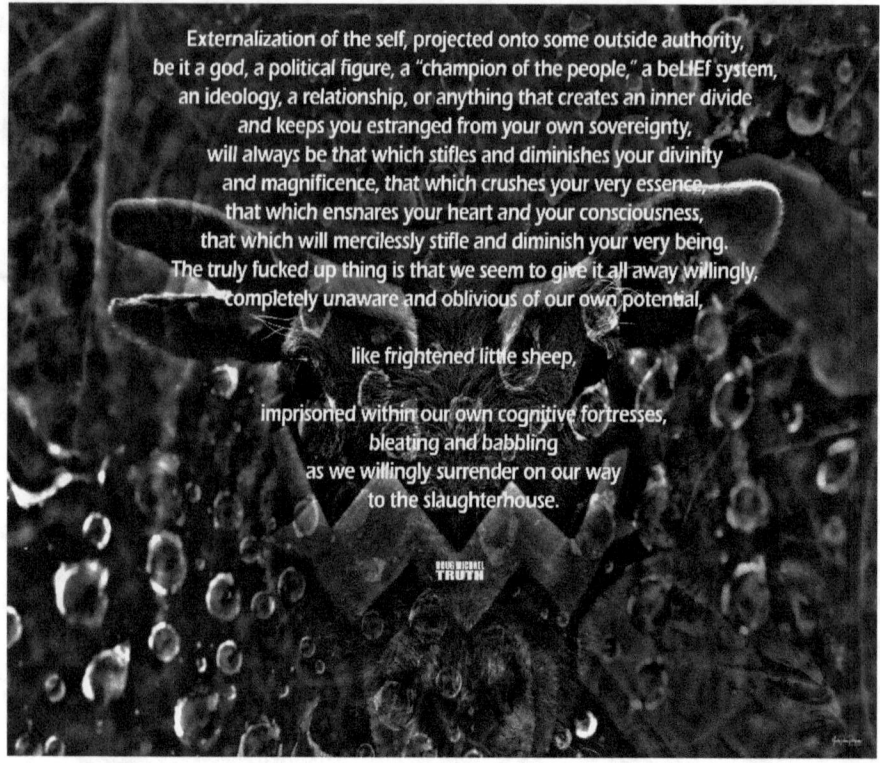

Externalization of the self, projected onto some outside authority, be it a god, a political figure, a "champion of the people," a beLIEf system, an ideology, a relationship, or anything that creates an inner divide and keeps you estranged from your own sovereignty, will always be that which stifles and diminishes your divinity and magnificence, that which crushes your very essence, that which ensnares your heart and your consciousness, that which will mercilessly stifle and diminish your very being. The truly fucked up thing is that we seem to give it all away willingly, completely unaware and oblivious of our own potential,

like frightened little sheep,

imprisoned within our own cognitive fortresses, bleating and babbling as we willingly surrender on our way to the slaughterhouse.

done it but isn't it about time that we gave it a try? What's the worst that could happen? You die so that your as yet unborn great grandchildren can possibly experience freedom? Something that the human race has never known is the true sense of what freedom actually is. We have only experienced the *illusion* of freedom.

We are slaves. Admit that to yourself! Until you can recognize that, how could you ever even begin to imagine what freedom is? Well, you can't because it's a foreign concept. We must venture into unchartered territories, into unknown waters. We must harness the reins of our own consciousness and guide it willingly into the next phase of our evolution or become extinct.

We as a species on this planet at this time, are faced with this choice as we stand at the precipice of annihilation, staring oblivion in the face. We face a monumental crisis at this time, but it's important to understand, that where there is crisis, there is also opportunity. If humanity, in its stubborn denial and steadfast arrogance, refuses to embrace this opportunity to create a new framework for what we may potentially become, then there will be no future generations left to clean up the mess; it will be game over! The ball is in our court in the here and now, and the decision as to where we are going, cannot be left to the psychotic rulers of the Earth Game, lest the world become a desecrated, strip-mined, barren lifeless rock. Ponder this:

The typical human body is made up of some seven billion, billion, billion atoms, each single atom resembling a miniature solar system. As above so below. Is our solar system simply a single atom in a universe of atoms? Is the microcosm a holographic reflection of the macrocosm? Are we embodiments of the entire cosmos?

It is estimated that the human body contains roughly 37.2 trillion cells. Each cell contains six feet of DNA. If the human body had only 10 trillion cells, this would mean that each human being contains 10 billion miles of DNA within them.

All life contains the same molecule coded within the DNA. We are truly all connected. For millennia, the symbol of the serpent was used to convey the animating life force, the DNA. Cultures the world over have used this symbolism for thousands of years and images of spiraling serpents can be found all over the planet. DNA wasn't officially discovered by western science until 1953 and yet the ancients were telling us all along what this building block of all of life is. DNA resembles two serpents spiraling and intertwined together. Proteins containing the exact same 20 amino acids make up all of life as we know it.

DNA is a massive storehouse of information. It is a living library contained within all of life. For billions of years it has replicated and recoded to form many different expressions of life, but it has stayed the same. The very same code of life that exists in bacteria, insects, plants, mammals, reptiles, sea creatures, trees and all other life is the same force of life that flows through you and me. All life shares this intimate connection, this spiraling, intertwining building block of creation.

DNA is crystalline in nature and emits electromagnetic frequencies and photons, which are the basic unit of all light. All life is thus made up of electromagnetic, light encoded filaments. We are made of light! The human body is composed of almost 50% hydrogen atoms, the same element that stars are made of. Everything shares an intimate connection, as above so below, as within so without. All life shares an intimate unity, and even material science has proven this.

How arrogant are the reductionists that seek to place the infinite into a finite box because they cannot escape the confines of their own limited egos? **Does not the entire universe dwell within? How can you possibly place infinity into a box? Separation truly is**

EVERYTHING THAT EXISTS;

WE CARRY IT!

THE TEMPLE
IS OUR OWN CONSCIOUSNESS
AND WE ARE THE CREATORS
OF OUR OWN EXPERIENCE
WHETHER WE RECOGNIZE IT
OR NOT.

YOU ARE AN EMBODIMENT
OF THE ENTIRE COSMOS,
SIMPLY PLAYING A ROLE
ON THE STAGE OF LIFE
IN THE CIRCUS BIZARRE.

YOU ARE ALL
THAT EVER WAS
OR CAN BE.

YOU WERE NOT CREATED,
YOU CANNOT BE DESTROYED,

YOU ARE!
YOU EXIST!

THERE IS NO EXTERNAL BIG DADDY
IN THE SKY
TO PAY HOMAGE TO.

THAT IS A HOAX.

WHAT YOU SEEK
IS ALREADY INHERENT
WITHIN YOU
DUE TO THE VERY FACT
THAT YOU EXIST.

INFINITE AND ETERNAL
CONSCIOUSNESS
IS OUR VERY NATURE,

BUT IN THE CIRCUS
OF THE INSANE,

THOSE WHO WOULD SPEAK IN SUCH WAYS,

THOSE WHO WOULD COME TO REMIND US
OF WHO WE ARE,

ARE CAST ASIDE OR GLEEFULLY MURDERED;

THEY ARE THE GREATEST THREAT
TO ILLUSION.

DAVID MICHAEL
TRUTH

but an illusion and yet humans in their unmitigated arrogance see themselves as above and separate from nature.

We are living breathing embodiments of the entire cosmos, each connected through the thread of life, the DNA. When you gaze out to a magnificent, starlit sky, immerse yourself in the beauty of nature or gaze into the eyes of a beloved pet, you are looking into a mirror. You are an integral part of the all that is, the self-aware in contemplation of itself, eternity is your playground!

The thread of creation flows through all life, each expression an aspect of the infinite. Can a finite mind even begin to grasp what it means to be infinite? How many have become convinced that what exists is relegated to the narrow frequency band of the five senses? That it's all purely physical? How narrow minded!

An entire microscopic world exists beneath the five senses. A special tool, called a microscope is required to see this. Is there a macroscopic world that is also invisible to the five senses? Everything in material existence is energy vibrating. What we call matter is mostly empty space. What is the energetic force that coalesces matter into apparent solidity? What is it that binds it all together? Consciousness!

It's not so much that everything is a product of consciousness; everything *is* consciousness, expressing and experiencing itself in infinite ways as it fragments into a multitude of expressions, each unique, yet existing within the wholeness that contains it. It is a grand paradox.

For many, intelligence is relegated to the world of the intellect. But there are many types of intelligence, intellectual, emotional, even cellular intelligence, down to the molecular level. The intelligence of the entire cosmos is encoded within.

And yet, rather than being in the mystery, we seek to reduce everything down to narrow confines, placing our understanding into the tiny little box of the ego. Everything that cannot be understood by this tiny aspect of the psyche is explained away, marginalized or outright ignored.

The self-aware spark of creation is inherent within you. It *is* you! Every breath is a gift, each instant is an eternity and we recreate ourselves with each passing moment, each thought and the emotions and actions that we bring into manifested reality, based upon how we think, how we feel and how we conduct ourselves as human beings. Are you ready to recognize your sentience, stand within sovereignty and walk the path of true freedom?

Everything that exists, we carry it! The temple is our own consciousness and we are the creators of our own experience whether we recognize it or not. You are an embodiment of the entire cosmos simply playing a role on the stage of life in the Earth Game.

You are all that ever was or can be. You were not created you cannot be destroyed; you *are*! You exist! There is no external big daddy in the sky to pay homage to. That is a hoax. What you seek is already inherent within you due to the very fact that you exist. Infinite and eternal consciousness is our very nature.

The time is long past for human beings to realize their fullest potential. It is time to reclaim the gift that is yours by your very birthright. It is time to stand within the light and magnificence that we are and to become all that we can be.

We are **not** powerless, unless we choose the role of the victim, which of course, is encouraged at every turn. Human potential is vast and remains largely untapped. What if the individual made a deliberate and conscious effort to tap into that wellspring of infinite potential? What may we accomplish? What may we become?

What if a certain percentage of individuals, deliberately detached themselves from the insanity and machinations of the Earth Game, the surreal, carnival bizarre, and instead, focused their energy on raising their awareness and expanding their consciousness as an act of will? What if large numbers of people did this? I don't see that happening, but perhaps it just takes a small percentage to start the ripple effect, like a pebble in a pond.

On the other hand, maybe human, third dimensional, physical experience has run its course in this plane of existence. Perhaps it simply is game over. Is it possible, that the long-standing suffering of this species, existing in this predatory, 3D world, has imparted all of the lessons that can be taught in this experiential playground full of schoolyard bullies? Can we take the final exam, and move on to the next level? If an individual fails, are they held back, to incarnate into another harsh, third dimensional experience until they get the lesson?

Perhaps we are creation in contemplation, and eternity is our field of endeavor. I like to think, that as conscious and sentient beings, that we may move on to bigger and better adventures. One thing that I feel certain of, in my bones, in my very being, is that we are far more than our physical vessels. To me, the body is nothing more than a ship navigated by consciousness, through the stormy seas of physicality, to explore, gather experiences and ultimately expand its understanding of itself. How many people in this world can even entertain that idea? Very few!

Until such a time that we realize that we are personally responsible, sovereign and self-aware beings, can we ever even imagine what it means to be the masters of our own destinies. This moment is calling us to do just that or perish. The realization of one's own sentience is the key to the lock on the door of captivated and enslaved consciousness. That is the way out of the mess and *that* is the solution.

The answer to your plight is found within what you carry with you, if only the individual could *inner*stand this and bring it fourth into the world. We are being called to do just that in this age of deception, this age of unveiling, this age of illusion. Will you answer the call? Are you even capable of doing so? These are the questions you must ask yourself, and you must answer them. Nothing external can or will do that for you, so stop looking externally for that which can only be found within the realm of your own consciousness. Stop giving it all away to the sickness of this world.

I strongly feel, that if we operate from that level of cognition, and spiritual knowingness, that we have nothing to fear at all, whether we decide to create a new template for human experiential reality in this plane, or we simply graduate and move on to the next level of our quest to understand ourselves and evolve to the next level of whatever is that we are to become. I think that either way, we win!

It's far past the time to cultivate the fruits of the spirit, you know, joy, compassion, honor, love, brotherhood, connectedness, peace, truth, passion, kindness and care! It's time to shake the chains of oppression and tyranny to the ground once and for all, the chains that shackle your heart and your mind, indeed, your very spirit. It's time to walk in the fire of the true magnificence that you already *are* by your very existence.

I don't think the Earth Game will ever be transformed into a utopia but as self-actualized and conscious beings, we might navigate the tides of consciousness to maximize our experience and advance our perceptions, never forgetting that it is a willful act. And who knows, maybe we can at least create a model that operates based on cooperation and common sense. Perhaps we can work to heal all of the division, but I feel that begins by first reconciling the inner divide, which entails a process of total deconstruction. It is navigating the ship into the stormy seas of the unknown, where so few dare to tread. Again, from Becoming:

"If what is known is deception, then will pursuing opposite concepts result in knowing truth? Indeed it could. For example, if benevolence has been sought from outside sources, is it indeed available from within one's own awareness? If freedom has not been found in either authoritarian systems or in the pursuit of individual freedoms, then where is it to be found? Could it be obtained within moral and ethical standards that gift the individual within an agreement made by co-operating groups? Could the size of the groups also be arranged by agreement? Could the groups find common ground for agreement within common desires for similar defined freedoms? If co-operation was the key ingredient rather than competition and the need to be/feel superior, then all things are possible. If common interest and desire were the defined beginning point around which all else is drawn by attraction to intended definition of desired experience, successful interaction is

possible. If freedom to withdraw and find a more adequate experience within another group was encouraged and allowed, successful adventure in self-definition would be assured. The experience of the search for the most perfect expression could be an end unto itself."[3]

As I've always stated, this is a willing and individual effort to shift the perceptions and evolve our cognition. That does not mean that we cannot assist one another in the process. Sharing information and ideas while we still can is probably a good idea. I think that deliberately working towards transcending the victim consciousness is critical in the beginning stages of facilitating this shift in consciousness. The victim is exploited and if we hold the idea of ourselves that we are victims, it will attract a victimizer to fulfill the other end of the spectrum. Humanity has been operating as victims for long enough. It's time to rise to our feet for a change. This must begin with an individual transition; it's a willful act! We're staring our very extinction in the face and I feel that it's important to consciously remove our consent and agreement, to rise above our current perceptions about who and what we are and what we are capable of and to begin to operate as sovereign beings. We need to manifest the change we wish to see and be what we are and that has to begin with you, the individual. I know where I stand, and I will not go into the world of Artificial Intelligence and become a digitized slave to the hive mind. It's a choice. What do you choose?

AFTERWARD

I've been going down the rabbit hole for nearly 20 years now and it just keeps getting stranger and stranger. It's like a massive labyrinth that just keeps expanding. Along the way, I have met some amazing fellow travelers, and this has shown me that we are not alone. I've gotten to know many of my supporters on a personal level and they are amongst the greatest people I could've ever hoped to have met. I extend my deepest thanks and appreciation to each and every one of them.

One thing I've discovered over the years, is that when you are on a journey of self-discovery, and searching for answers as to what is going on behind the scenes in the Earth Game, you can't expect much support form your family or "friends," and certainly not from coworkers or the people down at the local pub. Remember, when you are on this journey of self-actualization, you are a threat! Your cognition is moving away from the perceptual prison and those still hopelessly stuck in their cognitive fortresses may not be ready to be unplugged, and your bold courage, your

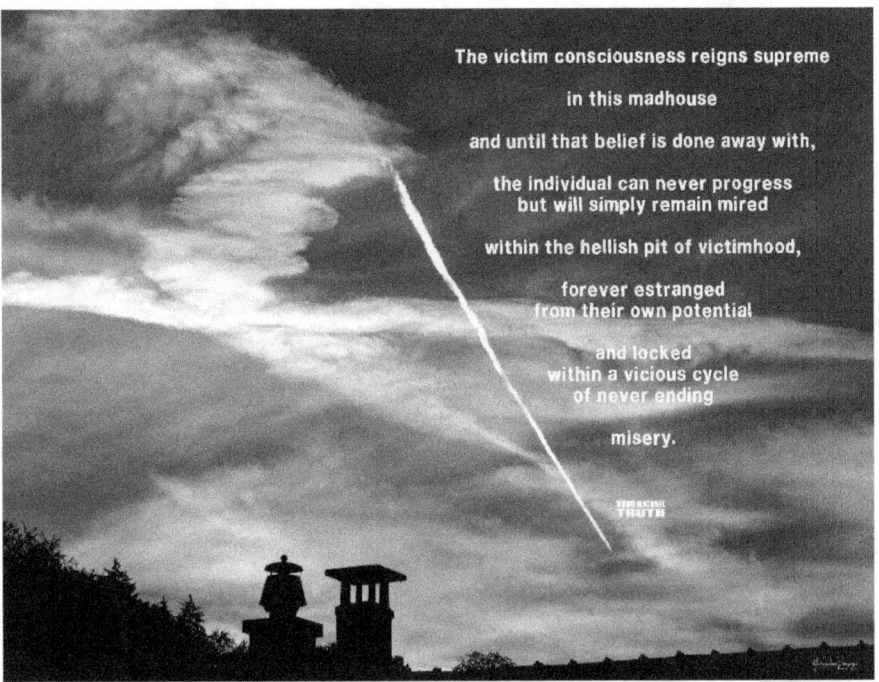

The victim consciousness reigns supreme

in this madhouse

and until that belief is done away with,

the individual can never progress
but will simply remain mired

within the hellish pit of victimhood,

forever estranged
from their own potential

and locked
within a vicious cycle
of never ending

misery.

daring to be different and to think for yourself poses an enormous threat to their carefully constructed perceptual illusions.

Don't let that get you down. Remember, you may feel lonely at times, but you are not alone! We are scattered around the world and there's a good chance that people of like mind and like vibration will appear in your life as others fall away from your experience. I've experienced this quite a bit over the years. Trust the process! Like energy attracts like energy!

At times, the road will get very bumpy, and when you find yourself overwhelmed, I suggest doing something that brings you enjoyment or laughter. I've found that having creative endeavors has really helped me to stay balanced. Creative expression has been such a gift to me in this crazy world, and in the days ahead, we are really going to need to tap into our creative natures to manifest the change we wish to see in the world.

I truly do appreciate everyone who has taken the time to read the books, view the videos and listen to the podcasts over the years. The positive feedback has been enormous, and words cannot describe my gratitude. Thank you! I will continue to share information in writings, audio presentations and in other ways for as long as I am able to do so. For access to more information, please see my website at: www.dougmichaeltruth.com

To be honest, some of the work on my website appears in this book, but I included it here because it fit in so well with the information I was trying to convey. There are no advertisements on my site and much of the information is available to download for free.

Again, I extend my thanks to everyone who has taken the time to read this and to those who have stood by me. All the best to each of you! May the light of good fortune forever shine upon you! Walk in peace!

Doug Michael.

Other books by Doug Michael:

We are born into an artificial, overlaid superimposed reality, an illusory, psychological prison, a simulacrum. Our entire lives are guided by unseen forces which through perceptual conditioning and the manipulation of human consciousness, have erected a control paradigm that enslaves the mind from cradle to grave. This book examines aspects of this manipulation and offers ideas as to how one may achieve cognitive freedom and transcendence of the control structure.

The Carnival Outré

Jamboree of Deception

Doug Michael

Welcome to the carnival of the insane, the blood-soaked madhouse where the lunatics have completely taken over the asylum. Within the walls of the surreal circus bizarre all things are allowed, and all manner of decadence is on open display for all to see and experience Witness the lunacy and immerse yourself within the madness that captivates the senses and winds its contorted designs around the very consciousness. This book takes a macabre look at life in the Earth Game and strikes a balance between being informative and just plain creepy without leaving the reader in a state of hopelessness. It exposes the machinations of the current superimposed reality from a unique perspective and examines the situation that surrounds the inmates and threatens their very extinction and yet, offers ideas as to how one may free their consciousness from the confines of the psychological and emotional prison paradigm.

End Notes:

Chapter 1

[1] *Becoming*, Bridger House Publications Inc.

Chapter 2

[1] https://ir.charter.com/static-files/1446750d-6d85-4e23-8746-37e56a565e81

[2] https://www.statista.com/statistics/263828/revenue-of-general-electric/

[3] https://www.statista.com/statistics/273555/global-revenue-of-the-walt-disney-company/

[4] https://www.statista.com/statistics/193440/revenue-of-the-cbs-corporation-since-2006/

[5] https://www.statista.com/statistics/273689/viacoms-annual-revenue/

[6] https://www.statista.com/statistics/692155/global-revenue-news-corp/

[7] https://en.wikipedia.org/wiki/Crowd_psychology

[8] https://en.wikiquote.org/wiki/Edward_Bernays

[9] Ibid

Chapter 3

[1] https://www.dictionary.com/browse/schism

[2] https://www.merriam-webster.com/dictionary/persona

[3] https://rationalwiki.org/wiki/Willful_ignorance

Chapter 5

[1] https://www.dictionary.com/browse/demoralization

[2] https://www.youtube.com/watch?v=XP_o5bDrq2o

[3] https://refugeeresettlementwatch.wordpress.com/author/acorcoran/

[4] http://www.allenbwest.com/ashleyedwardson/mainstream-media-wont-tell-you-why-sweden-is-now-rape-capital-of-the-west

[5] http://www.wnd.com/2016/03/swedish-rape-crisis-boils-over-as-media-stays-silent/

[6] https://sputniknews.com/us/201903061072986968-southern-border-breaks-record-migrants/

[7] https://bit.ly/308jB5o

[8] http://www.breitbart.com/london/2016/01/12/federal-police-break-ranks-complain-orders-from-above-ban-them-from-dealing-with-migrants/

[9] https://founders.archives.gov/documents/Jefferson/03-10-02-0378

[10] Ibid

[11] https://www.washingtonpost.com/powerpost/trump-to-make-new-offer-to-democrats-as-government-shutdown-drags-on/2019/01/19/2cde029e-1bf3-11e9-9ebf-c5fed1b7a081_story.html?utm_term=.e5fc60680015

[12] https://www.washingtonpost.com/news/wonk/wp/2015/09/28/why-one-of-the-worlds-worst-human-rights-offenders-is-leading-a-un-human-rights-panel/

[13] https://en.wikipedia.org/wiki/Totalitarianism

[14] https://www.merriam-webster.com/dictionary/totalitarianism

[15] http://www.hangthebankers.com/george-soros-admits-to-funding-the-ukraine-crisis/

[16] https://en.oxforddictionaries.com/definition/us/false_flag

17https://www.commondreams.org/news/2015/03/26/body-count-report-reveals-least-13-million-lives-lost-us-led-war-terror

18https://www.theguardian.com/us-news/2017/aug/21/donald-trump-expand-us-military-intervention-afghanistan-pakistan

19https://www.usatoday.com/story/news/politics/2017/08/27/trump-expected-lift-ban-military-gear-local-police-forces/606065001/

20http://abcnews.go.com/Politics/wireStory/trump-set-roll-back-limits-military-gear-police-49462793

21https://www.theguardian.com/us-news/2015/jan/31/detroit-aiyana-stanley-jones-police-officer-cleared

22https://www.boston.com/news/local-news/2014/04/18/eerie-photos-of-boston-on-lockdown-during-the-marathon-bombing-suspect-manhunt

23 https://docs.house.gov/billsthisweek/20180723/CRPT-115hrpt863.pdf

24https://journal-neo.org/2017/06/16/syria-iran-and-n-korea-will-trump-attempt-to-finish-the-neocon-hitlist/

25https://www.usatoday.com/story/news/politics/2017/08/25/executive-order-trump-imposes-new-round-venezuela-sanctions/601667001/

26http://geab.eu/en/top-10-countries-with-the-worlds-biggest-oil-reserves/

27https://www.theatlantic.com/national/archive/2013/02/tsa-pat-down-wheelchair-children/318100/

Chapter 6

1https://www.thedailybeast.com/elite-campuses-offer-students-coloring-books-puppies-to-get-over-trump

2https://www.youtube.com/watch?v=KXzjkVbZSjw

3 https://www.merriam-webster.com/dictionary/homogenize

4 https://www.youtube.com/watch?time_continue=6&v=jkaU9t9LByw

5https://www.christianheadlines.com/contributors/scott-slayton/elementary-schools-using-drag-queens-to-teach-kids-about-gender.html

[6]https://www.rt.com/op-ed/453680-air-pollution-racist-science-ideology/

[7] https://en.wikipedia.org/wiki/Nosedive_(Black_Mirror)

[8] goo.gl/bDNgsS

[9] http://www.fox5ny.com/news/nyc-gender-x-birth-certificate-law

[10]https://bit.ly/2DdXwbF

[11] https://www.merriam-webster.com/dictionary/gender%20dysphoria

12https://www.dailymail.co.uk/news/article-6700975/Florida-family-raising-11-month-old-baby-gender-neutral-calling-theyby.html

[13]ttps://www.usatoday.com/story/news/investigations/2019/01/10/american-psychological-association-traditional-masculinity-harmful/2538520002/

[14] https://singlemotherguide.com/single-mother-statistics/

[15] https://thefatherlessgeneration.wordpress.com/statistics/

16https://www.psychologytoday.com/us/blog/the-new-resilience/201508/women-initiate-divorce-much-more-men-heres-why

[17]https://www.theguardian.com/global/video/2019/jan/15/new-gillette-ad-tackling-toxic-masculinity-receives-harsh-backlash-video

[18]https://www.nbcphiladelphia.com/news/local/Charges-Upheld-for-Philly-Woman-Accused-of-Attacking-Police-Horse-433138913.html

[19]https://www.forbes.com/sites/theapothecary/2018/02/26/how-american-citizens-finance-health-care-for-undocumented-immigrants/#72519eff12c4

[20] https://www.quora.com/What-was-the-Kalergi-Plan

21https://archive.org/stream/PracticalIdealism-EnglishTranslation/Practical%20Idealism%20%E2%80%93%20English%20T ranslation_djvu.txt

Chapter 7

[1]http://en.wikipedia.org/wiki/False_flag

[2] http://en.wikipedia.org/wiki/RMS_Lusitania

[3]http://en.wikipedia.org/wiki/Operation_Northwoods

[4] Ibid

[5] *Body of Secrets: Anatomy of the Ultra-Secret National Security Agency,* James Bamford, Anchor publishing, 2002.

[6]Video documentary *JFK Conspiracy: Final Analysis*:

http://video.google.com/videoplay?docid=7457650579849429062

[7]http://kentroversypapers.blogspot.com/2007/06/dealey-plaza-esoteric-freemasonic.html

[8] *JFK Conspiracy: Final Analysis*

[9] *The Biggest Secret*, pp. 408.

[10] Ibid pp. 410.

[11]http://www.archives.gov/research/jfk/select-committee-report/summary.html

[12] *The New York Times*. April 25, 1966.

[13] Carroll and Graf publishing.

[14] Warner Brothers Pictures, 1991.

[15] *Reasonable Doubt: An Investigation into the Assassination of John F. Kennedy*, New York, Holt, Rinehart & Winston, 1985 pp. 99.

[16] Paul Joseph Watson: www.prisonplanet.com

[17] *The New York Times*, 10/28/93.

[18]*Waco: The Rules of Engagement:*

http://video.google.com/videoplay?docid=4298137966377572665

[19] Ibid

[20] *Waco: the Rules of Engagement*

[21] Ibid

[22] Ibid

[23] Ibid

[24] Ibid

[25] *Conspiracy Files*: Oklahoma City Bombing: http://video.google.com/videoplay?docid=5977554184697409940

[26] http://www.youtube.com/watch?v=NWwrEEP8EBk

[27] Ibid

[28] Ibid

[29] http://www.opednews.com/maxwrite/diarypage.php?did=6900

[30] Logical Figments Books, June, 1996.

[31] http://www.mindcontrolforums.com/hambone/okmc.html

[32] Bombing manhunt goes on," Associated Press, April 23, 1995

[33] Article: "Multiple Blasts: More Evidence," William F. Jasper, *the New American*, 3/31/97: http://thenewamerican.com/node/1356

[34] Ibid

[35] "Multiple Blasts: More Evidence."

[36] Documentary:http://freedocumentaries.org/theatre.php?filmid=131&id=953&wh=1000x720

[37] *Ludicrous Diversion*

[38] Clip from BBC Radio: http://www.youtube.com/watch?v=sEbUQiYOGjU

[39] Numerous sources exist for this fact. Fox News reported on this on 7/29/05 in their *Dayside* program. Also see: http://www.infowars.com/articles/London_attack/new_criminologist_aswat_mi6.htm

[40] Cambridge Evening News, 7/25/05

[41] *The Associated Press*, 7/7/2005

[42]Article: "Suppressed Details of Criminal Insider Trading

Lead Directly into the CIA's Highest Ranks," Michael Rupert, 2001, FTW

Publications:

http://whatreallyhappened.com/WRHARTICLES/illegaltrades.html?q=illeg altrades.html

[43]Article: "Suppressed Details of Criminal Insider Trading

Lead Directly into the CIA's Highest Ranks," Michael Rupert, 2001, FTW

Publications:

http://whatreallyhappened.com/WRHARTICLES/illegaltrades.html?q=illeg altrades.html

[44] British newspaper: *The Independent*, 8/23/05

[45] Video Documentary: *Terrorstorm,* Alex Jones, 2006.

[46]*The Guardian* 10/14/2008:

http://www.guardian.co.uk/uk/2008/oct/14/3

[47]Article: "30-year Anniversary: Tonkin Gulf Lie Launched Vietnam War," Jeff Cohen and Norman Solomon, Fairness and Accuracy in Reporting, 7/27/94.

[48] *London Times,* June 21, 2004.

[49]http://www.infowars.com/chinese-professor-threatens-third-world-war-to-protect-iran/

[50] http://www.strategicstudiesinstitute.army.mil/pdffiles/PUB890.pdf

[51] *Washington Post*, December 1, 2008:

http://www.washingtonpost.com/wp-dyn/content/article/2008/11/30/AR2008113002217_pf.html

[52] http://en.wikipedia.org/wiki/McCollum_memo

[53]http://www.activistpost.com/2011/08/tsa-molests-small-boy-contrary-to-their.html

[54] http://www.naturalnews.com/032757_TSA_surplus.html

55http://articles.economictimes.indiatimes.com/2010-07-01/news/27569308_1_body-scanners-skin-cancer-head-and-neck

56http://www.guardian.co.uk/world/2012/may/09/underwear-bomber-working-for-cia

57 https://www.youtube.com/watch?v=LVKFE1fUlLM

58 https://www.youtube.com/watch?v=IyTrFaUKwu4

Chapter 8

1http://news.bbc.co.uk/1/hi/world/middle_east/1559151.stm

2http://www.prisonplanet.com/articles/september2004/080904wargame scover.htm

3http://www.prisonplanet.com/agency_planned_exercise_on_sept_11_built_around_a_plane_crashing_into_a_building.htm

4 http://www.prisonplanet.com/011904wtc7.html

5 http://www.securecom.net/

6http://www.prisonplanet.com/suppresed_details_insider_trading_cia.html

7http://www.pnionline.com/dnblog/extra/archives/001139.html

8http://www.reviewjournal.com/lvrj_home/2001/Sep-16-Sun-2001/news/17011253.html

9 http://archives.cnn.com/2001/WORLD/meast/09/18/inv.terror.jarrah/

10 http://www.prisonplanet.com/041203metwithbinladen.html

11 ttp://observer.guardian.co.uk/magazine/story/0,11913,738196,00.html

12 http://www.youtube.com/watch?v=zrTjPGy2k_U

13http://www.prisonplanet.com/articles/june2005/240605officialstory.htm

14http://www.prisonplanet.com/articles/april2005/090405gotwarning.htm

15 http://portland.indymedia.org/en/2006/06/341238.shtml

[16] http://www.controlled-demolition.com/

[17] http://prisonplanet.com/us_agents_told_to_backoff.html

[18]http://propagandamatrix.com/willie_brown_got_low_key_early_warning.html

[19]http://prisonplanet.com/multimedia_priorknowledge_firefighterstape.html

[20] http://www.prisonplanet.tv/articles/may2004/050504bombsinwtc.htm

[21] http://www.prisonplanet.tv/articles/march2005/100305strategicexplosives.htm

[22] http://www.chiefengineer.org/article.cfm?seqnum1=1029

[23] http://www.prisonplanet.com/articles/november2004/281104anotheraccount.htm

[24] http://www.youtube.com/watch?v=BxdttHY59b4

[25] http://911research.wtc7.net/wtc/evidence/moltensteel.html

[26]http://www.youtube.com/watch?v=C7SwOT29gbc&feature=player_embedded#!

[27]http://en.wikipedia.org/wiki/Project_for

Chapter 9

[1]http://en.wikipedia.org/wiki/Cognitive_dissonance

[2] http://rationalwiki.org/wiki/Confirmation_bias

[3]https://educateinspirechange.org/alternative-news/non-conformity-questioning-authority-now-considered-mental-illnesses/

[4] http://en.wiktionary.org/wiki/consensus_trance

[5] http://en.wikipedia.org/wiki/Stockholm_syndrome

[6] https://www.wanttoknow.info/050331behaviormodificationtv

[7] https://www.statista.com/topics/979/advertising-in-the-us/

[8] http://www.youtube.com/watch?v=RRiILStjZWE

9http://articles.nydailynews.com/2008-11-28/local/17910475_1_wal-mart-worker-long-island-wal-mart-jdimytai-damour

Chapter 10

[1] https://bit.ly/2yaGEgz

[2] https://www.lifezette.com/2019/05/our-veterans-hungry-homeless-yet-lawbreakers-given-shelter/

[3] https://www.pgpf.org/chart-archive/0053_defense-comparison

[4] https://bit.ly/2MqAXrB

[5] https://bit.ly/2VL25S0

[6] https://www.dea.gov/factsheets/fentanyl

[7] https://bit.ly/2POaOAS

[8] https://www.youtube.com/watch?v=vWU_Df1Hz18

[9] https://bit.ly/2VIVyKP

[10] https://bit.ly/2V1DNCd

[11] Ibid

[12] Ibid

[13] Ibid

[14] https://bit.ly/2J31xo2

[15] https://bit.ly/2vFZ7Dc

[16] Ibid

[17] Ibid

[18] https://bit.ly/2DkRXZ1

[19] https://bit.ly/2K3OEtC

[20] https://cbsloc.al/2VXYgfA

[21]https://www.latimes.com/local/lanow/la-me-homeless-how-we-got-here-20180201-story.html

[22] https://bit.ly/2K3Xuav

[23] https://bit.ly/2QWQ76q

[24] https://bit.ly/2vOJoSa

[25] https://www.youtube.com/watch?v=bpAi7OWWBlw

[26] https://www.ipbes.net/news/Media-Release-Global-Assessment

[27] Ibid

[28] Ibid

[29] Ibid

[30] Ibid

[31] Ibid

[32] Ibid

[33] https://www.merriam-webster.com/dictionary/ecocide

[34] https://bit.ly/1JcVdQh

[35] https://bit.ly/1FA3iyi

[36] https://bit.ly/1s30HrE

[37] Ibid

[38] https://bit.ly/2Q8qyid

[39] https://bit.ly/1GFgl3U

[40] a becquerel is a unit of measurement for radioactive material.

[41] http://www.exposingtruth.com/fukushima-radiation-still-leaking/

[42] https://bit.ly/30qCMHR

[43] https://bit.ly/2VrGw89

[44] https://bit.ly/2w3quHd

[45] https://reut.rs/2V3lQUu

[46] https://bit.ly/16hn4kE

[47] https://bit.ly/1BiUCKg

[48] https://www.britannica.com/event/Deepwater-Horizon-oil-spill

[49] Ibid

[50] https://www.dosomething.org/us/facts/11-facts-about-bp-oil-spill

[51] https://www.huffpost.com/entry/corexit-bp-oil-dispersant_n_3157080

[52] Ibid

[53] Ibid

[54] https://www.britannica.com/event/Deepwater-Horizon-oil-spill

[55] Ibid

[56] Ibid

[57] Ibid

[58] https://bit.ly/2CBK0PP

[59] https://on.wsj.com/2YG2BSk

[60] https://www.history.com/topics/1980s/exxon-valdez-oil-spill

[61] Ibid

[62] Ibid

[63] Ibid

[64] https://www.theoceancleanup.com/great-pacific-garbage-patch/

[65] Ibid

[66] Ibid

[67] Ibid

[68] https://bit.ly/2wnqbY2

[69] https://bit.ly/2zGir6e

[70] Ibid

[71] Ibid

[72] *The Columbia History of the World*, 1981, page 54

[73] http://www.eazysmoke.com/marijuana-quotes.htm

[74] http://en.wikipedia.org/wiki/Hemp

[75] http://medical-dictionary.thefreedictionary.com/Cannabinoids

[76] http://norml.org/library/item/introduction-to-the-endocannabinoid-system

[77] https://bit.ly/2YYYRvs

Chapter 11

[1] http://www.wayofthefuture.church/

[2] https://bit.ly/2IyPyNi

[3] https://www.livescience.com/22694-global-sperm-count-decline.html

[4] https://bit.ly/2fFJO5F

[5] https://www.neuralink.com/

[6]https://www.rt.com/news/464373-elon-musk-unveils-neuralink-implant/

[7] Ibid

[8] https://bit.ly/2IYWX9f

[9] https://www.livescience.com/65585-ufo-sightings-us-pilots.html

[10] https://bit.ly/2Nv8y48

[11] Ibid

[12] https://bit.ly/2RRCHrJ

[13] https://bit.ly/32abZk2

[14] https://bit.ly/2xuuKAv

[15] https://bit.ly/2JlFVky

[16] https://bit.ly/2RZFe49

[17] Ibid

[18]http://themillenniumreport.com/2019/01/well-whaddya-know-no-5g-for-israel/

[19] https://www.ncbi.nlm.nih.gov/pmc/articles/PMC4503846/

[20] https://en.wikipedia.org/wiki/Programmable_matter

[21] https://bit.ly/32ttT1d

[22] https://nyp.st/2LnZOLc

[23] https://www.cnbc.com/2017/08/11/three-square-market-ceo-explains-its-employee-microchip-implant.html

[24]https://www.theatlantic.com/international/archive/2018/02/china-

surveillance/552203/

[25]https://www.zerohedge.com/news/2019-05-23/darpa-wants-create-mind-controlled-weapons-war

[26] Ibid

[27] Ibid

[28] https://www.youtube.com/watch?v=HTPIED6jUdU

[29] https://www.dougmichaeltruth.com/artificial-intelligence-singularity/

[30] https://bit.ly/2Gh79rw

[31] https://carnicominstitute.org/

[32] https://bit.ly/2XOElSn

[33] https://bit.ly/2SlJqeN

[34] Ibid

[35] https://bit.ly/2XNGbTn

[36] https://carnicominstitute.org/wp/morgellons-growth-captured/

[37] https://bit.ly/2xPZ48T

[38] https://bit.ly/2IYWX9f

[39] https://www.youtube.com/watch?v=Ag44dRO8LEA

[40] https://www.space.com/ufo-sightings-us-pilots.html

[41] Ibid

[42] Ibid

Chapter 12

[1] *Becoming*, Bridger House Publications Inc.

[2] Ibid

[3] Ibid